9-99

LACAN

AND THE

SUBJECT OF

LANGUAGE

LACAN
AND THE
SUBJECT OF
LANGUAGE

EDITED BY ELLIE RAGLAND-SULLIVAN AND MARK BRACHER

ROUTLEDGE

NEW YORK AND LONDON

Published in 1991 by

Routledge
An imprint of Routledge, Chapman and Hall, Inc.
29 West 35 Street
New York, NY 10001

Published in Great Britain by

Routledge
11 New Fetter Lane
London EC4P 4EE

Library of Congress Cataloging in Publication Data

Ragland-Sullivan, Ellie, 1941–
    Lacan and the subject of language / Ellie Ragland-Sullivan, Mark Bracher.
      p. cm.
    Includes index.
    ISBN 0-415-90307-6.—ISBN 0-415-90308-4 (pbk.)
    1. Lacan, Jacques, 1901– —Contributions in philology.
2. Philology. 3. Psychoanalysis. I. Lacan, Jacques, 1901–
II. Bracher, Mark, 1950– . III. Title.
P85.L34R35 1990
150.19'5—dc20   90-48416

British Library Cataloguing in publication data also available

Contents

Acknowledgments

The essays in this volume were presented as keynote addresses at a conference on "Lacan, Language and Literature" held at Kent State University, Kent, Ohio on Memorial Day weekend in May of 1988. The two addresses not included in this volume were "The History of the Anecdote: Fiction and Fiction" delivered by the late Joel Fineman and "R.S.I. in Freud's *Project*" delivered by Richard Klein of Oxford, England. Although Joel Fineman did not contribute his essay to this volume, the editors wish to pay homage to the excellence of his scholarship and the complexities of his work, standing as it does at the interfaces among literature, rhetoric, and psychoanalysis. Richard Klein, M.D., has chosen to give his essays to those publications not supported by institutions, a political decision we respect. We also thank the co-sponsors of the conference, the Center for Literature and Psychoanalysis at Kent State University and the *Newsletter of the Freudian Field*. We also thank David Metzger and Heidimarie Hayes for their assistance in the final stages of editing this volume. But most particularly we thank those speakers who came here from Paris to give us the benefit of the groundbreaking work you will read in this volume, work that is now changing the face of theory and practice in the analytic clinic. These theories regarding what knowledge is, what language is and does, and why gender makes a difference, are only a few of the effects of Lacan's teaching.

Ellie Ragland Sullivan
Mark Bracher

Introduction

Ellie Ragland-Sullivan

The essays in this volume are organized into three sections: Lacan and the Subject of Language, Lacan and the Subject of Psychoanalysis, Lacan and the Subject of Literature. Yet, such an organizational strategy does not truly divide the essays into discrete, separate subjects. For all the essays work from the same complex and ever varying teaching, that of Jacques Lacan, each essay shedding a bit more light on Lacan's innovative theories of what language is and what a subject is. Given that the essays all work from the teaching of one man, their diversity and open-endedness may seem surprising. Perhaps it is not an altogether impossible hope that the essays printed here will give a new focus to the meaning of pluralism itself, when differences are seen to be grounded, not by the figure, the mark, historical context or economic class, to name a few, but in the object *a*.

This Lacanian naming of an object that both causes desire and also intervenes in all human acts to produce discontinuities in them, adds something new to histories of meaning. Here meaning is grounded in heterogeneous objects that are not themselves grounded. In *L'acte psychanalytique*, Lacan's unpublished Seminar of 1967–1968, Lacan referred to three poles that constitute knowledge. The first is the symbolic order signifier that joins the world of language to that of images and objects, creating a subject. The second is the unary trait which links an imaginarized-symbolic subject to others and to the world via the projections that constitute the process of identification. The third is the object *a* which may be described as a falling of a piece of the real onto the vector which runs from the symbolic to the imaginary. "The signifier can, indeed, manipulate such material, despite the apparent hindrances the latter could cause in imaginary functioning, that is to say in the most fragile and difficult thing to grasp as far as man is concerned; not that there are not in him primitive images destined to give us a guide in nature, but, precisely since the signifier takes [the primitive images] over, it is always very difficult to pinpoint them in their raw side" (December 6, 1967). The third pole that is knowable, then, is what emanates from this object *a*, *jouissance*. Lacan envisioned the analyst at a delicate point in the middle of *jouissance*, knowledge (an imaginary function of idealization), and truth, at the place of a hole in knowing, being and feeling he called the place of desire.

Addressing the issues of knowledge, desire, *jouissance* and truth, in an effort to build up a picture of the Lacanian subject and a Lacanian theory of language, the contributors address contemporary debates, as well as those that are age-old. Most particularly sexual difference, creation, the referent, the symptom and invention delineate the concerns of these essays. In a sense, addressing the old and the new differs little when one marches the debates across a stage. But Lacan claimed to have added something new to old debates. And these essays attempt to show aspects of what that might be. Stuart Schneiderman replies to Jacques Derrida's critique of Lacanian analysis in *La carte postale*. Lila Kalinich interrogates Nicolas Abraham and Maria Torok's supposed exposure of a textual unconscious to be found in the traces of the Wolf-Man's various childhood languages. Colette Soler and Slavoj Žižek pick up the issue of Aristotle's difficulty in finding an order of the particular in their precise renderings of Lacan's order of the symptom, taken as that which invents, selects. The symptom, for example, would point to a new theory of the artist as someone without a symbolic father, someone who tries to escape the social perversion of the normative which Lacan wrote as *nor-mâle*. Herein the heterosexual is itself a symptom of what Ellie Ragland-Sullivan seeks to clarify in her discussion of Lacan's axiom: "There is no sexual relation." Ragland-Sullivan, Willy Apollon and Henry Sullivan join hands in working with this axiom, derived from a simple drama. Interpreting a slight anatomical difference between the sexes, members of a given culture imaginarily mythologize this difference in language, constructing myriad masquerades around the lack of a solid symbol or adequate signifier to re-present sexual difference in the Other, the place from which we speak and know.

Ragland-Sullivan argues that the blurred lines between the genders create an artificial division between the sexes such that culture and language themselves are masquerades adorning a minimal imaginary difference, language becoming not only a field of decorative tautologies, but also a life preserver surrounding the real of lack and loss. Apollon shows that in some subjects the signifier for gender difference—or identity—is so minimal that they can easily fall out of the social order, the result being a collapsing together of language, identifications and sexual identity. Lacan called this condition psychosis. In his contention that efforts to account for sexual difference intersect with anthropological attempts to discover a missing link, Henry Sullivan takes up Lacan's challenge that the beginnings of language are lost in the dawn of history. Sullivan investigates the representation of sexual difference depicted in cave drawings 24,000 years prior to standard anthropological accounts of the appearance of recorded culture, thought to coincide with the beginning of writing around 6,000 BC. Such drawings depicted horse/man alongside bison/woman as early as 30,000 BC. Moreover, these are co-simultaneous with the appearance of cro-Magnon man or *Homo sapiens* in 35,000 BC. Sullivan's argument thus takes issue with biological evolutionary arguments that claim to have finally answered the question of what human intelligence is and how it came to be constituted. Darwin's evolutionary man becomes another myth trying to explain origins, like the theological one that preceded it.

Sullivan develops his argument around a theme central to Lacan's teaching: that Descartes' founding the "I" in reason gave birth to modernism and contemporary science. But a post-modern *episteme*, Sullivan asserts, would be based on Lacan's discovery that human mentality is not fixed in an *a priori* Cartesian reason, nor is it determined either by a biological (Freud) or an economic (Marx) first cause. As stated in Lacan's quote from *L'acte psychanalytique*, the agencies that constitute mentality and identity are the signifier, the unary trait, and the object *a*. Giving body to Lacan's mapping out of the agencies of causality, Sullivan points out that animal cries are enmeshed in the real, but not in the symbolic. Moving Lacan's theory of language away from the realm of the semiotic where it is sometimes reduced to a Peircian theory of signs and away from the Saussurean linguistic reduction of the Lacanian signifier to sound, letter or acoustic form as well, Sullivan links the theory of natural selection of language-facilitating features (where *homo sapiens* becomes *homo loquens*) to cave paintings. He asks if such paintings are not a methodology or effort to symbolize "the thing" that divides us from ourselves? If so, cave paintings would embody this Lacanian paradox: art seeks to close out a void that can only be silenced by efforts to represent it or its effects. In a surprising conclusion, Sullivan argues that the "missing link" in evolutionary theory is the mystery of when and how language was born, rather than the mystery of natural selection. That is, we owe our symbolic being to the movement of the phallic signifier at work, delineating differences, inferring order, even in the form of the early tools of material culture, rather than to an evermoving continuum of gene-pool evolution.

Many essays in this volume reconsider the issue of creation. What creates the lack that in turn gives rise to creative efforts to suture lack? Language names things and thus murders them as full presences, creating an alienation between the word and the thing, an alienation that infers gaps or a ternarity into language itself. In this context, aesthetics (*qua* perception) becomes the effect of distance (called perspective in the Renaissance) that mirrors back to spectators, readers and auditors a resonating wall, not a mirror. So language gives rise to a void, as a lack of all things *qua* immediately graspable or knowable. We cannot be whole. Nor can anything else. But, paradoxically, the gaps in language give rise to the desire for closure or resolution, lest lack or loss be experienced in the body as doubt or anxiety.

Jacques-Alain Miller says the root of reference itself is creation. And reference, both ambiguous and vacuous, is reference to the void. "Benevolent neutrality" means keeping distance from the reference *qua* void, Miller explains, while creation becomes linked to cause when one considers that language is not only never equal to itself, nor is it ever the thing itself. Basing his discussion of the themes of creation and cause around word and object problems long studied by Anglophone language philosophers, Jacques-Alain Miller offers a new theory of the word and of the object in "Much Ado About What?" Having defined the referent of language as the void, Miller links Lacan's clinical valorization of impasses in psychoanalytic talking to his own distinction between theories of communication and theories of meaning. Miller, thus, clears the way to speak of a Lacanian theory of the disappearance of reference. Lacan's "creationist" theory of language—unlike theological and evolutionary "creationist" theories which are myth, myth being that which seeks closure, unity and resolution by naming the unnameable—is not a myth, but rather the discovery that myth itself works from and by structure. What is structure, then? Lacans's topological structuralism is certainly not a closed system structuralism à la Lévi-Strauss or Saussure.

Miller's elucidation of Lacan's theory of language answers those many readers of Lacan who have mistaken his "linguistic" return to Freud for a simple lumping together of Freud and Saussure. Rather, Lacan evolved a novel theory of representation where words and images negotiate desire and project identification while also carrying the drive energy that seeks *jouissance*. The purpose of language, then, is a multilayered performance. Lacan's theory of language, as clarified and developed by Miller, does not depend on Hegel or Saussure in the ways that have become commonplace assertions about Lacan's teaching. Rather, Miller points out Lacan's dependence on Hegel's dialectic as the discovery of the disappearance of reference and to Lacan's debt to Saussure's insight that words depend on other words. Miller's suggestion that American theorists and critics have found themselves new deadends because they have jumped into continental philosophy and political theory, while sidestepping American and British analytic philosophies of language, finds a strange resonance in the "new historicist" claim that Americans have turned to French theory out of a love for the exotic. The new deadends to which Miller refers appear as the dismantled language of deconstruction placed alongside a desire to find the safety of a seeming factualism or objectivity in historicizing and contextualizing anew.

But, as Miller shows, neither deconstruction nor new historicism has worked with the problematic of referent. Deconstruction has opted for a Kantian-Nietzschean solution of "undecidables," coupled with a poetic sense of the plural. New historicism has fought back with only a context of the visible or the "reported" for referent. In these discourses of the master—discourses that aim to disambiguate language—the time of anxiety or uncertainty that attends any search to know is exchanged for yet one more death of alienation into and by the signifying chains that have weighed subjects down throughout the time and space of history.

Russell Grigg's "Signifier, Object and the Transference" joins hands with Miller's "Much Ado About What?" to plea for a new analysis where the analyst's position should be that of a holding place for an unarticulated referent. While holding, the analysand awaits a new referent. Thus, transference and mastery are indeed connected. An analyst is in a position to impose his or her views of what is "good for" the analysand, an alienated situation that is paradigmatic of how a subject is constituted from the start. Since there are no guarantees that an analyst will not yield to the narcissistic pleasure of being the one who knows, Lacan elaborated an ethics of psychoanalysis to at least name the forces in play. "The transference is the point at which the analyst as signifier becomes the object of the analysand's desire," Grigg writes. Moreover, the analyst is not external to the analysand's unconscious, as Freud thought, but internal to it. Miller concludes that reference to the analyst, like reference to nonentities produced in language, is the same act. You always lose something, whether referring to something or someone, Miller says. If the root of the referent is creation, it is not surprising, then, that the goal of language is simply to replace what is lost, again and again. Loss is indeed the human *cause*. Moreover, the first creation is lack, itself created co-simultaneous with language's nullification of the referent. That is, lack is created in the very act of someone's trying to express something. And that which is not assimilated into language constitutes an order(ing) of the real.

In "Truth Arises from Misrecognition" Slavoj Žižek points out that the unconscious is made up of imaginary fixations. Thus, symptoms or the real—meaningless traces not assimilated into language that, nonetheless, constitute a return of the repressed as effects preceding their cause—can only be deciphered retroactively through imaginary relations: i.e. transference. "Truth" is the symbolic meaning given imaginary fixations in analysis, a knowledge constituted after the fact. In this Lacanian sense, actualizing the unconscious means putting ourselves into the future, not the past as post-Freudians claim. But, Žižek points out, we can only constitute this rewriting of history by supposing that the Other already knows and by believing that we are discovering this. An internal condition of truth, then, is the logic of the error of believing ourselves to have gone astray somewhere. "Truth," which Žižek describes as the *supposed* right way, is constituted through misrecognition, through the illusion proper to the transference that produces the meaning of a symptom. Žižek emphasizes a stunning Lacanian find. In trying to evade our destinies, we provoke them. The unconscious, the *Unbewusste* is a *bévue*, an oversight, an overlooking of the coinciding of truth with our own path toward it. The imaginary fantasies that guide our lives themselves have the structure of paradox.

The real was first named by Lacan as a palpable order of effects which persist in language and being although it lacks in imaginary-symbolic language consciousness. Entering the world as negativity, the real introduces disorder, then disappears, or as Millers says, if reference is finally reference to the void, it will necessarily be linked to creation. Henry Sullivan queries the issue of a void in being and knowing when he asks how desire as lack gives rise to *homo loquens* in some creative moment when man became a symbolic animal? How does a speaking animal go from uttering sounds and fragments to speaking discourses in one fell swoop, as if by magic? At the end of Section I, Ellie Ragland-Sullivan picks up Miller's question—"Much Ado About What?"—to contend that the "about what" is the divide between the sexes, a difference which exists only as an effect of the real Lacan called the phallus, not as a biological or moral necessity. Indeed, the burden of this difference carries with itself the anxiety of the drives. It is impossible for humans not to fall into the fissure made up of lures and gaps that surround the sexual difference.

If a simple divide between the sexes were the issue in the constitution of subjects, as Jacqueline Rose has argued, or if differences were only accretions of signifying traits as post-structuralist feminists maintain, there would be little "ado" about this difference. Lacan locates its limit in psychosis, where the lack of a founding signifier for identity means there is no innate myth for gender identity either. Not only does a person lose his or her name in a psychotic episode, this person also loses the imaginary myths that constitute an illusion of having or being one gender or the other. Neither everyday bi-sexual confusions or choices, nor the relation of the "drives" to a kind of normative polymorphous perversity, is available to the psychotic who lacks a founding signifier to provide the "necessary fiction" of a harmonious relation among being, body, language, desire and *jouissance*. The torment of being transsexual—neither clearly male nor female— unveils the grotesque effects of psychosis as a lack of knowledge. The psychotic does not know his or her gender clearly enough to lean upon that knowledge as the basis of an identity, not even as the basis of an either/or gender choice. In psychosis the parts do not cohere in any viable imaginary unity one might call a negotiable self symbol. Instead, delusional reformulations of the universe bring agony and despair, often suicide, rather than the supposedly joyful pleasure to be found on *mille plateaux* in an imaginary poetic weave of being to language and sexuality.

Ragland-Sullivan takes Lacan's picture of the unconscious—an effect produced by the culturally imposed divide between the sexes— to mean that the masculine, the signifier of difference *qua* difference, is itself an excess. The feminine is a name, not for woman, but for a reminder that something is missing in its opposite, the masculine. Feminine and masculine are used here to refer to traits, not to men or women. While the masculine masquerades around the feminine and vice-versa, men (normatively speaking insofar as norm means the greater number) masquerade around Woman, man's symptom. Woman is man's symptom of a refusal to believe he is not whole. As such, Woman bears the projection of man's essentialized unconscious fantasy. In "Truth Arises from Misrecognition" Slavoj Žižek unveils the symptom at work in culture to argue that totalitarian power is feminine, in the sense that *jouissance* is the fading beyond meaning *qua* logos that Lacan calls Woman. Ragland-Sullivan follows Marie-Hélène Brousse's "Feminism With Lacan" from the May 1989, Kent State, Ohio Conference on "Lacan, Discourse, and Politics," to say there is no feminine in the real of *jouissance* because such transgression of law will always pertain to the masculine, to the *père-version* that disturbs the feminine in culture. If there is no signifier for Woman, Ragland-Sullivan suggests, there is no place for man. The feminine (not correlated with women) is an identity position which will always interrogate loss while the masculine will reject or deny it. Žižek's and Ragland-Sullivan's essays, therein, open new vistas to a cultural critique of the patriarchy and to current theories of aggression, both personal and political.

Far from the binarist or phallocrat that feminists have accused Lacan of being, Ragland-Sullivan argues that he shows the precise building blocks of patriarchy in three linked, but differing, orders of knowing, being and affect. These are knotted (or not) to produce a fourth order of the symptom under the bias of sexuality. Colette Soler links the symptom to the sexual relation, to show the symptom as itself a denial of the reality or the truth of Lacan's axiom: there is no underlying symbol of symmetrical opposition adequate to the making of a sexual *relation*. Insofar as there is no signifier for sexual relationship, this particular foreclosure in the symbolic returns in the real of the symptom. Herein patriarchy itself can be seen as a symptom, continually confronted and duped by Woman who is co-extensive with the question, the enigma, the sublime object, all of which smash LANGUAGE, LAW, and LOGOS. Woman mocks human myths of a smooth sexual divide, a symmetrical binary, a paradoxical possibility of limitless narrativity or rhetorical tropes, as well as the possibility of metaphysical closure along lines of a non-contradictory logic or language taken to be coherent with a subject.

Stuart Schneiderman stresses one particular feature of Lacan's theory of language. The *true* destination of most letters (*lettre/l'être*) is obliteration, the garbage can. Many messages—a message containing truth—are sent for the purpose of not being received, or at least not understood. Once messages have accomplished their signifying effect, circled the chain of desire that caused them to be emitted to start with, they are destroyed. The letter becomes litter. This, says Schneiderman, is the secret concealed between the legs of the fireplace in the guise of a fictional female nude body Lacan imposed on Edgar Allen Poe's story of *The Purloined Letter*. It is the Woman secret contained in notions such as fading, void and hole, notions that have nothing to do with the vaginal part of female anatomy. Put another way, narration—like the human ego—tries to get away from enigmas, away from the symptom, to avoid the anxiety which designates a lack. Messages of desire appear only in lapses, then, revealing symptoms as inscriptions of unaccomplished speech acts that appear only as effects in or on the body.

One may well wonder with Russell Grigg if, in analysis, a message unheard by the analysand is, then, inscribed on the analyst's body? Whatever the case may be, Grigg writes that the asymmetrical relation between symptom, other and hearing means that analysis cannot function ethically if it functions as suggestion, re-education, or advice, and this because such analytic injunctions do not engage an analysand to act on his or her own desire. In line with Grigg's thinking, Schneiderman suggests that Derrida, like some analysts, fears that something might be *spoken* that would require him to act. By reading the Poe story as a dramatization of words spoken (or not), Lacan demonstrates a staple of his teaching; that action is always in accord (or disaccord) with desire. Whether the desire is admitted to, rationalized, denied, idealized, or whatever, Lacan's interest in the Poe story concerns desire. He did not look to this story out of interest in the purloined letter *qua* letter, nor to guess at the letter's contents. Rather the actual letter was a signifier, moving from place to place, leaving an impact of real effects in its wake.

By linking the signifier—whose function it is to hook subjects to language, thus making a symbolic—to the proper name, Schneiderman argues that proper names are deconstructed only at the price of cancelling a person *qua* identity. If this is so, only Dupin in the Poe story is a privileged character, because only he has a proper name. The narrator is anonymous, doubling the text, says Schneiderman, as a nominalized verb. Indeed, the referent of Dupin's name becomes the purloined letter, his own note left behind in the Minister's chambers, unsigned, a message to be destroyed, itself pointing to the ultimate referent, the void. Derrida's error in his critique of Lacan's *Seminar On The Purloined Letter* resides in his claim that the "distinctive feature" of the signifier lies in that it not be an identity, but a *différence*. Not only do signifiers mark opposition, they also mark relation within opposition. Even more importantly, names refer anti-descriptively to objects. That is, whatever lies beyond descriptive features constitutes an identity or an objective correlative of a rigid designator through the retroactive effect of naming, itself a radical act.

Poe's story fascinates Lacan, most probably, because it is empty of content, laying bare the path of signifying effects that catalyze the desire to narrate as itself a defense against desire. Neither Lacan, Poe, nor Dupin seek to know what is in the letter (an imaginary fiction). Rather, the story demonstrates how suspicion destabilizes the illusion of social continuity in a fiction, as in life. The female body the narration wants to cover up is the ego we all try to hide behind, lest we reveal to ourselves or others the fragility of wanting, with its attendant and potentially dissatisfying, unsettling effects. We read for the purpose of identifying with proper names. Even fictional proper names designate rigidly, Schneiderman says. We do not read for purposes of falling into a superego abyss where Law is the Derridean command to ENJOY WRITING. In surveying the Minister's Chambers, Dupin triumphs by looking to see what is not there. Like Dupin, we also look beyond our identification with character names in reading, to seek a piece of desire in a fiction, an object *a*, even a lost part of our own bodies. Put another way, we seek an exit from identification with our own imaginary signifiers.

Russell Grigg's paper addresses many of Schneiderman's concerns, but in terms of identificatory transference with an analyst, not transference to the proper name in a textual fiction. In analysis, desire becomes attached to the analyst's person, or to the signifier "analyst" who stands in for the Other as a place of knowledge posited within the transference relation. But one cannot transfer onto a text, except by remaining attached to one's own imaginary signifiers, Grigg says, pointing out that Lacan departs from Freud on this issue. Lacan searched for why repetition blocks memories rather than insisting, as did Freud, on the similarities in various forms of repetition such as transference, resistance, and so on. In Lacan's hands, Freud's diverse forms of transference become suppositions that assume or presume a subject who "knows". Grigg emphasizes the link between love and knowledge, pointing out that transference love arises out of a structure where one person talks to another person whom he or she does not know, making the demands of transference love automatic, not particular as are the demands of love in everyday life. Grigg, Apollon and Kalinich maintain that, given such a context, any analyst who believes he or she "knows" what is good for the analysand will create textual mirrors that may quickly turn into fascistic (rather than objective or correct) interpretations, indeed, into indoctrination. At the very least one confronts the alienating effects of suggestion where another's desire tries to take the place of one's own.

But just as "correct interpretations" of texts are thought to exist, so do supposedly correct ideologies arise in relation to powerful leaders who command group identification on the side of superego authority. Grigg reminds us that wherever the superego reigns, it reigns in tandem with the death drive. Unlike post-Freudians who take the superego as adaptive reality, Lacanians see it as enjoying obscenely. An agent of repression cannot undo repression, Grigg argues. For example, the social weight of institutions—where time is money—is removed when time boundaries of an analytic session are focused on what is said, rather than on the time of the ritual. Lacan's analytic goal was not narcissistic, Grigg maintains, but a desire to modify the ego/narration—whose fixity makes it an agent of resistance—by helping an analysand address desire instead. Willy Apollon also points out that the resolution of transference affects is a secondary, not a primary, effect of analytic interpretation.

In the determination of what the "Ways, Means, and Ends" of analysis are, Jacques-Alain Miller says the *means* are speech. But this produces a paradoxical meaning. The means of analysis are speech that cannot be verified or satisfied by material evidence. The only internal coherence in analysis occurs, rather, through gauging the coherence and inconsistency of speech. The *ways* of analysis lead to its ends, Miller says—hysteria, obsession, phobias—all curable by analytic results that lift inhibitions, increase pleasure, cause the disappearance of symptoms. But the how is the mystery of all this, how analysis can affect libidinal displacement—surplus *jouissance*—through speech. In hysteria, for example, thought is paralyzed. In obsession, mental illusions persist. How can speech unload the rifts of *jouissance* ore that paralyze an hysteric's language? How can speech convince the obsessional he need not split hairs infinitesimally in order to avoid imaginary punishment for the unbearable crime of being wrong? Nonetheless, speech, transference, interpretation and maneuver are all tools of analysis, not "scientific" theories used in a supposed correction of behavior or biology. Willy Apollon pushes the significance of the analyst's responsibility all the way to the potential for enduring the horror and futility of psychosis which Lacan determined as caused by language, not biology. While neurosis is concerned with the Other's desire, Apollon says psychosis must treat of the Other's *jouissance*; that behind the symptom which is made up of unspoken words or things too traumatic to inscribe in the Other, which indeed tell the story of efforts to annul the Other and erace traces of past *jouissance*.

Echoing Ragland-Sullivan and Henry Sullivan, Apollon brings the matter of what *causes* psychosis back to the cultural injunction to identify with sexual difference itself. To learn and live sexual difference operates a madness on everyone, a madness we try to negotiate with words. Sociological forces do not repress us, Apollon says, but rather our encounters with sexuality. Divided between demands addressed to others (a subject position) and answers awaited from others (an object position), any subject is divided by loss itself insofar as loss is caught up in the drive. The innovative point made by Apollon is that for a psychotic, not only for a neurotic, the analyst's presence guarantees that speaking into a void has a meaning, even before the analysand knows that speaking will open onto truth about his or her desire.

It becomes clear in Apollon's essay that Lacan parts company with post-Freudian analysts and literary critics, not only by viewing listening and speaking as acts—whether spoken or written—but in seeing them as asymmetrical acts. If the analyst does *not* answer questions, the question will become the structure of all questions: what does the Other want of me? The analysand will begin to act out (of) his or her own answer and only then will be able to constitute a new path—new desires—as a way of walking away from an old path that offered irresolvable impossibilities.

Unlike post-Freudian analysis where the analysand is supposed to learn something new from the analyst, Lacan saw analysis as ending in a paradox. That is, it ends after transference, only when the analysand refuses the analyst as an answer, a master signifier supposed to know. Echoing Schneiderman, Apollon points to the power of the symbolic order consequences of language effects that show up as ambivalent, opaque desire; desiring effects that seem not nearly so reliable as the knowledge one has or can glean from another. Yet desire has the structure of language. It can, therefore, be deconstructed and reconstructed. The end of a Lacanian analysis for a neurotic requires a placing of limits on the Other's desires. On the contrary, analysis ends for a psychotic when signifiers are added, not subtracted, and when body images are remade. Only in those ways can any limit to the Other's *jouissance* be installed.

Apollon's essay is a passionate attack on the biological materialistic theories that inform most of contemporary Western thought. Following Lacan's teaching, Apollon argues that the effects of *jouissance* are written on the body as meaning, not as organic causes or effects. Invaded by an excluded *jouissance* with which he or she identifies in a delusional state out of efforts to stop up the hole in being/knowing, a psychotic is submitted directly to the real, which has returned bearing the concrete realities of the death drive. Indeed, psychotics often destroy themselves in order to destroy their past: to destroy the Other from which they cannot bear to live. Here the body—as separate from the biological organism—is an exquisite writing where time and space are intertwined with voices and gazes, voices that arise from the lack in the Other and wander through language, carrying the charge of *jouissance*. Language guarantees neutrality, distance, a consistency to being, a consistency of meaning, of speech acts, of ideals and descriptions of events. This normative consistency disappears when the psychotic confronts the lack of an identifying signifier for a proper name and for a gender identity. Although most children and adolescents question the foundation of law in questioning authority (a signifier for a father's name), the psychotic lives the destitution of having no law, no name that gives him the illusion of being a singular (whole) identity, i.e., one who differs from the others. Foreclosure of an identifying signifier for name (lineage), for a rigid designator, opens onto the void which Jacques-Alain Miller calls the referent of language itself. Living within the void, the psychotic has no recourse to the distance Lacan translated by the social. He or she lives in a no man's land.

Judith Miller opens the section on "Language and the Subject of Literature" by turning upside down Buffon's famous Enlightenment dictum: "Style is the man himself". Just as Lacan's rethinking of representation makes of the image a cover over the void, so does Judith Miller's depiction of style as the "thing" itself destroys the apparent, transparent meaning of this phrase—long cited by thinkers, chic dressers and aesthetes—as being self-explanatory. Judith Miller shows how Lacan's rethinking of this *bon mot* takes us in the opposite direction from Michel Foucault's thinking. People do not, as Foucault opines, invent a self that they in turn control or master. Rather, one's style is determined by one's response to the Other's gaze, the Other being extrinsic to a subject *qua* subject.

Although Buffon tried to invent an adequate image of creation by fashioning language around nature, Judith Miller speaks of the inadequacy of language to describe nature or creation. Because language is linear, it is limited by its own nature. Literary texts and their interpretations, like Buffon's gardens, dwell under the gaze of whatever authorities support them, *as if* they were imaginary signifiers to be approved or disapproved, supposed bodies of totalized unity and perpetuity, like the *Académie française* whose very insufficiency to itself Buffon explodes by the paradox of giving it body through the idealizing, distorting mirror of speech.

Judith Miller's conclusion constitutes a surprise. The object *a* occupies the place of man in Lacan's definition of style. Man becomes the idealizing, judgmental object *a* Lacan called the gaze. But what is this object *a* we might seek *in* a garden, in an address to an august body, or in a fiction? Slavoj Žižek explains Lacan's idea that the surplus in an object *a*—that which stays the same as an irreducible kernel—positivizes discontinuity in reality insofar as the signifier has already constituted the object itself. If the signifier constitutes the object, then the signifier also locates or designates what a subject is. A subject, says Žižek, is *the failure of substance* in the process of self-constitution. Similarly, Russell Grigg points out that the subject of the signifier is dead: $. The subject is spoken about as *hypokeimenon*, lived as the object *a* at the level of *jouissance* ($◊ *a*). This "function" occurs through unarticulated and unarticulable fundamental fantasies whose paradoxical goal is to hold onto *jouissance*; to hold onto death. By burying one's head in the sand one can hide in language and, thus, avoid confronting the real of the already constituted—thus recognizable—excess in *jouissance*.

In varying ways, Apollon, Kalinich and Žižek all argue that the object, whether the *a* Lacan called the gaze or another *petit a*, cannot be destroyed in life or in analysis. Signifying chains circle around an irreducible kernel, ensuring that there be no "post" to any moment or movement in language, no Abrahamian, Torokian final textual solution coincident with one phoneme ineluctably slipping into another. The object *a* intervenes to make discontinuities of phonemes, and of idealized self-fictions as well. Kalinich points to the quintessential object *a*, death itself. Calling into question "Derrido-Lacanian" cryptographers, Kalinich's particular target are the analysts Nicolas Abraham and Maria Torok. For Abraham and Torok Freud's Wolf-Man case is a text driven not only by the *Stoff* of old-fashioned Freudianism: castration anxiety, primal scene, obsessional neurosis, and so on, but also by phoneme traces—the Derridean mark—that melt finally into noise.

In Kalinich's view, the point of Abraham's and Torok's game is to experience the joy of finding new wine for old bottles; to retain the old-fashioned Freudian reading while dressing it up in contemporary Derridean clothes. Pankiev's sister becomes the desired sex object, not his mother, and so on. No "instinctual" id is in question, just phonemes charting a path to the meaning of the Wolf-Man's neurosis: "Come Sis, rub me". The Canadian analyst and literature professor Patrick Mahony likes the bridge Abraham and Torok build between a classical-drive-theory Freud and the language Freud used to describe this case. Indeed, Mahony has argued that Freud and Pankiev shared important signifiers (signifiers thought of à la Saussure as acoustic sounds). Kalinich points out that Mahony uses Abraham and Torok to propose a "supposed" Lacanian theory of readability regarding analytic classics; "Supposed" because all three analysts read in terms of a conservative Saussurean theory of the signifier, not only misunderstanding Lacan's redefinition of the signifier away from the idea of alphabetical letter or acoustic sound, but also missing Lacan's clinical find. The phoneme is itself an Ur-object of desire, part of the pre-specular real that lines the subject, making of voice a writing *in* language, rather than of LANGUAGE a WRITING of voice.

Kalinich's contribution to Wolf-Man scholarship shows the advances made in Lacanian analysis over other theories that take language into account, by tying it to praxis. Kalinich not only convincingly shows the numerous errors in Russian that led Abraham and Torok astray in their efforts to decipher the Wolf-Man's desires in a phonemic text, but also addresses another issue in this case hotly debated since Freud's day. Was the Wolf-Man neurotic or psychotic? Rather than link up phonemes in a supposed literal decrypting of sexual desire, Kalinich argues that one can follow Lacanian theory on psychosis to read the Wolf-Man case differently. If phonemes for the actual father's name are found in even one signifying chain that makes up the Other—even in phonemic elision—Pankiev had to have been neurotic, she says. Repression triumphs over foreclosure of the symbolic father. Her reasoning is the following: if the symbolic father has no place in the Other, then no substitute (no movement of metaphor) can occupy his place. Kalinich's discovery that Pankiev's own proper name is a Cyrillic version of *Wespe* and of the word for the son of God—Pankiev who was deeply rooted in beliefs of the Russian Orthodox Church—leads her to argue that Pankiev has an identificatory place as a son of God the father inscribed in the Other. As such he is a Name, not just a phoneme. Yet one may ask whether signifying as a spiritual son is the same as identifying with a symbolic father. Interpreting texts—to learn whether Pankiev was psychotic or neurotic, for instance—can only occur under the aegis of our own illusions that in mastering a text, we master death, Kalinich concludes.

Whether or not Kalinich is correct in thinking phonemic elisions could constitute a rigid designator, a signifier for the name of a father, her arguments could be linked to Žižek's discussion of associative series. Rereading Hegel à la Lacan to show Hegel searching for a lawlike series arising from apparent lawlessness, Žižek emphasizes Lacan's discovery that external exclusions are internal to the Other itself. That is, one *both* misses the truth *and* it can only arise from misrecognition. The Other's defects reveal one's own subjective position; i.e. our secrets lie—not in any other's knowledge—but in our own desires. So, we are a part of the Other's games, a reflexive determination of the Other. In this sense the Other, nonetheless, exists insofar as we overlook it, do not give it *esse*, refuse to acknowledge the obvious; that nothing—our speech, our being, our desires—comes from nothing. But if the Other *qua* repository of missing material is absent, a deadend, then what has Lacan left analysts or epistemologists that is new?

Žižek points to Lacan's discovery that the only findable absolute in psychoanalysis concerns the particular logic of a given subject's enjoyment. Beyond the deceptive lures of the Other is the *plus-de-jouir* which appears as a negativity or discontinuity in human *Umwelten* where positivity always comes from imaginary consistencies. Too much knowledge about the *anderer Schauplatz* suggests that we might lose our very beings insofar as such knowledge requires abolishment of the only "substance" Lacan recognized: *jouissance*. Working with anecdotes, historical events, anything at hand, Žižek argues that not only does truth arise from misrecognition, but *the symptom is the real*. The fascination of speaking about the wrecked Titanic lies, for example, in a *jouissance* symptomatic of the "more in us than us" lured by the death that resides in us as an irreducible kernel of pain and enigma. This, says Žižek, is an answer to those who ask why there is something rather than nothing, even if the something is the enigma of a symptom? This nothing binds our *jouissance* to a certain meaning of being-in-the-world. When this comes unbound, the world (and word) quite literally come apart. Lacanian analysis ends when an analysand identifies with the real of his symptom as the support of his being; a kind of "I am this, but you need not be."

Žižek insists on the hard Lacanian truth, a truth that dismantles the title of this collection of essays. Not only does the given world of objects not exist, neither do language, nor the subject. Only the symptom confers a consistency to things, thereby implying the Other as a complete system containing its meaning. Žižek argues that post-structuralism can never succeed in its efforts to dissolve every substantial identity into a network of differential relations because the symptom, penetrated with *jouissance*, will always remain as a real kernel. It remains as the necessary counterpoint where differential language play is structured around bodily *jouissance*. The alternative reality to post-structuralist dissemination is, then, the burden of language with which we must, nonetheless, live, in tandem with the heaviness of the real that the symbolic, imaginary and symptom continually negotiate.

Yet people cling to the symptom at all costs because its *jouissance* organizes the suffering in which they believe. The symptom is mythologized, allegorized and enshrined in religious myths, in nationalist myths, in biological myths, in egoistic narratives. Lacan saw discourse as structured from and around the fantasy which opposes the symptom. Even though the fantasy is inert, blocked, barred inconsistency, it nonetheless, fills out the void in the Other. But the fantasy remains unanalyzable. The symptom, by contrast, overtakes itself on the way to its own interpretation, and so can be analyzed as a signifying formation with the independent existence Lacan wrote as ex-sistence. Yet as we interpret our symptoms, lovingly, we cannot do so except by traversing the fantasy we hide at all costs, the fundamental fantasy which masks our symptoms and blocks the movement of interpretation. Not only do we *not* wish to lift our masks to see our fundamental fantasies as illusions, neither do we want to let the symptom go, to let it "fall" as Lacan says. Because the *jouissance* to which it gives rise is the only positive support of our being. Its seeming consistency, which Lacan called a *semblant*, helps us all avoid madness. Žižek points to Lacan's conclusion that truth and *jouissance* are, however, radically incompatible. And truth is preferable, engaging as it does, the ethics of psychoanalysis. But paradoxically, truth can only open up through our misrecognition of the thing—the object *a*—that embodies our impossible *jouissances*.

Colette Soler's dense essay concludes the section on "Lacan and the

Subject of Literature" that ends the book. Explaining Lacan's reversal of Freud's position on art, Soler points out that while Freud applied psychoanalysis to art works, Lacanian analysis cannot be "applied" to artistic texts insofar as *they* are not products of the unconscious. Picking up a theme which runs throughout the first and third sections of this book—that of creation—Soler argues that creation works with the object *a*, while interpretation comes from the unconscious. After a critic has exhausted psychobiography, a piece of art still remains; novel and enigmatic. Why do we read, look, listen? Because, Soler answers, language has a hold on the symptom, itself an invention that imposes itself on the body. Like the symptom, literature is an invention that interpretation will not change, If interpretation does not give the truth of a work, nor change its language or life, then what does it do? It is social, Soler says, joining ego discourses where thinking and bodily feelings *can* be changed by speech. The text can lead to love (hate) and desire.

But interpretation does more. Insofar as literary creation brings something into place, thus marking the place it creates as empty, interpretation responds to that loss, to the empty set. Thus, no Lacanian reading of a text would search for an originally lost object. Rather a Lacanian reading would play on the lack which always pushes humans to seek objects. Why "objects"? Because all subjects are fixed by the enjoyment of their symptoms, a *jouissance* that makes them singular, limited by the particular "object" fixities which stand as a limit, as an exception to the infinite ciphering of the unconscious. While Freud thought symptoms revealed libidinal satisfactions engendered by fantasies—compromise formations where the repressed returned—Lacan argued that if something can be de-ciphered, it was formed in the first place and, thus, has the same nature as language (substitution, referent, etc.). Yet symptoms are not easily deciphered because they bear the inertia of the marriage of signifier to fantasy. Nonetheless, "literature" beckons us because it serves as a *jouissance* vehicle. Moreover, literature provides a *jouissance* of meaning *per se*— meaning that speaks a strange truth. The creator is one who has no "good enough" father, and only retains imaginary consistency by making meaning (something novel or dramatic) and by working with the real outside meaning (symptoms). And poetry differs. There *jouissance* plays on the literal level, subverting intention. Like analysis, literature operates by *sens*, that is, by an implied meaning that stands outside grammar proper. Each new artistic creation, like the end of each analysis, produces an invention; a new symptom.

I

Lacan and the
Subject of Language

1

Language: Much Ado About What?

Jacques-Alain Miller

That's a sentence with a question mark. As a matter of fact, it could be an interrupted sentence: much ado about what happened yesterday, what might happen tomorrow. You know how prominent interrupted sentences were in the experience of the distinguished late President Schreber. But "Much Ado About What?" is not an interrupted sentence. It is a question. It is a question about what? The answer would be: It is a question about what. Danielle Bergeron just some minutes ago asked, "What are you going to speak about?" I told her: About "what." Which is not very informative. That is a question mark, which is a queer sign. In Spanish, which is the language and literature taught by Henry Sullivan who will speak later, you use two question marks, one being an inverted question mark. And if I had answered Danielle Bergeron in Spanish, probably I would have put this Spanish sign there to say in an unambiguous manner: "I am speaking about language. Language is much ado. And the question is much ado about what?" But the clearer point of the question is that there is much ado about language itself.

I have been speaking now for about five minutes and I imagine you wonder, what is he talking about? You are wondering what I am talking about in spite of the fact that—I believe, I hope, I am sure—you understand every sentence that I have said. Am I right? That is to say, you may understand every sentence I say, even if my English is not perfect, but that does not mean you know what I am aiming at. You understand what I say because it is in English, more or less, so in effect you understand the literal meaning. You may even see that there is for me much ado in that I am moving my body: there is some energy there. You know it is not my own language, but you do not have what we may eventually call the contextual meaning, what I am aiming at. That is an experience which is, I believe, fairly familiar at such a conference. That is, you listen to speakers who look like they understand themselves, and you understand them because it is English, but at the same time you may nonetheless wonder, what was the speaker aiming at? So eventually you may come to a point where you say, "Aha! That's what he had in mind!" That is, sometimes you get this meaning of aiming at from the supposed literal meaning.

We can say that this difference is very present, very obvious in every human communication. We might say it is the difference between literal meaning and textual meaning. We could also say with the philosopher Paul Grice that it is the difference between what the words mean and what the speaker means with his words on a given occasion. And we might even distinguish between the semantic reference and the speaker's reference. When you introduce this distinction into the logical analysis of language, you have already introduced something very complex. As a matter of fact, you have introduced the difference between signifier and signified, and more than that, between signifier and signification.

When a sentence goes on, and a whole discourse goes on, or let us say when a chain of signifiers goes on, it would be fine if this language were doubled exactly at the same time by signification. It would be very fine if a constant relationship existed between a chain of signifiers and a supposed chain of signifieds. That would be a valuable relationship: the marriage of signifier and signified.

What we know is that, on the contrary, meaning has a sense of aiming. But actual meaning lags behind the letter of aim. And the way meaning works is not better, or clearer. It leaves you in the dark. For instance, perhaps you understand just a little better what I am aiming at now. But it is still lagging behind. It is better that meaning lag behind a bit, however. It is much more boring when meaning is ahead, when you can anticipate, even before someone has begun to talk, what he or she is aiming at. And you know, when you already know what he is aiming at, you do not pay attention. Sometimes, in spite of my personal quest for clarity of thinking, I like to delay the understanding effect a bit. In the analytic experience—because all that I have said refers to an analytic experience—you have no idea of what the patient means by what he or she says. And even if you have some idea, it is better to forget it, better not to understand or believe you understand a single word. You have no idea of what your patient is aiming at, and he comes to see you because he does not know what he is aiming at in behavior that could be strange even to himself, in the strange things that happen to him with some participation from himself.

So in an analytic experience you suspend the connection between signifier and signified. You keep them separate. If your would-be patient says "depression," which is a common word, you are not quick to translate the depression of this patient into what another means by depression. Or if he says "love," you immediately translate the use of that word precisely for only one subject. For instance, love means fucking for one person, but for another, love explicitly means not fucking. You can discover this only after some time. The obsessive patient will help you to understand what he is saying, if you spend a lot of time, take much trouble, and go to much ado to clarify what he says, what it is all about. And he clarifies all the more when what he is aiming at becomes even more obscure for himself. And that is why—precisely because he is lost in what he is aiming at—he generally takes aim at one or another of his fellow creatures. Aiming at one's fellow creature is a shortcut in this search for what one is aiming at.

But, let us get back after this little introduction to "much ado about what." Perhaps we could write it as a pre-logical sentence, a sentence with a hole inside. Much ado about "x." This leaves a place for substitution, for trying out some answers. It is already a logical form. We could write Fx, the capital letter F being a summary of the expression, "much ado about." We are going to try some different answers, very simple answers, to this hole in the sentence.

I believe there is an answer which is already in everybody's mind, because we all hear it: Shakespeare's comedy. There is a sentence that is already lexicalized for you, which is one possible answer. One possible value of "x" is, as you know, nothing. Since I am advancing a theory that language is much ado about nothing, and I intend to consider this Shakespearean text, I would like also to talk about "ado." "Ado" is a wonderful word, which is a contraction of "at-do," which means "to do," but in a contracted way: dealing, concern, trouble, labor, fuss, exertion, or *le souci*, that by which someone is occupied or pre-occupied. And generally it is as occupied and pre-occupied that someone comes to the analyst.

I

But before getting to this value where x equals nothing, let us first take a simple answer. Because the idea that language is much ado about nothing is not the first idea one has. The first idea one has may be: it is about something. Perhaps we could give as a first answer: it is about noting. And as a matter of fact, there is a literary critic, Richard Grant White, who noted in 1958 that in the phonetic pronunciation of Elizabethan England, "nothing" and "noting" sounded much the same. So we believe that in the very title of Shakespeare's play there is a pun, a play between "nothing" and "noting." And you find, in fact, various puns on "nothing" and "noting" in *Much Ado About Nothing*.

So that is the first idea: language is for denoting. That is, language is chiefly referential language. Language is here among us to help us express our thought, but chiefly to indicate the right way to someone else, to direct someone to the object we have in mind. As in: "Bring me this!" And supposedly, in this imperative use of language, I have to select an object in the external world so that someone can bring this object to me without ambiguity. But to have no ambiguity, you would need targeting in the word itself, and it would be something like: "Bring me item number three," as they say during the judicial process. The very object is already targeted in a way that disambiguates the use of language. So let us say—I shall not expand on this point, which is the clearest of points—language is for reference, for referential use.

That is not to say that in psychoanalysis we have no use for referential language. Surely we have. For instance, a main topic of psychoanalysis is the question of how to give appointments. If you do not give appointments—and with some success, without ambiguity—then there will be no analytic session. And the topic of appointment—that is, how after an analytic session, to bring back, I would say, the use of referential language—is always a very delicate matter. When you say "Come back," you may solve the problem by having an unmovable timetable, so that you will never again have to give another appointment, because it will all be set up for seven years. But generally, that is not the case.

So analysts also have a use for referential language. And we might wonder, in that case, what the reference is. What is the object that has to be met? The object is the analyst himself. He has to use language to enable the other to meet him, and that is why he moves very little. When he moves himself to go for a holiday to another country, it is the main topic of the sessions. The analysand is awaiting the reference. For this reason one needs the analyst as a reference in the analytic process. That is why analysands talk so much about him. Because he is in some way the reference of the analytic process. That is why there is so much ado, so much concern about the analyst. And in this way, for the obsessional subject, it is very important that the analyst not move. Sometimes if he merely speaks, it is too much. The demand that the analyst be lifeless can be understood in this way. For the hysterical subject, on the contrary, to make him move, to make the immovable reference move, is a goal, and that is why eventually the hysterical subject will give much ado to the analyst about himself and will try to elicit a testimony that there is life in that subject.

Since, in some sense, the analyst *is* the reference of the analytic process, he may take a very simple way of interpreting what the patient says. No matter what the patient tries to say, the analyst can always say: "You are aiming at me. You are speaking of nothing else than me." That is transference interpretation. Transference interpretation gives the solution to the question of interpretation, an instant know-how for would-be analysts: for any references the patient is presenting you, always substitute yourself as a reference, and you will never err. I am not recommending that. I am trying to show how the idea can occur.

So in this first answer to the question, we suppose that language is an apparatus, a machine, a tool for reference. And what must be said is that in the philosophy of language—which is in your country, as in Great Britain, the mainstream of philosophy—language is considered, is analyzed, chiefly as an apparatus, a machine, a tool for reference. And there is some truth in seeing language as a tool for reference. In our language, in the discourse of the master—that is what I demonstrated in the example of the imperative—the necessity of disambiguation is a necessity. To give orders, or even to make people produce—and thus for the management of production—it is all a question of mastering the ambiguities of language such that the employee will know exactly what he has to do. Language seen as a tool for reference takes on all its meanings in the discourse *of* the master *for* the master.

(Something really curious to understand is how the Japanese have mastered the disambiguation of language so well, when there are many more possibilities for ambiguity in their tongue than in ours.)

But what we learn through those who analyze language as a tool for reference is precisely that it is not such a good machine for reference. If language were really a tool dedicated to reference, the conclusion would be: it does not fit. If we spoke in quantification language, in quantification logic, then everything would be fine. But on the contrary, when you read a logical analysis of language, what you find on every page is, on the contrary, misunderstanding, and pages and pages are written about various misunderstandings and how to resolve them.

As a matter of fact, a true master does not take so much time to disambiguate language. Think of Napoleon who said that a good drawing is better than a long discourse. A true master does not take time to speak. He shows by the famous ostentation gesture what you have to do. So there is a connection between referentiality and mastery. Indeed,if time is money, space is also money. Everything has to be in a true or precise place, for instance, to be fetched.

II

And so the analysis of language, which is now dominant in your country, can be said to have begun with Bertrand Russell in 1905 with the theory of description, the same year as the "Three Essays on the Theory of Sexuality" by Freud. Russell sought to disambiguate language, considered as a tool for reference, along the line of Gottloeb Frege. At that time Russell said in so many words: "I use Frege to disambiguate language." That is, what problem do you come to at the very moment you try to figure language as a tool for reference? Immediately—that is in 1905—you see the problem: that you can speak of something that does not exist. The obvious problem is, as a matter of fact (this is not a contrived Lacanian trick), that there are empty, vacuous descriptions in language. You know the example of Russell, which he pondered about so much; a short text which is really the father of all philosophical literature in your country since then. His example was: "The King of France is bald." The sentence, "The King of France is bald," retains all its meaning for an Englishman. Englishmen know about France very well, and about the political regime of France.

When you are an analyst you always give more weight to the example than to what the rule is. I could expand a lot on Russell's "The King of France is bald.." As a matter of fact, it is a double example; not only does the King of France not exist, his hair does not exist either. So the example has something to do with the idea that the King is naked, or the Emperor has no clothes. That is clear. He is not only without a crown, he is also without hair. So he could say, "My kingdom for my hair," but never mind . . .

I have been talking for quite a while about this King of France who does not exist. You can do that. It is an example of what Russell immediately encountered: that in language, you can have much ado about nothing. And in this case, you are speaking about something, in the saying of it, as you would speak about the President of the United States who exists. But by the form of the sentence language does not enable you to know if what you are referring to exists or not.

So there comes disambiguation; that is to say, trying to do things with language, such as in an electric game where you know you have to give answers. So you pull the plug and put it inside the game, and either a red light or green light goes on to tell you whether your answer is true or not. Well, the effort to make a logical analysis of language is to get to that. That is what Rudolf Carnap tried with Martin Heidegger in the same way. He believed that if he translated the sentence by Heidegger logically, he could ascertain that it did not mean anything.

So that is the first conclusion you come to, not with psychoanalysis, but with a logical analysis of language: that language produces reference to nonentities. And that is why, for instance, an adversary of Russell's who is called Alexius Meinong had the idea of distinguishing two categories of objects—objects which exist and objects which do not exist—to extend a bit our ontology. He even had the idea that all those objects which did not exist could be situated in the null set, i.e., were like the population of the null set.

The whole philosophical logical analysis of language is grounded on nothing other than errors of reference. This philosophy breeds on errors of reference. For instance, I have here a text by Saul Kripke that Stuart Schneiderman has given me. That is the kind of problem you find inside this text, a problem advanced by Keith Donnellan. Suppose someone at a gathering, glancing in a certain direction, says to his companion: "The man over there drinking champagne is happy tonight". Suppose both the speaker and hearer are under a false impression and, rather, that the man to whom they refer is a teetotaler drinking sparkling water. Not drinking champagne, but drinking water. That is an example of the kind of problem Kripke and Donnellan refer to.

So it is a plague with language, the fact that language which is supposedly meant to refer to things generally fails to. In fact, you have to use very stringent means to obtain a clear univocal reference through language. The most intelligent of logicians clearly has the notion that reference is not at all primary within language. Willard Van Orman Quine does not have the idea, for instance, that the child saying "milk"—or someone showing the child a glass of milk saying "milk"—would be the primary use of language. Quine knows well, indeed, that to say the word "milk" when looking at a glass of milk is very ambiguous. The word "milk" could signify the glass itself, or the bottom, or the table on which the glass is sitting. Or "milk" could mean: "I want to drink what is inside". Or, for instance, a child might say "milk" to refer to other liquids or other things to eat.

So, you note Quine does not entertain the idea that the chief use of language is to say "milk" when you have a glass of milk in front of you. He knows that you need a sentence. Donald Davidson, his pupil, goes further, saying you do not only need a sentence, you need all language to be able to really connect the word "milk" with the glass of milk. And even then it is not so sure you will manage it. For instance, if it is sparkling milk, there could be some discussion about whether it is milk or not. Or, for instance, people who like pure milk directly from the cow and are given pasteurized milk instead would say that *this* is not milk.

The problem is very difficult. And already you have to admit that sentences—at least sentences—are primary in semantics. That is to say—and Quine says it, not Lacan—words are dependent on sentences for their meaning. First Jeremy Bentham—and Frege himself—knew very well that you do not have any direct connection between words and reality, because words are dependent on sentences; that is, on articulation with other words. And the question of reference for some-one like Quine comes after sentences, when you get to isolate the predication of individuated words in sentences; there you can begin at the summit. You can begin to wonder if something corresponds to it. And when Quine wondered if something corresponds to it, his answer was that the reference of language is always inscrutable. That is to say, there is no way to tell what the singular terms of the language refer to. That is a thesis advanced prior to the idea of an indeterminancy in translation. This means that we ought, as Quine says, to observe the behavior of our neighbor in order to know what he means in what he says. But even the totality of behavioral evidence, actual and potential, will never enable us to ascertain with complete certainty what the referents are of what our neighbor says. Tremendous. If someone goes to Quine—not to the logical apparatus of Quine, but to those passages—one finds him completely subversive.

It is through Quine that you can get to Lacan, I would say. The conclusion of Quine's ontology, as a matter of fact, is that there is no absolute reference, only a related reference. And at the end of our quests, he says, we acquiesce in our mother tongue and take its word at face value. At the end, with language, there is a point where one must desist from one's inquiry and accept something at face value, for what it is.

III

Before Quine, Frege had already invented a simpler way to proceed. He did not get into questions concerning various references. His simplification was to say that there were two references for all language, that language was much ado about two references only: the true and the false. And he considered that a true sentence had as a reference, not the object of which we talk, but rather the truth. And a false sentence has a reference of false. There is already in Frege, then, the idea of how we can eventually simplify what the reference of language is. We may consider various objects as references, existing or not, but Frege himself considered the reference of language to be the true and the false.

Let us say that with Lacan we proceed only one page further, and already we begin to understand, perhaps, that the question of reference cannot be solved in terms of correspondence—that is, a correspondence between milk in my mouth as a word and milk in the glass as a substance. The next time "milk in my mouth" might be a drink. On the contrary, when you are at the level of sentences, what are the referents of sentences—not of names, not of words—but of sentences themselves? The problem with sentences is that some are true on some occasions. The same may be true on one occasion and false on another occasion. Quine called these "occasion sentences."

That is also Hegel's example at the beginning of *The Phenomenology of Spirit*: I say it is daylight. But when I am here at Kent, Ohio, there is no way of knowing it, because one cannot distinguish the difference between daylight and night very well in this auditorium. But let us suppose we see the daylight, and even say it is daylight. It is a true sentence. And when I speak, there is always a reference to the present. Hegel's example is very clear. You write it down, but immediately, when you write down "It is daylight," the reference evaporates because the sentence remains at the same place, with the same meaning. When the day ends and night begins, this sentence which was a true sentence grows into a false sentence. So writing has this immediate consequence in Hegel: that the reference of language evaporates. So writing is much ado. But in this sense, writing is much ado about nothing. And that is why Mallarmé, who was Hegelian, thought precisely that writing was writing about nothing—that language considered from the point of writing was in itself a dissolution of the reference, and even of the writer himself. "*La disparition elocutoire du poète*" (the elocutory disappearance of the poet) says that 19th-century literature is hounded by the idea. Flaubert wrote a book about nothing, Mallarmé a book about everything—both of them in this post-Hegelian sense of considering writing.

And so from this point of view, correspondence is not the keyword of the theory of language—not correspondence theory, but rather a disappearance theory as a theory of language. From this point on, if you extend to speech itself what is so clear when it is a question of writing, you no longer say that language expresses something. On the contrary, you say that language nullifies the referent. You say that language erases the reference. You draw the theory of language from writing as such, saying that one always speaks of what does not exist, because even if it exists, the very fact of speaking of it makes it disappear. It does not exist because you speak of it. The real is what it is, but when it is represented, expressed, referred to, connected in some way or another to language, the real begins to be what it is not.

Thus, I would say that the nullification of reference is the dialectical conclusion, the dialectical Hegelian conclusion, of language. It is fundamentally through language that negativity enters the real world. I would say that all this logical analysis of language done by people who despise Hegel illustrates this very fact: that in language you immediately introduce into the world an incredible disorder. Through language you regiment champagne drinkers and teetotalers, and wonder if they are happy or not, and so on.

That is the example Lacan gave in his first seminar. He takes the example of the elephant and says that the most important accident that happened to elephants in their lives was something they never knew: that we have the word "elephant," and that the moment we have the word "elephant" elephants begin to disappear. Because we are now killing them, systematically. We are taking aim at them. That is the aiming I am talking about: the taking aim of reference is the taking aim of suppression, of erasure of reference.

And that is why Lacan could say at the beginning of his teaching that "*le mot est la meurtre de la chose*" (the word is the murder of the thing). One does not find the quiet cohabitation of word and object as you have it in Quine. In Lacan it is, on the contrary, a relation of murder: words replace things. And it goes very fast, this replacement of things by words. It goes up to the point of *jouissance*, in that you come to the point where you enjoy words instead of enjoying things.

This position on language is not pure Lacan. I would say it is chiefly an Hegelian consideration of language. It runs through all the literature of the 19th century. In France just after the war Maurice Blanchot was the chief proponent of this position of the theory of writing where writing is fundamentally an activity in a void, creating a void. Writing is always writing in the direction of an absence. In Blanchot it takes on Heideggerian overtones. But chiefly it is an Hegelian theory which even enabled certain thinkers to criticize Heidegger, where, in fact, the topic of presence is so insistent. Perhaps you might get an idea in what I am saying that you could use for an archaeology of literary criticism such as it is practiced nowadays in the United States.

IV

Now we are decidedly in the "nothing" area. Take, for instance, as a reference, the definition of a sign by Charles Sanders Peirce, an American linguist. You know the definition: the sign represents something for someone. The difference which is hereby introduced in this schema—something, someone, and the sign—is this: an erasure of the *some*thing. It is a fundamental difference, and it establishes the sign, we could say, as an entity which replaces and erases the thing. We could write it as a metaphor $\frac{\text{sign}}{\text{thing}}$, but with this proviso: that in this metaphor, the conclusion of the metaphor is the erasure of the reference.

So what we have as a point of departure for Lacan's teaching on language, I would say, is Hegel and Saussure. That is, the disappearance of reference is taken along with the fact that sentences are primary insofar as the meaning of the word is dependent on sentences—i.e., is dependent on language—such that the word is always dependent on other words. And that is precisely the concept of articulation. When you define a sign as such in Peirce's way you have only *one* to define: a sign, something, and someone. If you take seriously the proposition that the word has a meaning only in connection with other words, you can never define just one signifier. You always define two. So the minimum of the sign is one, but the minimum of the signifier is two. You can understand the difference between sign and signifier in this sense. A sign is supposed to take its meaning from the reference. A signifier is supposed to take its meaning from another signifier. So it takes two, and the minimum of signifiers, I would say, is S_1 and S_2 which you find as such in Lacan, as simple as that.

I have listened to many questions about the concept of the symbolic order. Well, the important thing in the symbolic order is the concept of order itself: that is, a dimension, a self-contained dimension. Symbolic order has no meaning if it is not the vacuousness of reference, such that a signifier is connected to another, and in the place of the reference we can put an object with a bar which looks like the signifier of the null set.

Lacan says that language is not a code. A code is computed by the fixed correlation of signs to the reality they signify. In a *language*, on the contrary, the various signs—the signifiers—take on their value from their relation to one another. That is the meaning of symbolic order. The symbolic order is effectively a self-contained dimension and is not grounded on correspondence, but on circularity. That is, a sign is defined through other signs. And when Lacan proposes a definition of the signifier, it is a circular definition he gives: a signifier represents a subject for another signifier. That is not a true definition, because in the definition itself, you have the word to define. This circularity is very well detailed by Quine who asks: "What is an F?" If I ask what is an F, the only answer is, "An F is a G." That is the structure of all answers to all questions about a word: you define a word by another one. And Quine says, the answer makes only relative sense, a sense related to the uncritical acceptance of G. That is the foundation. But if you stop here, it is the foundation of an infinite metonymy. What is an F is a G, and a G is something else, etc.

But do not forget that this infinite metonymy is based on the primary metaphor, the primary metaphor that killed the thing, as Lacan taught. And at the basis of this there is an erasure. So you see that we have now a new ternary. We had the sign before, the something, and the someone. Now we have something else. We have one signifier (S_1) and another one that is necessary for this one to have a meaning (S_2) and we have the suppressed subject ($\$$). That is our new ternary, replacing the Peircean ternary. Moreover, we are not only saying that reference is ambiguous, we are also saying that reference is vacuous, and to speak is always to speak about nothing. That is, nothingness enters reality through language. You can say that in another way: reference is the void. But this void is created by language. That is, we replace the correspondence theory of language by a creation theory of language, the first creation being a lack, and in this sense it is a lack of all things. On this I would differ with Professor Henry Sullivan when he seems to suggest that desire as lack could be a condition of language. I agree with the importance of desire as lack, but I would say that desire as lack has language as its condition. A void would be unthinkable in the real if not for signifiers. "Creation"—first of the void by the signifier—is the key word, not "correspondence."

And more than that, generally speaking, we do not take signifiers as that which describes reality. We take signifiers as what enters the real to structure reality. That is seemingly a basic structuralist point of view. That is, it is too simple to always speak like Quine of chairs and trees when we know from anthropology that the "supposed" savages have names for what we do not even see and for what we cannot name. In English we say "you" to everyone; to every man and woman we say "you." How poor that is as a language! In Japan you have one word for "you" when it is a woman and another "you," a different word, when it is a man. You have another word when it is a superior man, and yet another when it is a superior woman, or inferior, or when it is an old man, young man, baby—all those "you" 's. What is simplified in our language by a "you" is on the contrary pulverized in Japanese. Thus the Japanese translator of Lacan said to me once, because he was so sensitive to this: "When I hear people of the West, I always feel that perhaps they speak to God!" This pronoun problem of "you" is causing great difficulty for psychoanalysis in Japan, because the idea of the great Other is a difficult thing for them.

The consequence of all this is that an evolutionary point of view concerning language is very difficult to bring back. On the contrary, we cannot imagine the slow, gradual learning of language, but, rather, language created at one stroke. It is a holistic theory I would say. If a child can learn language, it is on the precondition that he is already in language. And in language, the minimal example, taken by Lacan from Freud, is the *Fort/Da!*, which is S_1/S_2. That is the minimum, which is sufficient to write the entire library of Babylon. So when Quine looks for the root of reference, the root of reference is creation. And it is in that sense that Lacan can say that the signifier appears *ex nihilo*. That is, it creates a void. But where does it come from? It comes from the void.

And you, the someone, where are you in this consideration? In this ternary, you are nothing more than the nullified object. What is possible to say is that you as a subject of the signifier are nothing more than a null set. You are equivalent to the bar or to the void, and it is in that sense that Lacan can say, that the subject is the effect of the signifier. That is the same sentence as "Words are the murderers of things". That is to say that what we call the subject in analysis is nothing more than a function of the combination of signifiers. You might think it is a very far-fetched idea, but it is an idea necessitated by the notion that speech in analysis and interpretation can change the subject. If we take as our point of departure the idea that speech and interpretation can change a subject, the simple way to formalize this is to say: The subject is nothing more than the effect of the combination of the signifiers. And so we say that is truth, truth as a *relation*, an *effect* induced by a combination of signifiers at a given time. That is why Lacan put the subject at the place of the truth value in his various schemata.

The gist of the question is this. Is it enough to recognize the vacuousness of reference? Is it enough to say, in some way, that reference is nothing more than this meaning, and that language does not refer to anything, does not describe? This could give credence to a kind of Zen analysis. Lacan begins his Seminar by alluding to the Zen practice which actually teaches pupils that language does not refer and does not describe. Zen teaches pupils to accept as the answer to a question, a kick, for instance, when they are looking for a reference. And there is something of that in psychoanalysis: a learning of the vacuousness of reference. But what is present immediately in analysis is already this vacuousness of reference. That is the first effect you are submitted to when you enter analysis. You are going to speak of a lot of things to your analyst. You are even going to ask for help, for comprehension. And the supposed "benevolent neutrality," which is a psychological way of saying things, is nothing other than keeping a distance from the reference and inviting the subject to see the pure combination of signifiers. "Benevolent neutrality," is the evacuation of reference. That is why you can make fun of an analyst who says: "You say that, but what do you mean by that?" But the gist of analysis is that it refers you to the pure combination of signifiers. It puts the reference or void at a distance.

Entering analysis is thus progressive evacuation of reference or void which takes the place of an object, a new object still broader. That is to say, language not only has effects of meaning, it also *produces*. And the secret of psychoanalysis is precisely how to get to this new kind of reference which Lacan called object, object *a*, which is a new kind of reference that analysis clarifies. And it is in this that we are at the same time in the vacuousness of reference, but as a condition for the emergence of a reference unheard of up until now. It is a kind of reference which is precisely something, not nothing, and which we cannot get to, which we cannot take as a member of the set of signifiers. Let us say that it is a remainder. Freud spoke of the quantum of affect, that quantum of affect which does not find a place. There are still people like Otto Kernberg who believe that Lacan does not speak of affect. Yet, that is the central point of Lacan's theory of psychoanalysis. But surely Mr. Kernberg cannot recognize affect under the guise of the object *a*. That is why we can say hysterics were at the beginning of psychoanalysis. Because the hysterical subject *par excellence* embodies this remainder which does not find a place.

Works Cited

Bentham, Jeremy. *An Introduction to the Principles of Morals and Legislation*. Ed. J. H. Burns and H. L. A. Hart. London: The Athlone Press, 1970.

Blanchot, Maurice. *La communauté inavouable*. Paris: Les éditions de minuit, 1983.

Carnap, Rudolf. *Meaning and Necessity*. Chicago: University of Chicago Press, 1947.

Davidson, Donald. "The Philosophy of Plato." *London Review of Books*. 1 August, 1985:3–12. See also "Une conversation avec Donald Davidson." *L'Ane* 39 (July–Sept. 1989): 28–34.

Donnellan, Keith. "Reference and Definite Descriptions." *Philosophical Review* 75 (1966): 281–304.

Flaubert, Gustave. *L'éducation sentimentale*. Paris: Centre de Documentation Universitaire, 1974.

Frege, Gottloeb. *The Basic Laws of Arithmetic*. Trans. and ed. Montgomery Furth. Berkeley and Los Angeles: University of California Press, 1964.

Freud, Sigmund. "Three Essays on the Theory of Sexuality." *S.E.* 7. London: Hogarth, 1962.

Grice, Paul. *Studies in the Way of Words.* Cambridge: Harvard University Press, 1989.

Hegel, G. W. F. *The Phenomenology of Spirit.* Trans. A. V. Miller. Oxford: Clarendon Press, 1977.

Kripke, Saul A. *Naming and Necessity.* Cambridge: Harvard University Press, 1980.

Lacan, Jacques. *The Seminar of Jacques Lacan. Book I: Freud's Papers on Technique* (1953–1954). Ed. Jacques-Alain Miller. Trans. with Notes by John Forrester. New York: W. W. Norton & Co., 1988.

Mallarmé, Stéphane. *Poésies.* Ed. Carl Paul Barbier and Charles Gordon Millan. Paris: Flammarion, 1983.

Meinong, Alexius. *On Assumptions.* Ed. and Trans. James Heanue. Berkeley: University of California Press, 1976.

Peirce, Charles S. *Philosophical Writings of Peirce.* Ed. Justus Buchler. New York: Dover Publishing, Inc., 1955.

Quine, Willard Van Orman. *Word and Object.* Cambridge: The M.I.T. Press, 1960.

Russell, Bertrand. See Whitehead.

Schreber, Daniel Paul. *Memoirs of My Nervous Illness.* Trans. and Ed. Ida Macalpine and Richard A. Hunter. New Intro. by Samuel Weber. Cambridge: Harvard University Press, 1988.

Shakespeare, William. *Much Ado About Nothing.* Ed. Barbara K. Lewalski, The Blackfriars Shakespears. Dubuque, Iowa: Wm. C. Brown Company, 1969.

White, Richard Grant. *Studies in Shakespeare.* 5th Ed., The Riverside Press. Cambridge: Houghton, Mifflin & Co., 1891.

Whitehead, Alfred North and Bertrand Russell. *Principia Mathematica.* 1, 2, 3. Cambridge: Cambridge University Press, 1968.

2

Homo sapiens or *Homo desiderans:* The Role of Desire in Human Evolution

Henry W. Sullivan

The thoughts offered in this paper are an attempt to address that aspect of our Congress's thematic entitled "Lacan and Language." More specifically, I have chosen to engage the thorny question of the origins of language, inasmuch as this is inseparable from the origin of man. This latter subject, however, is one on which Lacan himself seemed expressly to discourage speculation. Objecting in 1946 to Freud's own "sociological" interpretation of his discovery of the Oedipus complex, Lacan wrote: "I do not think that the Oedipus complex appeared with the origin of man (*if indeed it is not completely senseless to try to write the history of that moment*), but rather at the dawn of history, of 'historical' history, at the limit of 'ethnographic' cultures" (my emphasis) (*Écrits* 1966, p. 184)

It is notorious that Lacan's teachings on language or on other subjects have been applied or adapted by others in ways that might seem completely senseless. Yet my purpose is not to suggest lines for writing the history of the origin of man; rather, I succumb to the irresistible temptation to wonder what may have been the role of desire in the origins of human language and, hence, of human evolution. Lacan's teaching, in my personal view, is not merely a fundamental renewal of thinking about psychoanalysis—it is the articulation of a new *episteme*. I would go as far as to say that he stands as founding theoretician of a post-Modern Age, much as Augustine laid out the City of God blueprint for the Middle Ages, or as Descartes mapped out the preoccupations of the Modern Age. The intractable problem of writing about human culture in a prehistoric era (which left no written record) may yield a little, I submit, by being examined in the light of a Lacanian *episteme*.

The continual note of caution that I sound in this beginning will advisedly be maintained to the end. I should wish you to receive the following not as a series of statements but as a series of questions, which, I trust, will have their effect. Above all, I wish to cast doubt on the almost universally accepted assumption nowadays that human mentality takes its origin from biologically determinist, first-cause explanations. Respectable authorities writing on the subject in such areas as physical anthropology, palaeontology, or, more recently, sociobiology, typically begin by raising the issue of human mental evolution or cultural development and then proceed to talk immediately of brain size, neurons, frontal lobes, gene pools, and the like. This, I submit, is looking for the right answer in the wrong place. Mental evolution must also be studied with reference to the logic of the signifier and to what Alexandre Stevens calls "the Saussurean cut" in linguistic epistemology (47). Above all, no account of human language and mind can make sense without reference to Lacan's theories on desire as the sign of a lack out of which representation and meaning are created.

I Sign Systems, Primate Vocalization, and Human Language

In the first place, I wish to clarify the limited sense in which I am using the terms "speech" and "language." It is an error, or at best a metaphor, it seems to me, to construe the sign systems employed by bees, ants, birds, and other species lower in the evolutionary scale than primates as a language. For this view we have the support of Lacan. In his Seminar on Poe's "Purloined Letter" of 1956, Lacan referred to his disagreement with the linguist Emile Benveniste over the latter's comparison of "Animal communication and human language." Lacan observes: "Those who are here know our remarks on the subject, specifically those illustrated by the countercase of the so-called language of bees: in which a linguist can see only a simple signaling of the location of objects, in other words: only an Imaginary function more differentiated than others" (35). Lacan's fuller answer to Benveniste occurs in the "Discourse of Rome" (1953), where he draws this distinction: "But is [the bee code] a language? We can say that it is distinguished from language precisely by the fixed correlation of its signs to the reality that they signify. For in a language signs take on their value from their relations to each other in the lexical distribution of semantemes as much as in the positional, or even flectional, use of morphemes, in sharp contrast to the fixity of the coding used by bees. And the diversity of human languages (*langues*) takes on its full value from this enlightening discovery" (*Ecrits* 84).

Though they display no creativity, animal sign systems work well enough however. Rituals such as the mating of birds through ostentation of plumage, calls, or dance movements illustrate this. Sign systems also illustrate the absence-presence polarity with regard to referents often thought of as a unique property of human language *sensu stricto*. In baboon colonies on East African savannah plains, for example, an outer ring of male guards will protect the females and young at the center. Should a predator approach, a guard baboon will signal this danger by drumming on the ground with its back feet. The semiotic interest in this example is that the guard animal, or encoder of the signal, has the object or referent *present* and in view. The predator cannot therefore be termed an absent representation in the baboon's "mind." To the fleeing females, however, for whom the predator is absent to view, the drumming sounds signify its *presence* or imminence. But, as Saussure observed of all semiotic codes (including human language), this sign is both *fixed* (it always means danger) but also *arbitrary* (some kind of shriek might serve just as well). Or as Lacan has it, the sign is something which means something for someone.

My point is that for the destinatee of the sign or signal—the protected female—the sign refers to an object in its absence. It is one of many signs operative in this animal colony. But these do not constitute a symbolic order. In his commentaries on Lacan's use of the term "holophrase" and its possible relation to the origins of language, Alexandre Stevens comments on images perceived by animals as follows: "But this preciseness of the image does not make it into a signifier. That is why, if holophrases exist—and they assuredly do exist—they are not a transition from an animal cry to a signifier in language. It is just the opposite; the image, in the animal—as well as the animal cry, which falls within the same field of reference if it assumes a specific function—far from blending into the world of symbol, remains enmeshed in a real situation" (57). This is a capital distinction to which we will return, but it is interesting to observe for the moment that two aspects of semiosis that will reappear in human language—the fixity-arbitrariness relationship and the absence-presence polarity—already have ample precedents in animal sign systems.

But is "nonhuman primate speech" a form of language? I do not think so. Indeed, I think "speech" when applied to pongids such as the chimpanzee, gorilla, or orangutan is also a term to avoid in favor of "vocalization." "Speech" in English (and even more so *parole* in French, with its strong Saussurean and Lacanian associations) confuses the issue before us by begging the question of language origins. But nonhuman primate vocalizations can and have been studied by the linguists R. J. Andrew, Philip Lieberman, and others. These studies show that while such primates do possess physiological apparatus potentially capable of producing a wide range of sound contrasts (such as voiced versus unvoiced, phonation onset and stop, etc.), they underutilize them or employ them only in part.

The principal thesis of Lieberman's *On the Origins of Language: An Introduction to the Evolution of Human Speech* (1975) concerns the physiological production of sound in *Homo sapiens.* He argues that the supralaryngeal vocal tract (the long, tube-like cavity above the human larynx that facilitates complex sound production) is inefficient for purposes *other* than speech. The human larynx is thus adapted for efficient phonation at the expense of respiratory efficiency (27). Interestingly, the air passages of a newborn human and an adult chimpanzee resemble each other much more than either resembles those of an adult human. In the newborn and the chimpanzee, the soft palate and epiglottis can be moved together, whereas in adult humans they are widely separated. Consequently, the adult epiglottis cannot close the oral cavity off from the airway leading to the lungs (108–09). This increases the adult airway's flow resistance: good for phonation, but bad for breathing. In nonhumans, the sealing of the oral cavity aids the sense of smell and allows an animal to breathe while its mouth contains a liquid (for example, when a dog laps water). The adult human supralaryngeal airways, however, also increase the risk of asphyxiation; food lodged in the pharynx can block the entrance to the larynx (177). Similarly, the greater selective advantage of enhanced sound-production ability places less value on chewing, causing the prognathous lower jaw and teeth (typical of Neanderthal man, for example) to be retracted below the upper jaw. Reviewing these inefficient aspects of adult human anatomy, Lieberman concludes that: "The selective advantages of communication would be overwhelming only when the value of communication in the total hominid culture outweighed these disadvantages" (177).

So far, we have established that many species employ sign systems; that many nonhuman primates have a great vocalization potential that is under-utilized; and that *Homo sapiens* has exploited vocalization or speech potential to such a degree that it has led to the natural selection of supralaryngeal features that would never otherwise have been preferred. In a word, the human sign system has been welded to an acoustic speech system aided by natural selection to form a *Homo loquens.* But are we now in the presence of human language as Lacan would understand it?

The answer must still be no, since we have made no mention of desire which, Lacan says invoking a text of Spinoza, "is the essence of man." (*Seminar VI, Le Désir*, Vol. I, p. 5). Lacanian desire concerns a "lack in being" (*manque-à-être*) and is apparently not so far from the etymological sense of the pedantic English cognate "to desiderate": "Feel to be missing, regret absence of, wish to have" (*OED*). But desire in Lacan is more fundamentally something lacking: the unconscious, which is itself built up around loss. Desire is also a principle of struc-turation in the genesis of the subject. It points to that void or real in human existence around which interpretation in the registers of the imaginary and/or symbolic grows up. Desire-as-lack, in other words, is contributary to human representation and the making of meaning. The adventure of making meaning of their existence-as-lack is what drives human populations to fashion imaginary and symbolic repre-sentations into the uneasy cohesiveness of culture. This, I submit, is a far cry from animal sign systems or even evolved hominid speech. A crude equation to illustrate my meaning might be the following: sign system + primate speech + desire = human language.

II   Human Culture and the Sexual Difference

The Lacanian Juan-Carlos Indart once defined culture as "a set (*ensem-ble*) of men and women and the representations which inhabit them." I think this is a useful definition that may help answer the question: is it possible to study the presence of human language in a prehistoric culture which has left no written record? The earliest written record, as you know, only goes back as far as about 6,000 BC in the shape of Egyptian hieroglyphics and Sumerian cuneiform. But there is an alternative route. Stone Age cave paintings date further back in time than writing. And representational art, I venture to suggest, must have human language as a *conditio sine qua non*, since it operates pictographic functions similar to those that language operates in its systems of signifying chains. I shall advance Lacanian support for this position in a moment.

We are fortunate to know from the work of Ann and Gale Sieveking of over a hundred sites in Western Europe where Palaeolithic cave paintings have been discovered. Altamira in Northern Spain and Las-caux in the Dordogne are perhaps the most famous. From archaeologi-cal data and carbon–14 determinations, it is possible to date the time span of Palaeolithic parietal art as about 30,000 to 10,000 BC. This corresponds to the appearance of Cro-Magnon man (*Homo sapiens sapiens*) in Western Europe in about 35,000 BC, during the fourth and last of the Ice Ages (the *Würm* glaciation). Whereas the evidence for the crudest stone implements goes back approximately 2,000,000 years to the pebble tools of *Homo habilis*, there now occurred a tremendous acceleration in cultural evolution in the Upper Palaeolithic for which no one to date has offered any satisfactory explanation. By 32,000 BC, the first known musical instrument, a bone flute, appeared; by 29,000 BC, the cave art under discussion; by 23,000, the sewing needle; by 17,000, the first spear thrower, and by 12,000, the bow and arrow. This brings us close to the beginnings of early urban civilizations and the dawn of history.

As mentioned above, the appearance of cave paintings by 29,000 BC indicates for me that human language, as strictly defined in this paper, had already existed for some time. The inspiration for this view is to be found in Lacan, and Lacan himself devoted some illuminating pages to Upper Palaeolithic art in Section XI of his Seventh Seminar, *L'Ethique de la psychanalyse* (1959–1960). Now after the discovery of the first decorated Palaeolithic caves in the middle of the nineteenth century, the central interpretive enigma has always remained: what purpose did they serve? Successive theses have suggested that the depictions of bison and wild game were an example of Stone Age leisure and art for art's sake; or for purposes of sympathetic magic and totemism; or, again, of fertility magic (Ucko and Rosenfeld).

The Frenchman Leroi-Gourhan, employing a kind of structuralist hermeneutics, is responsible for the first systematic analysis of the distribution of animal species in the caves. Basing his analysis on the facts of the art rather than on ethnographic parallels with modern-day primitives, Leroi-Gourhan drew up a detailed inventory of over sixty-five caves. He showed that well over half the animals shown are horse and bison. By the frequency and spatial distribution of these and other animals, he concludes, these signs in Palaeolithic art must represent two coupled or juxtaposed themes, "A" and "B" respectively. For the analysis of the distribution of the animals, he divided the caves up into seven different regions: 1) the first point where representations begin; 2) passages and shafts which connect up large galleries; 3) points at the beginning of fissures, diverticules, and alcoves; 4) the furthest region which is decorated; 5) the central part of decorated walls in large galleries; 6) marginal zones around the central part; and 7) points inside fissures, diverticules, and alcoves. He finds that all animals can be divided into the A (or horse) group and B (the bison) group. These in turn correspond to the human sexual difference, male and female. Group B animals (which are bison, aurochs, and women) are found regularly in the central panels (category 5 above), while group A are found in the six remaining areas only. The special distribution of the horse, in particular, forms the basic theme of man-woman and/or horse-bison (140–41).

Though Leroi-Gourhan supposes, probably correctly, that the caves must have been systematically organized sanctuaries, I believe this structuring of species and space around the human sexual difference is less the methodology of the art than its actual goal of expression. Lacan frequently points out that a given structure itself sends a message. In particular, the human sexual difference is for Lacan an impasse or irreducible real which resists satisfactory symbolization. The effort of culture is to try to express this difference anyway, and the successive efforts to express it might, in one sense, be considered the history of culture.

More importantly still, the attempt to interpret the real of sexual difference confronts us with the void which Lacan, in another turn, has also called the "Freudian thing" or simply *la Chose*. In his own remarks on Ice Age parietal art, Lacan took up precisely this thematic. (*L'Ethique*, 167–69). His concern is anamorphosis in art. Anamorphosis, technically speaking, is a distorted drawing appearing regular from one point. The cuttle fish-like ellipse that is a distorted drawing of a skull in Holbein's *The Ambassadors* (1533) is a good example, and it decorates the cover of Seminar XI, *The Four Fundamental Concepts of Psychoanalysis*.

Lacan duly notes that underground caves, being dark, were precisely the worst site in which to view paintings. But while the walls provided successive artists with the opportunity to try out or test their creative potential in a subjective sense, in an objective sense the paintings were also tests or trials: " . . . for these images cannot not seize us as being at the same time profoundly linked to the closest tie in the world—I mean to the very subsistence of populations which seem to be composed essentially of hunters—, but also to that something which, in its subsistence, assumes for itself the character of a Beyond the Sacred; which is exactly what we are attempting to determine in its most general form by the term 'the Thing.' This is primitive subsistence, I would say, from the angle of the Thing" (168).

This relationship—the depiction of natural objects of subsistence from the angle of the ultimately unspeakable void—is the beginning of anamorphosis in art as it came to be expressed formally in the early seventeenth-century Baroque. Stone Age art had an orienting function at the junctures of inside and outside. Lacan continues: "Just as the exercise on the wall consists of situating the invisible inhabitant of the cave firmly in place, we can see a chain forming itself from the temple, viewed as an organization around this void which exactly designates the locus of the Thing, to the representation of the void on the walls of this void itself, in so far as painting progressively learns to master this void, to hug it so close that it becomes dedicated to anchoring the void in the form of spatial illusion" (168). Finally, Lacan notes that it is a gross blunder to think of pictorial art as simple, one-to-one mimesis. He states: "Of course, works of art imitate the objects which they represent, but their purpose is precisely not to represent them. In giving an imitation of the object, they make of this object something else. In this way, they only pretend to imitate. The object is installed in a certain relation to the Thing, which is designed simultaneously to encircle, to make present and to make absent" (169). The primary goal of art is "to project a reality which is not at all that of the represented object" (170).

These extensive remarks on cave painting should suffice to show that Upper Palaeolithic art was grappling with the same dilemmas of representation's trying to symbolize the void or the Thing and thereby account for the real which permeates and gives rise to human language in the fullest sense of the term. We can, therefore, logically infer backwards the existence of such human language in Cro-Magnon man prior to his appearance in Western Europe around 35,000 BC: language which was an acoustic or phonated sign system laced with desire.

III *Homo sapiens* or *Homo desiderans*?

The term *Homo sapiens* is one of a plethora of fanciful names coined in the 1800s to describe postulated species of prehistoric man. Its customary translation is "wise man." Yet one does not need to be a Latinist to recognize here the root of *sapio*, the common Latin verb "to know." But what precisely was *Homo sapiens* supposed by nineteenth-century anthropologists to know? Are we perhaps in the presence of one reading of Lacan's formula *le sujet supposé savoir*: a prehistoric subject who is supposed as knowing something?

Only the human species accumulates knowledge and finds methods—pictorial, notational, mnemotechnic, alphabetic, archival, etc.—for transmitting this knowledge across the generations. But this knowledge also arises out of the human sexual difference, because according to Lacan there is no signifier in the unconscious for Woman. As Jacques-Alain Miller expresses it:

> The unconscious knows nothing of the relation of man to woman or of woman to man. Provisionally it can be said that the two sexes are strangers to one another, exiled from each other. . . . Indeed, there is a signifier for the male and that is all we've got. This is what Freud recognized: just one symbol for the libido, and this symbol is masculine; the signifier for the female is lost. Lacan is thus entirely Freudian in stating that *woman* as a category does not exist. . . . The

absence of the signifier *woman* also accounts for the illusion of the infinite, which arises from the experience of speech, even while that experience is finite. . . . The analysand therefore appears as a kind of Diogenes with his lantern, but in search of *woman* rather than a man. . . . The passion for things Symbolic has no other source. Science exists because *woman* does not exist. Knowledge as such substitutes for knowing the Other sex. (Miller's emphasis) (2)

When we consider the quantum leap in knowledge and technique exhibited by Cro-Magnon culture, is it conceivable that the full features of human language, such as the unconscious, the quest for woman displaced as a quest for knowledge, the stimulus of desire as a sign of lack giving rise to representational meaning, and so on, were all already operative? Were we to answer yes to this question, then technical knowledge should be viewed, even in that remote time, as arising out of unconscious *savoir*. And unconscious *savoir*, in its quest for missing objects, is a manifestation of Lacanian desire. We may, then, have the key to the famous Great Leap Forward of the Upper Palaeolithic: desire is the motor of human history, but also of human prehistory. Before there was *Homo sapiens* there must have been *Homo desiderans*.

IV   Desire as the Motor of Human History

I have tried to lay the preceding groundwork so as to suggest that the "missing link" of evolution lies not in biology, but in language. We have pushed this origins-of-language moment further and further back in time to the middle Pleistocene (Buettner-Janush, *Origins*, 26). We have connected desire with primitive technology as a precondition of human language and sapient man. But are the most elementary stone tools to be regarded as indications of human desire? Stone tools first appear in the archaeological record as crude pebble choppers with no more than a few flakes removed from one side; they have been found at sites with fossils that date to 2,000,000 years ago. By the middle Pleistocene the tools had developed into finely made, symmetrical ovate-shaped handaxes that were flaked on both sides and carefully trimmed or retouched to produce straight edges. These are the first standardized artifacts (that is, objects made systematically to conform to a pattern preconceived in the maker's mind) and are the first to show that the toolmaker's considerations were aesthetic as well as functional (Buettner-Janush, "Hominidae," 1028). Now these biface and flake tools were made by Pithecanthropines from perhaps as long ago as 500,000 BC (*Origins*, 26). Is there anything in Lacan's theories which can connect these with the first appearance of desire as lack in hominid culture? Is there anything there that can explain standardization of artifacts hewn from nature and a concern for aesthetics?

In the mirror stage, Lacan argues, prespecular objects of desire (namely, the breast, faeces, imaginary phallus, urinary flow, the gaze, voice, phoneme, and the void) provide a lining to the subject. Already in the first six months of extra-uterine life, the infant has connected need (for food, fluids, etc.) to demand in its cry to the other. The objects named above are both the cause of desire and the objects of desire; but *desire as lack* supervenes when the mirror stage comes to an end at approximately 18 months. The first pure signifier of lack, which divides the subject (the S_1) and creates the conscious-unconscious division, is the phallic signifier. Though a very bulky treatise could be written on the ramifications of the phallic signifier, I should like to draw attention here only to its civilizing effect in standardizing and regularizing the randomness of nature. As Jacques-Alain Miller once said, you can note the fleeting evanescence of the phallic signifier in its residuum or effect, for example in the huge rectilinear, North-South pattern of streets and avenues in an American city. It seems to me that a regular and symmetrical, biface flaked tool must exhibit the passage or flight of the phallic signifier over the formless stone object.

V Conclusion

We have established a distinction between animal sign systems, primate vocalization, and hominid speech in order to show that human language *sensu stricto* is all these things, plus something more: the desiring, representational element that is the true mark of humanness. We have emphasized that this human language grapples with the real of sexual difference in order to try and conceive the ineffable relationship between unconscious structures in man and the created nature that is both his habitat and body; between that which is already concrete or full and the void. These relationships, for Lacan, are already depicted in Stone Age parietal art, and I have argued, further, that those black, red, yellow, and white representations prove that human language was fully developed before 35,000 BC; perhaps as long ago as 70,000 or even—a riskier speculation—before 100,000 BC. This language was the first superior technology; one which permitted the advance of what archaeologists term "material culture" (artifacts, tools, fire pits, burial sites, etc.). The advantages of language as technology determined a selective preference for many developments in the supralaryngeal vocal tract which are inefficient for survival in the ordinary animal sense and inexplicable by any other means.

Now we should not be surprised to think of human language as the cause of advances in material culture. It may sound very Hegelian and un-Marxist to reason this way. But is it really a coincidence that physical anthropoid evolution came to an end when language and superior technology took over? It is from this point forth, I would suggest, that language and tools do the work of adaptation to new conditions. Indeed, many organs—the vermiform appendix, the tonsils, central wrist bone or *os centrale*, the cutaneous reaction that causes "goose flesh" or even nipples in the male—are vestigial structures that are now meaningless, since further adaptation has taken place outside the body. Language and technology mark the point where material conditions cease to impinge on anatomy, and the hominization of the planet begins.

I quarrel, then, with what might be termed the "absolute materialism" or "monomaterialism" of contemporary accounts of human evolution. Modern biologists and sociobiologists readily agree that language is the characteristic *par excellence* of man's mental evolution and cultural development. But from the optics of a Lacanian *episteme*, statements like the following by the German Bernhard Rensch strike one as naïve: "As his most essential characteristics—speech, insight and purposeful actions—depend upon the development of his brain, it is apposite to ask whether these typical features could have developed had his size been different" (128). To talk of "insight" and "purposeful actions" places us immediately in the realm of interpretation and intentionality (aspects of humanness inseparable from unconscious desire and Lacanian drive theory), considerations which figure nowhere in Rensch's calculations. Similarly, in the gene-culture coevolution theory of C. J. Lumsden and E. O. Wilson, we may read statements like the following: "The mind springs from a machinery of neurons created according to the genetic blueprint, but it grows in an environment created by the preexisting culture, which is a particular history embedded in the memories and archives of those who transmit it" (77). The problems arise here with "memories and archives." Are we talking of unconscious memories? Of lost objects? Of the attempt to interpret loss and lack culturally, as described above? Are we talking of cultural memory as preserved in the symbolic order and language? Are not these "archives" really the unconscious memory-bank that founds the subject in relation to the signifier and the Law of the name-of-the-father? And what, pray, do all these secondary cultural characteristics have to do with some animistic "machinery of neurons" or "genetic blueprint?"

I am not an absolute Idealist trafficking in spiritualism and mysticism. I see clearly the physical-anthropological, Darwinian and material-genetic factors in human evolution. But these fail badly if proposed as the unique causality of *Homo sapiens*. For there is also a materiality of language: not visible writing; not spectrograms measuring human voice signals; nor even the language materials stored in libraries and archives. I refer to language that is material in its effect or impact. Language which, in this fifth dimension of phallic cause and effect, has the power to move mountains and has indeed done so in every corner of our planet.

Works Cited

Andrew, R. J. "Trends apparent in the evolution of vocalization in the Old World monkeys and apes." *Symposium of the Zoological Society of London* 10 (1963): 89–101.

––––––. "The Origin and Evolution of the Calls and Facial Expressions of the Primates." *Behaviour* 20 (1963): 1–109.

Benveniste, Emile. "Communication animale et langage humain" [in *Diogene* no. 1]. Reprinted in *Problems in General Linguistics* [1966]. Trans. M. Meek. Coral Gables: University of Miami Press, 1971: 49–54.

Buettner-Janusch, John. *Origins of Man: Physical Anthropology*. New York: Wiley & Sons, 1966.

––––––. "Hominidae." *Encyclopedia Britannica* (15th edition) 8 (1983): 1023–30.

Condillac, Etienne Bonnot de. *Essai sur l'origine des connaissances humaines* [1746]. Ed. Raymond Lenoir. Paris: A. Colin, 1924.

De Man, Paul. *Allegories of Reading: Figural Language in Rousseau, Nietzsche, Rilke, and Proust*. New Haven and London: Yale University Press, 1979: 140–56 [on Rousseau's *Essai*].

Derrida, Jacques. *De la Grammatologie*. Paris: Editions de Minuit, 1967: 272–78 [on Rousseau's *Essai*].

Herder, Johann Gottfried. *Ueber den Ursprung der Sprache* ("Essay on the Origin of Language"). Berlin, 1772.

Lacan, Jacques. "L'amour courtois en anamorphose." Section XI in *Le Séminaire. Livre VII: L'Éthique de la psychanalyse (1959–1960)*, Texte établi par Jacques-Alain Miller. Paris: Seuil, 1986: 167–84.

––––––. *Le Désir et ses interprétations (Seminar VI, 1958–1959)*. 3 vols. Typescript: n.p., n.d. Unpublished text.

––––––. *Écrits: A Selection*. Trans. Alan Sheridan. New York: W. W. Norton, 1977.

––––––. *The Language of the Self: The Function of Language in Psychoanalysis*. Trans. Anthony Wilden. Baltimore and London: Johns Hopkins University Press, 1968.

––––––. *Le Séminaire, Livre XI: Les quatre concepts fondamentaux de la psychanalyse (1963–1964)*, Texte établi par Jacques-Alain Miller. Paris: Seuil, 1973. See also *Seminar XI: The Four Fundamental Concepts of Psychoanalysis*. Trans. Alan Sheridan. New York: W. W. Norton, 1978.

———. "Seminar on 'The Purloined Letter.' " Trans. Jeffrey Mehlman. *Yale French Studies* 48 (1972): 38–72. Reprinted in Muller and Richardson 1988: 28–54.

———. "Propos sur la causalité psychique" [1950]. In *Écrits*. Paris Seuil, 1966: 151–93.

Leroi-Gourhan, André. "Le symbolisme des grands signes dans l'art pariétal paléolithique." *Bulletin de la Societé Préhistorique Française* 55 (1958): 384–98.

———. *Art et Religion au Paléolithique Supérieur*. Paris, 1963.

———. *Les Religions de la Préhistoire (Paléolithique)*. Paris: Presses Universitaires de France, 1964.

———. *Le Geste et la Parole*, 2 vols. Paris: A. Michel, 1964–65.

———. *Préhistoire de l'art Occidental*. Paris: L. Mazenod, 1965.

Lieberman, Philip. *On the Origins of Language: An Introduction to the Evolution of Human Speech*. New York and London: Macmillan, 1975.

Lumsden, Charles J. and Edward O. Wilson. *Promethean Fire: Reflections on the Origin of Mind*. Cambridge: Harvard University Press, 1983.

Miller, Jacques-Alain. "Another Lacan." *Lacan Study Notes* (New York) 1.3 (February 1984): 1–3.

Muller, John P. and William J. Richardson. Eds. *The Purloined Poe: Lacan, Derrida, and Psychoanalytic Reading*. Baltimore and London: Johns Hopkins University Press, 1988.

Newsweek. "The Way We Were" [on the New York City exhibit "Dark Caves, Bright Visions" at the American Museum of Natural History, November 1986 to January 1987]. *Newsweek* 108.19 (November 10, 1986): 62–72.

Rensch, Bernhard. *Homo Sapiens: From man to demigod*. Trans. C. A. M. Sym. New York: Columbia University, 1972.

Ruspoli, Mario. *The Cave of Lascaux: The Final Photographs*. New York: H. N. Abrams. 1987.

Rousseau, Jean-Jacques. *Essai sur l'origine des langues* [1754]. Paris: A. Belin, 1817.

———. *Essai sur l'origine des langues*. Facsimile of 1817 edition published by Jacques-Alain Miller. Supplement to "Cahiers pour l'analyse" no. 8. Paris. Bibliothèque du Graphe, 1967.

———. *Essai sur l'origine des Langues, ou il est parlé de la mélodie et de l'imitation musicale*. Ed. Charles Porset. Bordeaux: Guy Ducros, 1970.

Sieveking, Ann and Gale. *The Caves of France and Northern Spain: A Guide*. Philadelphia: Dufour, 1966.

Stevens, Alexandre. "L'holophrase, entre psychose et psychosomatique." *Ornicar?* 42 (July–September 1987): 45–79.

Ucko, Peter J. and Andree Rosenfeld. "Historical review of interpretations." In *Paleolithic Cave Art*. New York and Toronto: McGraw Hill, 1967: 116–49.

3

The Sexual Masquerade: A Lacanian Theory of Sexual Difference

Ellie Ragland-Sullivan

The term sexual "masquerade" comes from an article written by the psychoanalyst Joan Rivière in 1929 to refer to a woman taking herself for a man disguised as a woman, and thus masquerading as a castrated woman ("Womanliness as Masquerade"). Rose writes in *Feminine Sexuality* that Lacan placed feminine sexuality under the sign of the masquerade, proposing the masquerade as the very definition of "femininity" precisely because it is constructed with reference to a male sign ("A Love Letter," 57). In the same introduction Rose links Lacan's theory of the meaning of sexual difference to his inversion of the Saussurean formula for the linguistic sign, sticking close to the idea that the linguistic signifier holds sway over the signified in creating meaning. By arguing that the relation of a signifier to a signified is not as arbitrary as Saussure's sign implies because meaning is made by oppositions, Rose redraws the picture Lacan used in his 1957 essay "The agency of the letter in the unconscious or reason since Freud." By replacing Saussure's model of the TREE (*Tree*) with another model,

Lacan questions the relation of a word to its image, the relation between words and things with LADIES   GENTS. Rose reads this

diagram from 1957 within the realm of the binary, as a simple opposition. This would be an imaginary reading.

She supports her interpretation of the 1957 essay by quoting the Lacan of 1973, from "A Love Letter," a chapter in *Séminaire* XX, as if the early Lacan were identical to himself sixteen years later. But Rose conflates the 1957 and 1973 texts in error, not only because the later

Lacan has changed from earlier positions, but because his early text, nonetheless, spells out the theory he will develop in detail in *Encore*. Rose's Lacan sees the sexual divide as determined by the biological literalism of having or not having the phallus *cum* penis. That is, anatomical difference *figures* cultural interpretation of sexual difference. According to her gloss, Lacan supposedly said in 1973: " 'Any speaking being whatever' must line up on one or the other side of the divide" ("A Love Letter," 67). But even in 1957 Lacan did not portray the sexual difference as a simple division where *organs* give rise to cultural signifieds.

What Lacan actually says in *Séminaire* XX is that males can make the error of believing they are whole simply because "male" signifies that which opposes itself to female. The idea of a symmetrical opposition is founded on the mistaken assumption that the male/female opposition also gives rise to a relation. Men can have the illusion they are everything (Φ_x) because the visibility of the phallic image gives rise to imaginary identifications based on the illusion they are members of a set of all those who are not the same as the primordial mother, the one who does not count because she is pre-social, evocative of a bond that lies, in part, beyond or outside the social. In this context, she becomes the empty set, the void, or the one who does not count because she is lost to memory at the level of *la langue*, although the masculine is defined as that which differs from her. But nothing is ever *nothing* in Lacan, thus never a universal. The primordial mother, lost to memory, always remains (for both sexes) as the real of effects relived in relation to part objects which become partial drives. Thus, all subsequent relatings of males to females rely on an un-relation. Although the phallic signifier has no literal signified—not even the anatomical one—it is, nonetheless, the first countable symbol of the effect of difference as a signifier referring only to itself, the signifier that delineates difference from sameness, order from chaos, law from nature.

Feminist readings of Lacan that focus on anatomy lead to confusion regarding his theory of sexual difference which takes the economy of psychosis as the proof of its logic. Lacan taught that sexual difference gives rise to gender ideologies which appear in multi-variations of a cultural taboo against an identificatory fusional relation between mother and infant, most particularly between mother and son. This does not mean that female infants are closer to psychosis, merely that they are enjoined by language and imago to identify with similarity rather than difference. Thus, the incest taboo is not so much a biological "no," as it is a strong cultural injunction to boys to identify away from the maternal and the feminine, to substitute the name of a lineage to the desire of a mother. If no "incest" taboo *qua* Freudian Oedipus complex is in play, what is at stake, then? Lacan points to the exceptional anxiety involved in taking on a masculine identification. Indeed, the figure of the male *qua* male might be called the cultural lie which maintains that sexual identity can be personified by making difference itself a position.

Lacan gives a name to this effect that does not exist as an entity or object, an effect he calls the law of the phallic signifier, a law whose effects apply to female as well as male. The paradox to be found in calling for such a "law"—law taken here as a cultural intervention that enables the social link to persist—is that gender identity fictions are necessary if subjects are to cohere in a seeming consistent alignment of desire, *jouissance*, body, being and knowing. A gender identity maintains the desire from which the individual and social reconstitute themselves structurally as metaphors. That is, persons can speak only because language is always already a substitute that refers to something else, the desire that gives rise to speech. One definition of psychosis, for Lacan, is the lack of the lack that gives rise to desire. And desire is the desire for being, not for knowing. Gender fictions are at the base of the illusion that one has or is a being. In psychosis gender positions are not nailed down. The psychotic suffers from not knowing what or who he or she is at the levels of being and *jouissance*.

Rather than simply opposing man to woman in *Séminaire* XX, thereby falling into the trap of the binary Lacan himself described as the imaginary, he argued that both men and women inscribe themselves under the *phallic* signifier which structures identity on the basis of differential identifications. Language and human culture also arise out of identification with this differential Lacan called the symbolic order. So identity is learned as a gendered set of fictions which bear the truth of one's desire whose polymorphous perverse *jouissance* is carved up by the effects of language and taboos written on the body. Although masculine and feminine traits characterize both sexes, ensuring that there be no pure feminine or masculine essence, the assumption of a gender identity elaborates fantasies around *jouissance* experiences that keep any subject from being fulfilled by her or his desires. Insofar as difference identifies itself to law—a no to the chaos of psychosis—it is what Lacan called the phallic part. "To any speaking being whatever," Lacan says, "as it is expressly formulated in Freudian theory, it is permitted, whatever the case, whether or not one is endowed with the attributes of masculinity—attributes which remain to be determined—to inscribe himself in this phallic part. If he, the speaking being, inscribes himself there, no universality will be permitted, he will be this not-all [*pas tout*], insofar as he has the choice to place himself in the Φ_x [phallic function] or to not be in it. Such are the only possible definitions of the part called man or woman for what is called being in the position of inhabiting language ("A Love Letter," 150; see also *Séminaire* XX, 74). If either sex is certain that he or she lacks nothing, then psychosis is the potential limit of that person's freedom. In the same context, one can not be psychotic, if one's desire is neurotic or perverse.

In 1973 Lacan clearly finds a great deal more in the sexual difference than merely a simple divide. But even in 1957, his ladies/gents anecdote does not suggest any simple symmetry between the two signifiers, ladies and gents. He describes the two children in a train rolling into a train station where the little girl saw "Gents" on a bathroom door from her window, and the little boy sitting across from her saw the adjacent door marked "Ladies." Lacan elaborated his statements about language in this essay in tandem with his evolving theory regarding sexual difference: "For this *signifier* [—what represents a subject for another signifier] will now carry a purely animal dissension. Ladies and Gentlemen will be henceforth for these children two countries towards which each of their souls will strive on divergent wings, and between which a cessation of hostilities will be the more impossible since they are in truth *the same country*" (258/my emphasis).

In 1968 in "Of Structure as an Inmixing of an Otherness Prerequisite to Any Subject Whatever," Lacan stressed, as others before him had, that sexual identity is culturally constructed: "The signifier intrudes into the signified, namely in a form which, not being immaterial, raises the very question of its place in reality" (294). In *Séminaire* XX the question raised about the reality of sexual difference comes back as an answer: the difference residing between "ladies" and "gents" is not only a signifying effect, but a *jouissance* effect as well, that neither "lady" nor "gent" can embody or express. Indeed such *effects* are produced by the impossibilities encountered in trying to identify with difference itself as an identify position. By conflating the 1957 and 1973 texts, reading both as descriptive of a simple binary split between the sexes, Rose misses Lacan's suggestion that it will be all the more impossible to stop a cessation of hostilities between these two countries "since they are in truth the same country" ("The agency," 295).

Lacan discovered a real impasse which itself creates the cultural necessity of inventing fictions to cohere with biology. The symbolic order parcels out its signifying myths between desire and *jouissance*, trying to explain to human "beings" their animality, mortality, the body (birth, sex, procreation, death), and so on. Explanations of origins appear as myth which are themselves proof, Lacan argued, of a split between the speaking being and the real "object" that causes his or her *jouissance*. But since the sexual divide is alienated behind cultural pre-givens (myths, fictions), yet paradoxically returns as a sexual unrelation, we can henceforth deny, idealize, ideologize, circumvent, miss it, and so on.

Lacan delineated the unconscious as an effect caused by this particular divide. The unconscious *is* sexuality insofar as something is lacking to define how two sexes—defined in degrees of opposition one to the other—might find a "natural" rapport or Oneness within the actual otherness or twoness out of which cultural mythologies and ideologies spring, essentializing an anatomical divide at the level of psychology, sociology and economics. In "Notes on Temporal Tension" Bruce Fink argues that truth "is primarily that, in a Lacanian framework, of the absence of *un rapport sexual*, a relationship one would be justified in characterizing as sexual" (28). So far-reaching are the consequences of this divide, that Lacan links Woman-writ-large to problematics posed over the ages by representation and knowledge. Moreover, content is irrelevant to the structure itself, elaborated as questions, doubts, enigmas, quest, affect. These all tell us something about why Woman has always been mythologized as knowing or being something other than purely rational.

In 1980 at the First International Encounter of the Freudian Field in Caracas, Venezuela, Jacques-Alain Miller addressed this problematic in a talk entitled "Another Lacan" (*Lacan Study Notes*). Explaining the importance of Woman as a position outside grammatical language and clear meaning—an *hors-sens*—in Lacan's return to psychoanalysis, Miller opened the way to an understanding, not only of Lacan's theory, but also to the threat presented to institutionalized frameworks when so-called feminine traits evoke Woman. Woman was Lacan's signifier for the anti-thesis of masculine certitude, based on an identification with rules, order, law. Miller's view presents the feminine as an attitude toward knowledge and procedure, rather than as a category strictly defined by gender. The feminine is on the side of Woman, an imaginary fantasy that calls into doubt "so called" rational logic as well as its step-child, "common sense." Miller's "Another Lacan" will probably surprise those who think Lacan's view on women has been faithfully reported by Luce Irigaray, Hélène Cixous, and others associated in varying ways with "French feminisms" or post-structuralist feminisms. Such feminisms lump Lacan together with Freud as an enemy of the female sex and share the view that Lacan was anti-woman, a phallocrat, a man who is derogatory of women.

Yet feminists who claim to liberate Woman to the potentials of her freedoms by positivistically reducing all women to a "class" defined non-dialectically, avoid seeing the power politics in play insofar as most women identify with the cultural myth that delineates the norm, or in Lacan's words the *nor-mâle*. This is an identity position which can be occupied by a man or woman who seeks to identify with difference where difference delineates the one who knows, the possessor of the law. The one who identifies with a position outside the law of man, whether male or female, occupies the position of "not all," the one who recognizes the lie in knowledge. Feminisms that ignore the ego fixity which anchors a gender position imposed by every cultural means, even long before an infant is conceived or born, may take a sociological point of view whereby women are victims awaiting liberation. Many feminisms envision woman's freedom as lying just around the corner. Freedoms will readily be won, for example, by our changing language lest language—itself the mask of patriarcy— appropriate womans' voice. And so on. But such one-dimensional terms do little to address the larger questions attached to women's and men's issues. In Lacan's clinical work, he came to understand that any dismantling of ego, language, or desire placed the analysand at the risk of death. The "self" may only be imagined, but individuals live from such "necessary fictions."

Propositions, such as Luce Irigaray's, that women should evolve a new writing, an anti-intellectual writing of the body where the feminine sexual masquerade be used as a counterfoil to masculinist imperialisms (and so on), are age-old devices, long used it the war between the sexes. Indeed, how is one to argue for change or "liberation" if one simply restates the tactics of one side against the other? When American post-structuralist feminists seek revolution by teaching certain reading strategies which equate reading with transference, and interpretation with a reversal of opposites, one wonders what new misrecognitions are in play? What do women gain by word play that has little to do with how they live their lives, or with the larger sufferings of women, children, or men? This is not to say that deconstructive strategies are not valuable tactics in helping male and female students who might never question their assumed roles become more attuned to the myriad differences that make up apparent samenesses. But finally, these strategies intended to disrupt the metropole in order to expose patriarchal mastery as the enemy within, do not, as Elisabeth Meese argues in *Crossing The Double-Cross*, "equip[s] us to detect and unravel our own and other's masquerades with a certain skill" by seeking the "otherness of texts repressed in interpretive or constructive acts" (xi). Deconstruction's blind spot centers precisely on the issues of text *qua* ideology. If texts and interpretations are assumed, à la Gadamer, for instance, to be ideological, one must ask what ideology is. Lacan saw ideology as an *imaginary* credo meant to critique the supposed masters of knowledge. In Slavoj Žižek's turn of phrase: "Ideology is not simply a false consciousness, an illusory representation of reality, it is rather *this reality* itself which is already to be conceived as "ideological" (*The Sublime Object of Ideology*, 21).

Either feminist position—reducing oneself to the sexual body as a way of attack, or inverting language to show that sexual differences do not really exist except in language—ends up in an *impossible* feminism that leads right back to the *real* as the encounter with an impasse Lacan calls the sexual non-relation. If males and females are "natural" enemies, as Irigaray and others argue, or if they only think they are enemies because they fail to account for the myriad traces of *différance* undercutting the binary (deconstruction), woman still remains in the position of victim. These theories fall into a progressivist fallacy that fails to account for why women ever merited an adversary in the first place, and why the battle has not yet been won, at least among the privileged. Yet post-structuralist feminism(s) consume vital intellectual and activist energy by keeping its advocates in the conscious realm, the imaginary circle of love/hate. Because love/hate (guilt/ blame) is a Sisyphean ritual whose repetition becomes its own *raison d'être*, imaginary logic prevails without anyone's asking what caused this paradoxical war? Or why narcissism is rigid, or why speech defies writing, or why *jouissance*, by definition, exceeds the law. What has not been measured in contemporary post-structualist feminism(s), in my estimation, is the initial necessity of assuming identity *qua* gender identity, the subsequent difficulty of changing that identity, and the permanent discontinuities produced by identifying as a gender—male or female—that is not One.

Post-structuralist feminists seem unaware of the "Other Lacan" who teaches us that the phallic signifier has no signified, that this signifier only symbolizes the learning of difference as an effect which posits a materiality in language which differentiates the word *qua* meaning from the word *as* the sense of its meaning(s). That is, meanings always point to other meanings, to missing pieces. From infancy on, we use language to fulfill our wishes. But immediate and total satisfaction of wants or desires are fleeting. Lacan's formula for drive shows the paradoxical canceling of the subject in its demand for its particular satisfaction ($\$ \Diamond D$): the subject demands because lack and loss keep the subject from being whole. Despite momentary satisfactions, lack and loss prevail, producing a kind of low grade dis-ease or even anxiety. Thus, any signifier tries to delineate itself as full, but always misses the referent it wants to find and pin down in the Other because full satisfaction or full meaning disappear even at the moment of experienced encounter. The niggling pull just beyond what we think of as reason—what Lacan called the Freudian unconscious—is one with the subject as metaphor, subject of desire who is subject to temporal tension. In this context, the unconscious *causes* us to speak what we think we know (*supposer/se poser*) in our quests to try to know for sure what we want, who we are, and so on.

Mireille Andrès argues that metaphor basically takes the place of the question concerning the mother, her desire, the énonciation which has no "language"—only a murmuring Lacan called *la langue*. The signifiers that seem to answer the question "what do I want/what does mother want" give a pseudo- or semi-answer She wants something that is referred to the father's name. Not his penis, *per se*, but whatever fulfillment he is supposed to provide for her unconscious desire. The unrelation here is the paradigm for the impossibility of attaining fulfillment through "right" behavior, human relations, material objects, and so on. Although these give momentary satisfactions, they do not extinguish lack. Thus, desire is for the impossible real: for *jouissance* or the expulsion of law. Lacan says the phallus *becomes* a signifier, not because of any male sexual superiority, but because it is submitted to the circulation or chaining of desire(s). The "name" the mother gives the signifier for father—the paternal metaphor—is always a name of the absence of plenitude (*Lacan et la Question du Métalangage* 170).

In this view of Lacan, the catch–22 for men and women alike appears as an irresolution that inhabits language, marking it with desire as a deficit in being and knowing which is ever present, but not fully spoken. Thus man fails to "colonize" the unconscious by controlling the feminine or women. He also fails to pin down his own masculinity as a fixed, permanent, natural fact. Instead Woman becomes his symptom, described by Gérard Miller in 1985 as "the response given by the subject to the question of knowing what he is for the Other" (84). But what is a symptom in Lacanian parlance? Žižek calls it "a particular element which subverts its own universal foundation, a species subverting its own genus" (*The Sublime*, 21). Symptoms speak the enigmatic structuring of desire while fantasy ($ \lozenge a$) bears on the cause of desire. Let us propose, that if Woman is *man's symptom*, essentialized in myth, she appears as a hole in his imaginary. As the symptom of his real—the unassimilated kernel of meaning around which he tries to close out desires circulate—she is not symmetrical to him. He becomes her problem but not her symptom. In this view, no interpretation of texts, of discourse, or of persons leads to knowledge of the unconscious, nor to exposure of ideology. Instead interpretation leads to the point where language or knowledge stumbles over Woman for whom there is *no* signifier in the unconscious. The unconscious, in turn, creates gaps and discontinuities in conscious life by injecting the realities of lack and fading into language and being. We usually take such aporiai as that which it is not given us to know when, in fact, they are ideals and wants that "drive" us and tease us with the refusal of a final solution.

In "Another Lacan" Jacques-Alain Miller took up Lacan's notion of the pass, the idea that one possible end of analysis is passing from the position of analysand to that of analyst. Lacan differs from Freud's idea of the end of analysis in "Analysis Terminable and Interminable" (1937) by bringing in Woman. Freud thought that at the end of even the best analysis, the "castration complex" presents an impasse or reef, making a cure impossible. Indeed, Lacan's thinking begins here where Freud's stops, making Lacan's importance for feminism the relevance of new theories of language and gender where the two are, moreover, co-dependent. Lacan read Freud's 1934 essay as an effort to answer another question, the one regarding the enigmas surrounding sexual difference, whose answer does not lie in any literal castration fear: How should a natural harmony arise from "two countries" derived from the same country, structured to be different at best, at war at worst? How does one suddenly become a man for a woman, or a woman for a man when no representation inheres in the Other to serve as an adequately truthful answer or model? Freud could not reply to his own question, Lacan maintained, because his cultural context allowed no answer such as "there is no sexual relation." If the cultural injunction to identify with difference is not, as Lacan claims, equal on both parts, then any subsequent divide supposed to be symmetrical rests on false premises. Put another way, there is no $\times$ which is not a function of $\times$ [the empty set] or the "same country" from which boys and girls start. In other words, thought is always inadequate to sex, structured as it is by a signifier that divides consciousness from its own cause.

The unconscious knows nothing of a *relation* between man and woman because relation only inheres between signifiers for opposition. While the masculine is defined in opposition to the feminine, the feminine is not opposed to itself. Although subsequent unconscious signifiers do imply relation based on opposition (S_1/S_2), the first universally countable signifier for difference *qua* difference is the signifier marking gender difference as a position taken toward language and law. The phallic signifier is the mark of opposition as the basis of cultural meaning, that which gives access to language over *jouissance*. The phallic signifier, thus, denotes difference as arising in reference to a null set, in reference to void or loss. Given this reality, the end of analysis can not be thought of in terms of a Freudian harmony, in terms of that which, by definition, even existed.

Indeed, the only place where the difference between the sexes disappears is the twilight zone of psychosis, whose structure derives from the foreclosure of a signifier denoting sexual difference as the basis for identity support. If Lacanian epistemology sheds new light on contemporary "cures" pronounced in the name of happy love relations or sexual pleasure, it is because Lacan refused to idealize human "relations." Lacan often said that "love" may *be* curative, but not because it is love (an idealized closure). Rather, because it allows us to give what we lack in the Other; to not give up on the Other; to not give up on desire. That Lacan finds a sexual un-relation at the end of analytic "cure" points to a path of freedom found along the byways of reconstituted desire and gradually assimilated bits of the real. Lacanian analysts aim for an uncoupling of the analysand from the circular Other (sex)—the unconscious—to which individuals aim their questions of love and desire in a closed trajectory of substitutive quest/ioning they only imagine to be aimed at the other of transference (love/hate) relations.

Lacan argued that there is no one countable symbol for Woman in the unconscious, although both man and woman are values or signifiers in the symbolic order. Very simply put, if man counts as the first symbol of that order because he is opposed *by definition* to the maternal nexus, males count as the Ur-symbol for culture itself. This is a matter of structure having little to do with masculine character traits, qualities, substantive concerns, or positive attributes of any sort. Yet, this masquerade, the charade of the happy couple is the social bond *par excellence*. "Normative" women, the *"nor-mâle,"* bow to patriarchal mythology in accepting to live by the masquerade of a master discourse: "I am what I am"; / "A man is a man"; / "A woman is a woman." Mastery is transparent narcissism: m'être / to be me. By contrast, female hysterics are constituted in opposition to a normative identificatory trajectory, their unconscious quest(ion), a search for a signifier for femininity. Having identified with the Other's lack, or with desire as lack, rather than with the ideal ego (the moi), the hysteric unlike her more socially mobile sister, (does not) believe in the roles prescribed for her. This latter, apparently, normative woman coheres as long as her desires, *jouissance*, beliefs, and ideals coalesce into a somewhat smooth alignment where her ego and desire and identified with collective social prescriptions for women in a given historical moment.

Yet, entry into analysis has the effect of hystericizing any patient— male or female, "normal," obsessional, perverse or psychotic—insofar as talking, questioning, trying to know, produces a search for the missing signifier for Woman. In "Another Lacan" Jacques-Alain Miller said Lacan might well have put over his office door: " 'Let no one enter here who seeks not Woman,' for whoever enters will seek her anyway." Any search opens to the search for an absent signifier where the inadequacy of signifiers for sexual difference finally bump up against a beyond in culture itself which Lacan names Woman. From the moment a question of the real (the impossible) raises its head as cause, Woman is no longer written as contingency but as the real, the impossible. Moreover, the passion of the signifier yields to the passion of the real whose cause is always on the slope of the feminine; the *pousse-à-la-femme*. And Miller takes Lacan's theory of inadequate signifiers for aligning sex, gender and identity so far as to claim that "knowledge as such substitutes for [our not] knowing the Other sex" ("Another Lacan," 2)

Although the anatomical difference does count, it counts in an imaginarized symbolic. In what ways will one identify with the *myths* that interpret anatomical difference, whether one means fantasy identifications with a little girl's supposed lost phallus, or with a little boy's phallic ghost? Whatever particular form his identifications take, the male confronts a difficulty females do not. Having seen visible proof that the other sex has no penis, he bears witness to the fantasy he can lose his, be castrated imaginarily. This is the (imaginary) phallus which is an Ur-object of the real and so marks the desire that supports the fantasy of loss, as well as loss of potency. One is familiar with the aggressive and narcissistic side-effects that accompany loss of face, there where phallus, penis, name, and social value compose some kind of masculinist ideology. By contrast women do not experience a fundamental castration anxiety since they cannot be deprived of a piece of anatomy that was never theirs.

Early in his teaching in "The Formations of the Unconscious" (1957–58), Lacan spoke of the masculinity complex as a problematic one which, curiously enough, results from a resolved Oedipal complex and bespeaks a closed subject. In this signifying nexus, males defend against imaginary castration anxiety by linking identity, discourse, and sexual apparatus to a fantasy of superiority *qua* difference. Such a position must then mobilize forces to shut out the feminine, telling the tale that something lacks in speech and being; i.e., the Other sex that bespeaks the unconscious. While this early Lacan reverses Freud, he finds support in the structure of Freud's argument. In "Desire and the Interpretation of Desire in *Hamlet*" (1959), Lacan referred to Freud's "Der Untergäng des Oedipus Komplexes" (1924) where Freud indicates that the aim of the Oedipus complex is not to kill the father or violate the mother. Rather the point is that this "complex" is unconscious (46). Lacan teaches that unconscious fantasy "drives" us toward objects whose cause is not only opaque, but lost *qua* content. In this context, the Oedipus "complex" becomes a structur(ing) of desire around a fundamental fantasy rather than a "complex" formed by repressed instincts. And objects may as easily be the promise of satisfaction, things or persons.

Although feminine and masculine sexuality are both similar and different at the level of gender identity, the *raison d'être* of the masculine *is* that it differs from the feminine. In this sense males may confuse their identity and sexuality with a universal by identifying with difference as itself a truth position ($\forall$x). The phallic image that marks a boy as differing from a girl will subsequently function in a third place in all three orders: in imaginary fantasy, as signifier or differential in the symbolic, as *objet a* in the real. Lacan cites Otto Fenichel's theory that woman = phallus ("The Symbolic Equation"). Like the penis which is perceptually detachable in fantasy, and thus beyond the law of the binary, the female body as the first, primordial object of desire, also takes on attributes of the phallus *qua* mark of lack, and as desiring or desired object. Even though the female body is first desired for food, warmth, etc., and only later partialized and fetishized into sexual organs and libidinal effects, this body, nonetheless, evokes desire at the level of a primordial void that belongs both to male and female. The point is not the mother as reified object, however, but that this body evokes desire at the level of a primordial link between the void— what is not there but produces palpable effects all the same—and the imaginary phallus, taken as the ghost of a visible imago. And as simultaneous object and cause of desire, the Lacanian Woman exceeds inside/outside distinctions that the imaginary reduces to the visible. Rather, she gives rise to structural positions where desire, language, and gender coalesce in recognizable relations to authority and knowledge. Both male and female are framed, then, not by language or biology, but by the desire that covers over whatever *jouissance* has been sacrificed, but remains in language or the body as an excess.

Because her very body serves as a lure to desire, Woman is essentialized by males as containing secret truths, the answers to enigmas, answers from, or to, the Otherness that the masculine denies and rejects and projects onto others. In this sense she is the phallus. Although gender identity evolves as an unconscious position taken toward the phallus, seen as an elemental effect emanating from an uninterpretable fundamental fantasy, such positions can only be deciphered through transference relations and in terms of symptoms whose cause(s) reappear, if at all, as transformed, distorted memories.

And beyond the signifying chains of memory, one encounters Lacan's insistence that there is no essence of the phallus, nor of the masculine or feminine, except insofar as *jouisssance* is a kind of substance.

So the penis is only one symbol of the phallus *qua* object of desire in the imaginarized-symbolic. But when correlated with any cut or mark of lack, the phallus becomes pure desire, a referent that annuls itself at the place where it points to the *jouissance* effects of the real. Other symbols of the (imaginary) phallus are the breast, the voice, the gaze, fragments and slits of the body, scents, and so on. These are all objects of the real that give rise to desire, but return discordantly in search of *jouissance*. Although the signifier "phallus" does not exist as a positive object, it signifies this fact: that the effects of sexual difference constitute the axis of the symbolic order. Images or visual differences quickly exceed their own reductionisms, opening onto the subject's division instead. Lacan called this division castration or the eclipse of a subject behind a signifier; that is, behind an image or word that re-*presents* a subject for another signifier. Yet the split is between an already alienated speaking being and the real effects that cause desire and return as symptoms. This experience of being spoken from Elsewhere produces the subject as an effect of alienation or castration. Language, thus, stands in for a subject, both as agent of the learning of difference, in the first place, and as the carrier of alienated desire(s) of the Other. In this sense, language is paradoxical, an index of its own negative function.

But beyond language qua *logos*, Lacan postulates a positivized negative—the Woman. As a referent, Woman opens onto the void of loss that dwells just beyond the doubts and fadings that arise from the lack of eclipse that is the absent Other for both sexes: S (Ⱥ). When film critic Laura Mulvey indicts Lacan in "Visual Pleasure and Narrative Cinema" for depicting Woman as the bearer of a bleeding wound, one who only exists in relation to a castration she cannot transcend, Mulvey reads Lacan as speaking a biological literalism. She, thus, confuses menstruation with castration, or castration blood and castration with cutting off the testicles. She has not taken into account Lacan's use of the word "castration" to say that language castrates all humans: "The Word kills the thing." For Lacan, woman re-presents a positivization of the real or void to which language refers. She does not represent a symbol of castrated deprivation, modeled on a biologically emasculated male.

Lacan gives us quite another idea of woman from contemporary critic David Macey's, as well. Where Mulvey sees biology, Macey sees mystics. In *Lacan in Contexts* Macey depicts Lacan as a surrealist who placed Woman in the position of mysterious Other. This, says Macey, makes him a sexist iconographer whose surrealist aesthetic—i.e. Baltimore in the early morning—points to a mystic iconography. Moreover, writes Macey, "Feminism and indeed any sexual politics, is constantly trivialized and dismissed [by Lacan] as pathological" (209) But Macey demonstrates that *he* has not grasped Lacan's theory that the imposition of gender difference on infants—culture imposed on nature—gives rise to identity as a problematic. Insofar as gender is an enforced ideology where an *idea* of the whole stands in for missing parts, gender is always already a politics where effect gives rise to cause.

But what determines whether a subject identifies as masculine or feminine? One answer is desire. This is strange, seeming to have no relation to gender identity. Yet, both males and females are effects of the phallic signifier, itself the effect of difference. A person's relation to the phallus or third term confronts each subject *beyond* the pleasure principle where the object a dwells as an irreducible weight. In the *jouissance* effects it produces, Lacan found a sense of spatial and temporal consistency that infers a kind of libidinal glue into meaning. And this consistency offers an anchor, a grounding in objects that are not themselves grounded. But our *jouissance* moments are bittersweet, our consistencies disrupted even as we declare ourselves sure. If, as Lacan argues, Woman identifies, more or less, with similarity rather than difference insofar as she is not asked to *be* in terms of *being different*, she will identify—not with a missing piece of anatomy, as post-structuralists have claimed, but—with the real which points to a hole in the absent Other. Splinters of the real return into language from this hole, materializing language with unassimilated kernels of *jouissance* that evoke a meaning outside meaning. The feminine—if not Woman *per se*—by definition admits of missing or weighty pieces more easily than the masculine, whether she knows it or not. The definition of the masculine (not man *per se*) is that which believes itself to be whole. But beware the paradox: whole in relation to what *he is not*—woman. That is, man is a failed woman. She knows no one is whole because she has not identified with difference as an imaginary universal, an identity fiction of autonomy. Rather, she has identified with similarity as an identity position that, in terms of its own logic, lies a bit outside culture and law ($\forall x$). Each sex, therefore, speaks a different language of identity and desire from the other.

It is not surprising that Lacan saw Woman as symptomatic, not only for man, but of a beyond or excess that niggles in reality and thought. A beyond that returns in language and *logos*. She counts by not counting. The "same way," the path of the all too familiar, casts no shadow in thought qua thought, but is discordant to it. It is, paradoxically, no-thing and that on which we count for our grounding. She counts in the same way the real does, as our very cause which is a lost cause. There where phenomenological objects are lost *qua* object, Lacan posits the *objet a* as a palpable effect. Marie-Hélène Brousse has suggested that the feminine is an impossibility in the real which—by definition—disrupts the feminine in culture (64). Put another way, the masculine effort to exist as difference personified means that he tries to live an impossibility, a lie. This intrinsic paradox of the masculine opens onto death and returns to haunt the feminine with the weight of its real. Beyond the position or failed autonomy, Lacan rewrites the position of Freud's mythical father in *Totem and Taboo*. The primal father's *jouissance* lies in its being the law of the other. This is the position of the Lacanian real father.

Males are enjoined by the incest taboo—the law itself, ultimately the law against psychosis—to identify image-inarily away from the mother's body and being. Identifying, instead, with the word for the father's name means a clinging to the symbolic realm of rules, strategies, and law. Language as a system of rules is indeed a prototype of a closed circuit whose self-sustaining *raison d'être* is not only to negotiate desire, but also to exclude disunities, inconsistencies, doubts, fadings, anxiety, *jouissance*. It becomes clearer what Lacan meant by locating the father's name as the first countable signifier of the symbolic order, that which counts on the side of culture and law, as opposed to the feminine side aligned with a "beyond" in law and culture. The Name triumphs over loss, over the empty set, and thus has the structure of the symbolic, of language, of metaphor; that which "stands in" for an absent ground, building identity on the quicksand of a void. Freud's mythic primordial father who becomes Lacan's real father is the *structure* that permits one to enjoy what he prohibits others. Yet prohibition yielding to excess opens onto the real, the void, the feminine. There where desire and law collide, the limits of the real appear as *jouissance* in the obscene form of total egoism or the death drive. Although masculine *jouissance* differs from feminine *jouissance*, except, perhaps, in the case of male mystics, both males and females are spoken by a real father, there where *jouissance* resides beyond the pleasure principle on the side of death.

Such a theory goes against post-structuralist feminist arguments that the Lacanian symbolic constitutes a patriarchal ideology. Rather myth—like Freud's myth of a primal horde—is the quintessence of the symbolic revelatory of language working from structure—R.S.I.—ordering traumatic (thus foreclosed) events, language, identity fictions in multi-layered associative signifying chains. Language and relations are interwoven, but also separable strands, insofar as they are ordered by *jouissance* and its excesses that desire tries to pin down. In trying to explain origins, myth tells stories that essentialize us. Yet, topological structure is not just another myth, but, rather, supercedes metaphor to show that we are surrounded by primordial losses that reappear as effects in every human act. There is no *the* symbolic order then, no totalization of anything, not even drives. Repetition proves that something was marked down. Otherwise, nothing could reappear in a network of culture-specific signifiers. Repetitions prove to us that we exist, although we fade from continuities. By retrieving pieces of thought from an Other, an opaque *savoir* just out of grasp, we speak and act, drawing on the signifying structures that in-form us in lightning flash instances. Yet, using words means canceling them from memory *as they speak us.* So where do we go from here? While gender fictions repeat themselves as ego myths that mutate in the symbolic and imaginary, symptoms appear at the impasse of the real where issues of sexual identity reveal subject limit as the limits of *jouissance* that mark any person's body, language and desire.

Lacan's teaching requires us to hold many conceptual balls in the air at the same time. How does one align myth, body, organs, cultural ideals, and ideas as they cohere and change in each subject? One answer is by thinking in terms of topological structure where the only grounding is the object *a,* itself not grounded. One would take account of the relationship of the subject to desire and *jouissance* in Lacan's four orders R.S.I. knotted (or not) by the *sinthome.* The hysteric's life question, for instance, is the very structure of the question: am I a man or woman? The obsessional's sense of identity and body is so confused with his mother's that he puts extra weight on words and thoughts, using language to build real fortresses against desire. Thus he tries to escape the gaze of the other—the effects of the real—but paradoxically remains faithful to the impossibility of seeking to be alive, but from a *jouissance* position of acting *as if he were dead.* Faithful to the Other whose slave he is, he tries to avoid others in order to attenuate the suffering that "enjoys" him. In the obsessional's illusion, he thinks himself to be master of the game that so brutally checkmates him instead. He is guilty of identifying with his mother's desire for him over the rotting corpse of his father. His "debts" to a denigrated father are debts he cannot repay, no more than he can repay a finally dissatisfied mother. Guilt and denial push him to wage battles around too little difference/distance from the feminine. It may seem paradoxical, but is actually logical, that language and law are often master signifiers for him. These signifiers stand-in for a weakly

inscribed signifier for a paternal name with which to identify in unconscious fundamental fantasy.

But post-structuralist feminists have not generally followed these
lines of Lacan's teaching. For example, in *Gynesis* Alice Jardine reads
Lacan literally. Pointing to his axiom: "There is no sexual relation,"
Jardine misreads his symbols of sexuation as a universalizing error.
By confusing the cancellation of *the* before woman, she says, sure,
there are no *women* if there is no sexual relation. Lacan has *discounted*
woman (164). Yet, the word "relation" is the operative word in the
axiom where "relation" does not mean sexual "act." In fact, Lacan
finds the universal error on the masculine side and further indicts
men for essentializing women. Jardine thinks Lacan has failed to
understand representation: "Representation is the condition that confirms the possibility of an imitation (mimesis) based on the dichotomy
of presence and absence, the dichotomies of dialectical thinking (negativity)" (119). Yet Lacan's theory of representation leads to a new
theory of dialectical thinking, neither of which Jardine takes into
account. In 1973 Lacan said: "If the MLF feminists were not so mad
at me, maybe I could say something new to them about feminine
sexuality" (*Encore* 54). The "new" concerns a knowledge women and
male mystics have, but that most men lack: a knowledge about *jouissance*. What they know—women and male mystics—is that there is a
pleasure and suffering beyond the *logos* and beyond lack, a *jouissance*
that concerns knowledge and being. This "knowledge," at odds with
what we call knowledge, subverts all myths of solution or resolution:
It is the knowledge that no One is whole (*Encore*, 69). Appearing in
myriad guises, this "knowledge" hides, for example, in the martyr's
superior smile masking the *belle âme* secret. She knows that she
"comes" from the real. Her *jouissance* contains the knowledge that
she suffers in serving the others who use her without knowing they
do so. Her secret is that she is superior to others because she suffers.

Lacan argues in the opposite direction of Jardine. Representation
is non-mimetic. The mirror-stage image proves to have been a falsifi-
cation, an illusion of Oneness, when reality is actually characterized
by a One-minus. Thus, the Ur-forms of representations are, rather, the
primordially repressed *objet a*, which return as *points de capiton* to
materialize language by eternal engagements of desire with *jouissance*
as encounters of body and libido, eternal clashes of the real with the
symbolic. These primary objects, primordially repressed and lost to
active memory—the breast, feces, urinary flow (imaginary) phallus,
phoneme, void, voice, and gaze—have a fetishistic quality that reap-
pears all the same to intervene in language as *das Ding an sich*. As

corporal objects the non-specular primordial object *a* gives rise to heterogeneous objects of desire around which "drives" cluster as partial drives. In this context, *hors-sens*, "drive" seems to elude meaning because its goal is the *jouissance* or satisfaction sought in the lure of objects.

Although the logic of the "drive" is not correspondent or coherent—because primordial objects are lost—there is, all the same, a logic of the drive ($ \emptyset $ D). In Lacan's elaboration of the order of the real, commonplace concepts of representations as mere images, flattened artifacts, or rhetorical tropes gave way to a picture of re-presentations or signifiers as masking or covering over presentations; i.e. the *objet a*. Lacan had already argued that metaphor was equivalent to Freud's idea of primary-process condensation, whose proximity to dreams and literary symbols suggests a greater meaning than that of simple trope. Indeed, if metaphor is a function (*functio* Latin for performance), then it is also a name for movement, for energy; that is desire as the residual left-over from an inert *jouissance*. If "true symbolism" is only apprehendable in the cadre of metaphor, as Lacanians stress, defined as signifying substitutions, based on oppositions and relations, that occur *as* language, one sees why Lacan did not have to divide mental processes (as did Aristotle) into logical propositions and rhetorical tropes within conscious life, and symbolic or mimetic ones in the unconscious domain (Bouquier et al., *Ornicar?* 38, 137). Rather, the learning of identity in terms of sexual difference and gender ideology automatically inserts metonymies (object *a*) into language *qua* cause and object of desire. The *petit a* creates gaps that reveal the play of *jouissance* effects in meaning. This is not to be confused with the Derridean lack of a center or origin that spawns a freeplay of linguistic "substitutions" limited only by the supplements that constitute a frame or context. What Lacan shows us is language reeling from the effects of drive that never quite reaches its object.

While the symbolic/imaginary realms of language and images try to hide the hole in the Other where "objects" are lost to memory, Lacan declares this hole the *raison d'être* of human knowing. If lack dwells on the negative side of desire and infers aphanisis into language, one can understand Lacan's claim that only the real or the void are certain. In this sense the real is positivizable in its production of *jouissance*. Addressing the Lacanian idea that some*Thing* is certain, Slavoj Žižek has written: "Psychoanalytic 'essentialism' is paradoxical insofar as it is precisely psychoanalysis—at least in its Lacanian reading—which presents the real break with essentialist logic" (*The Sublime*, 4).

While deconstruction and Marxim define themselves in anti-essentialist terms as affirming an irreducible plurality of theories and studies that depend on the radical contingency of the social-historical process, Žižek says that Lacan, by contrast, "enables us to grasp this plurality itself as a multitude of responses to the same impossible real kernel." (4). When Lacan spoke of the structure of the subject as topological, he described contradictory orders of meaning which reveal why clear and distinct knowledge is so difficult to attain. Humans deny inherent contradictions by clinging to fundamental ideologies, whether they be scientific ideologies that wed the true to the visible, or so-called radical intellectual stances where the supreme good is thought to lie in embracing a totalized Plural, a totalizing Indeterminacy. Yet, each circle of the Borromean knot holds only insofar as it is chained to the other, each contradicting the other, while tied to relations of *pure signifying* which find their limits in impasses and encounters where the object *a* is produced. Deconstructive theories that aim to subvert class and sex wars by opposing and then destroying hierarchies may lead to certain awakenings regarding the layering of networks of signifying associations, but they do not address the question Lacan asked after Freud: Why and how does the sexual difference make such a difference?

Early in his teaching Lacan said the purely topological origin of language—its resonance at the level of effect—lies in that "it is essentially tied to something which happens to the speaking being under the bias of sexuality" ("Ste Anne" 209) that creates a real palpable hole in being and in knowledge. One dreams over it, makes a center of it, whence all sorts of vocabulary and *jouissance* effects. This hole exists, not only because originary objects *are* lost, but because some experiences, too painful to articulate, are lost as memory, but remain as meaning effects registered in the body, as *objet a*. Psychoanalytic interpretation, dreams, the lack of harmonious sexual relations, and creative art itself, function at this interface where the orders (R.S.I.) circle around these remainders of the real, seeking satisfactory resolutions and conclusions. "Drive" aims at elusive *jouissance*, trying to force unity and eradicate anxiety, doubt, and questions. In turn, the real—the *object a*—appears as obstacles to the smooth movement of symbolization within language. Although drive tries to circumvent loss, no symmetrical response answers. Rather the Other exists outside us as a lack in whose center loss resides.

One proof that the Other is only "supposed" as a source of knowledge lies in Lacan's demonstrations of his axiom: There is no sexual relationship. That is, the relation between the sexes is by definition a place where lack and loss play out their effects in all the orders: real, symbolic, imaginary and symptom. No symmetrical relation between man and woman is possible. Rather one finds the limits of idealized relations in the reality of relations circling around the "impossible" antagonistic things. "There is no final solution," says Žižek, "and the only basis for a somewhat bearable relation is an acknowledgement of this basic antagonism or impossibility" (*The Sublime*, 5). Yet Lacan taught that giving up on harmony, on the ideal, opens us up paradoxically, to greater freedoms.

There is no *natural* sexual rapport, just as there is no transparent relation of the subject to the Other. But each person's identity questions means to deny an unsymbolizable difference—the difference where unity is sought. So, the sexual masquerade structures culture around pretenses, two can be one, the Emperor is not naked under his clothes, and so on. By hiding basic truths, people live by any ideology or ideal that offers resolution in preference to cuts, breaks and confusion. "When the subject takes the place of the lack," Lacan said in 1958, "a loss is introduced in the word and this is the definition of the subject" (Inmixing," 193). That is, lack may be localized in a mark the letter or *l'être* stands in for. Lack is what the subject stands in for. Early feminisms that totalize sexual ideologies, view sex as a commodity to be tossed back and forth to the correct team. But the teams keep changing, as do ideas about what is correct. If one looks at the sexual question from a Lacanian viewpoint, however, no one group has the right answer. Any of us who fashions our sexual *jouissance* into an ideology—heterosexists, heterosexuals, homosexuals, lesbians, married swingers, celibates, youthful experimenters, and so on—expresses desire with the force of a law imposed on others. Thus, any sexual ideology expresses a potential oppression of an other's desire.

But Lacan showed us how to exit from such imaginary prisonhouses, difficult as it is, because the imaginary hides the fact that subjects are split between language (alienation) and the objects that cause them to desire satisfaction, while also blocking satisfaction. Yet, these Ur-objects that cause desire have no signified, although they emanate from real objects whose first forms provide lining of the subject, and later metapmorphosize into myth, desire, *jouissance*. But the illusory consistency supplied by fantasy—an interweave of language and image—veils the linkage of desire with *jouissance*. Fundamental fantasies totalize, operating from "made" assumptions inaccessible to interpretation, while the "objects" of desire meant to satisfy fantasy splinter the misrecognitions of fantasy. Therefore, Lacan's matheme for fantasy is built upon a paradox:—$\$ \lozenge a$—in part because the objects sought replicate their own cause, but only partially. When objects represent the organ function that produces them, the split between the organ and its product (for example, between the eye and gaze) makes it clear why Lacan redefined the so-called part objects as partial drives that are always already libidinized in their search for fulfillment. Inscribed as "erogenous zones" on the body, desire zones are constituted as the mark of a margin or border. Lacan called this border a cut, such as lips enclosing teeth. "Observe," Lacan said in 1958, "that this mark of the cut is no less obviously present in the object described by analytic theory: the mamilla, faeces, the phallus (imaginary object), the urinary flow. (An unthinkable list, if one adds, as I do, the phoneme, the gaze, the voice—the nothing)" ("The Subversion," 314–15).

Lacan taught that analytic cure be directed toward a final, not entirely possible, goal: the braking or separating of a fundamentally unconscious fantasy from the object of desire that sustains it in the real. Fundamental fantasies are already organized around opaque and alien desires which satisfy themselves by clinging to symptoms that provide a familiar *jouissance*. Yet because language enables us to believe in narrative, in our stories, in deconstruction, linearity and progress, we are assured that answers lie "out there," or will eventually come to us through acquisition of desired objects, or yet another signifier, or a supplement, another research project, the method itself, and so on. It is difficult to see that the major function of language is not to find answers, communicate, or provide information, but to project narcissism, protect egos, mask *jouissance*, negotiate desire. Dreams, literary texts, sexual relations, analysis, pleasure, pain, symptoms, repetition, the feminine and religion all reside on the slope of fading, gaps, and questions. It is not closure or solutions that mark these phenomena, but mystery and enigma, marks of the fourth order Lacan named the symptom.

By now we see that Lacan's psychoanalysis *qua* theory of sexual difference is not Freud's. Lacan postulated a structural asymmetry that evolves in the constitution of sexual identity as masculine or feminine, not because of any gender requisite or innate character, not because of male superiority or female envy, but because the first countable signifier concerns the difference as a gender identity "cause." Gender identity will always take on symbolic and imaginary meaning in reference to a *signifier* for the name of a father (the paternal metaphor) and in correlation with a mother's desire *qua* primordial and ineffable metaphor. Thus, gender identification is not established only by the Other's desire, which is on the slope of *savoir* or knowing, but also in tandem with the imaginary where the subject's ego is fed by *jouissance*. In tandem, these produce the real as an order of leftovers, scars, debris. By turning the Oedipal construct away from the family *qua* family, Lacan was able to refer principally to cultural constructs or language conventions (the place of the Other) and *jouis-sance:* $\frac{J}{A}$ or $\frac{A}{J}$? Not surprisingly, the ideal ego—an unconscious formation—itself has the structure of the symptom. And the symptom has the structure of metaphor—that which can be seen only in its substitutes.

So what is the sexual masquerade? In Lacan's theory it means waltzing around effects of the real that places impasses and knots in the symbolic and imaginary, knots that constitute meanings (*sense*) impossible to articulate or assimilate. The *jouissance* effects we call antagonisms, conflicts, problems and paradoxes are, then, blockages we try to circumvent produced by the real which "drives" us to speak (or write) in an effort to "enjoy." One sees the hitch, the catch, the tautology. Lacan's real father denotes a paradox: the production of *jouissance*, which occurs at the moment desire becomes law. The real father at the heart of the sexual masquerade points to the impossibilities or impasses in being, knowing, and speaking the truth as pure CONTRADICTION. Put another way, the real *is* the structural impasse where *jouissance* effects evacuate law to create knots or double binds, pointing to philosophical double-bind chestnuts as tautological linguistic or mental efforts to re-present a palpable, yet impossible, place in knowing and being. The real is *not no-thing*, then. Known by its effects at the level of *jouis-sens*, bits and pieces of the real are always disrupting any smooth flow of language, or of supposed identificatory harmonies, producing the inconsistencies of wisps, sighs, fragments, glances. Yet since an irreducible kernel of the real always remains to be circumvented at the heart of every signifying chain, the real always weighs language down with its density which produces a new kind of materiality in language.

Moreover, the Lacanian sexual (un)relation gives witness to a conception of desire whose comings and goings adorn language, as do the enigmata of the "drives." The desired objects meant to provide "enjoyment" quickly become empty sets: the mouth trying to say, the ear trying to decipher the meaning of a word, the eyes seeking to pin down the meaning of a gaze, and so on. Walls, not mirrors. In April 1987 in New York City Jacques-Alain Miller said that this *jouis-sens* beyond language is not the unconscious, but nonetheless points to a "satisfaction of unconscious drives" (Jacques Lacan's *Television*, 41). If, as Lacan taught, unconscious drives do not always wish one's good, feminist theories that have equated *jouissance* with pleasure and the erotic pleasure of sexual freedom to gender liberation, have missed the meaning of Lacan's rethinking of the links between repetition, the death *beyond* the pleasure principle, and *jouissance*. The sexual (un)relation points, not to the pleasure obtained or the partner one chooses, but to "the drive" misrecognized by the ego. Indeed, the ego is not a "drive," but a fiction complicitous with its own deceptions. In this sense the ego might be called the site of ideology in the sense that ideology is narcissistic, a master (*m'être*) discourse whose goal is certainty and closure: "to be me."

Feminine sexuality—not necessarily correlated with gender—is a masquerade not only because s/he can disguise her desire, can fake it, can cover her body with cosmetics and jewels and make of *it* a phallus, but also because her masquerade hides a fact—that masculine sexuality is a tenuous matter. Things do not work so easily between man and woman, or between any sexual partners for that matter. If *only* this point were understood, Lacan's phallic signifier would not be read imaginarily—i.e. essentialized—as a privileging of the masculine. It would be seen, rather, as a dividing effect created by learning difference as gender difference. Counter-arguments by French feminists such as Hélène Cixous or Luce Irigaray that make of woman the first signifier, correlated with gender alone, would themselves be seen as totalizing and essentializing, reducing woman to an imaginary status of the visible and primordial. Yet even before the signifiers aligned in any identi-kit start a count where a subject identifies as man, woman, either/or, both/and, or neither/nor, the "*a priori*" objects of desire that produce *jouissance* effects intervene in the seeming unity of the imaginary where sex appears to cohere with gender and desire. Yet, the reality is that gender obscures the discontinuities in our knowing, being, intention, affects, and so on.

Because no one of us is finally partner to the other, we try all the harder to either claim sexual harmony or ego autonomy. Between any one and the other, each subject's partner is the Other sex. Yet between a subject's ego and the Other (sex) to whom that subject's question regarding sexual identity is addressed or dramatized, a dialectical war rages between desire, potentially enslaving or freeing, and narcissistic symtoms—subjectification—petrified into ego fictions from early in life. But in life, desire loses out to the fixity of the ego because desire is opaque and the Other, unreliable. Moreover, *jouissance* objects support the ego, placing death *cum* libidinal fixity at the very center of being. Thus, we love our symptoms even more than our potential freedoms.

Psychoanalytic clinics, literary texts, films, gossip chains, all tell the story of a real impasse in sexual relations. The phallic symbol is not an adequate representation for establishing rapport, nor does Woman contain the essences spoken in her name. There is no sexual harmony in the unconscious, then, only each subject's relationship to the phallus as the signifier of its own impossibility: a "negative version of truth as the index of itself" (Žižek, "Why Lacan is Not A," 35). Neither sex is the negation of the other, but the obstacle to the other. Nor does homosexuality offer an ideal Good in relationships anymore than heterosexuality. Every person always confronts the Other beyond the other.

Pointing to Aristotle's efforts to solve the problem of human *existence*, Lacan said that while Aristotle knew existence could not be established outside the universal, the particular gave him great problems, paradoxically leading him to reduce existence to the particular. Lacan tries to solve the problem of existence by his appeal to the structures of topology after basing his notion of language on the 20th-century mathematician Gottloeb Frege's discovery of the natural number, where zero grounds number one and implies one more. Language exists as a seemingly coherent system because it has a relationship to something else: *not* only to the next signifier *qua* word or sound, but more profoundly, to the void as the referent of language. Moreover, people seek others as referents in the hope of undoing knots, dismantling double binds, and finding unities, solutions and harmonies after all—despite the lacks and losses that drive people to repeat symptoms of which they understand nothing.

More precisely, Lacan names the place where the existence question can be re-examined Woman. Insofar as she represents an unhappy "structural" truth about the human condition, one learns that the existence of an identity depends on turning away from the Ur-mother. Everyone—who is not clinically psychotic—lacks, is not all (*pas-tout*). Logically speaking, if there is at least one symbol by which to represent difference, then "human existence" *qua* identity can be defined from there. Lacan takes the imaginary phallus as the "at least one' symbol of difference in the real order of primordial objects that line the subject. But it is not the visibility of this symbol that counts. Rather, the symbol gives birth to a signifier that positions a subject in culture insofar as he or she assimilates an imaginarized symbolic defined by a differential: the law of gender limits. So the function of the "at least one" repeatable symbol is paradoxical here. It both starts the count of culture and quickly becomes its own limit. This limit alone stops the infinitization in meaning that deconstructive dissemination describes as necessary metonymies—necessary, that is, to deconstructive theories of language. Indeed, the seeming impossibility of psychoanalysis rests on the disbelief that a minimal difference could give rise to maximal effects. Rather than heed such psychoanalytic "non-sens", men and women are duped into believing strange persistent myths: that man is "it" (the bearer of knowledge as truth) and Woman has "it" (truth that yields itself up) as a beyond in knowledge.

Insofar as the feminine has been mythologized on the side of shadows, desire, and dreams, if not as the very source of the enigmata of aesthetics, the masculine clings instead to *logos* and identifies knowledge with the visible, with method, the provable. Jane Gallop is on the right track in *Reading Lacan* when she links metonymy to the feminine and metaphor to the masculine, but not because of the biological literalism she implies (126). Metaphor and metonymy are not gender specific. Woman may *seem* universalizeable because culture identifies her with the silence of the drives that Lacan called the real, even if she does not recognize this as a knowledge about *jouissance*. Neither sex is assured of a universal function in terms of knowledge, then. Nor is there a consistency in gender identity, sexuality, body image, or even in surfaces, only in appearances. Freud discovered gender difference as the key to the *unnatural* way identity is constituted by the cultural, rather than by the animal natural. Lacan pushed Freud's confusion about this discovery—and particularly the role of the feminine within it—onto another plane where even Woman cannot answer the question *Was will das Weib?* in its most radical sense. Because the answer is the real where points of limit or impossibility within language, desire, sexuality, and meaning meet in contradictory understandings or collide at mysterious impasses.

Beyond appearance (the phenomenal), Lacan located both the phallus and the gaze on the slope of fading in a new reading of the noumenal. The phallus—taken as an effect, as the mark of lack—skews the binary opposition between the sexes that would reduce difference to interchangeable samenesses. Yet the difference opens onto limits, the impossible, and so is always interpreted again and again. But insofar as interpretation *is* the elaboration of desire, the phallus far exceeds any anatomical parameter, while still calling any interlocuter of Lacan back to the body as the source of meaning and "drive." Likewise, the gaze exceeds the ocular act of looking, although looking seeks to know or understand. Rather, the gaze turns us inside/out. Are we seeing, looking, or looked at? While looking certainly offers pleasure as Laura Mulvey and other film theorists argue ("Visual Pleasure," 200), Lacan's gaze is commensurate—not with the eye, but—with *jouissance* encountered on the side of anxiety and idealizations: judgment, narcissistic fantasies, threat, the presence of a void. The gaze and the voice constitute component parts, of a superego-like constellation Lacan called the ideal ego where unconscious fantasies dwell.

The ego is, however, susceptible of fragmenting back into its signifying components in art, psychosis, sexual acts, or certain uncanny moments of everyday life.

How, then, do individuals keep from feeling anxiety on a constant basis? We are *always* looked at, heard, or not heard; always detotalized. The answer is clear. We fill the void with all kinds of fodder to close out loss. We *identify* with things, but call ourselves interpreters of things: scientists and hermeneuticians. While artists—whom we do not know how to value—try to recreate or somehow embody the lacks and losses they know only too well, we, on a more mundane level, try to fill the void with beliefs and love. We write about love, talk about love. Each person loves in the other what he or she lacks in the Other. Love is a waltz around a non-relation, a sign of hope eternal that the void may be eternally and permanently closed. Yet, to stake all on love or on *an* interpretation is to opt for imaginarized symbolic answers that close out knowledge of the human masquerade going on before our eyes. Who *is* looking at whom, and from where?

Is film critic Laura Mulvey correct in "Visual Pleasure and Narrative Cinema" in describing woman as image and man as the bearer of the gaze? (203). In Lacan's teaching man is first represented in language by one unconscious symbol—the symbol for difference—and woman is not. Yet that re-presentation is a lie, a sham, a veil over a void. Rather, both sexes encounter the gaze of others, and of the Other. Woman masquerades around a gaze that re-presents the impossible real at the heart of the symbolic order, of patriarchy. She masquerades around a gaze that positions her as a desiring subject, a bearer of the ecstasy and agony of knowing *jouissance* all too well. Woman is a response of the real not because of gender *per se*, but because she points to a place in meaning where an exposed hole is in the Other. The real arises from this hole [(S$\cancel{A}$)], shedding its many skins.

I would place the obvious points of join between psychoanalysis and art alongside Lacan's fascination with Woman. The self-referential movement of the signifier was, for Lacan, the movement of an ellipse around a certain void created by the primordiality of loss as a positivizable cause of being and knowing. Although he did not romanticize this void, Lacan saw those inscribed on the side of the feminine as teaching some truth about it, a truth that explains the "logocentric" passion for systems of answers and closure. Such systems find their "truths" in appeal to objectivity, method, common sense, reality, cults of personality, and so on. The feminine truth that goes "beyond" writing, semiotic codes, or substantive answers joins hands, instead, with literary language that offers pleasure partly because the text is a kind of "body" where transference, narrative, repetition, and pleasure point to a "beyond." Writers know about this beyond because they write—not to express some transcendental unconscious, but—to try to make the object *a* (the real) appear, even as it escapes them. Similarly, when feminism celebrates hysteria, the female orgasm is not at issue, but the "beyond" in the feminine that links *it* to language and knowledge and representation. Woman lies at the heart of the human "drive" to hide, not to know. Yet, we try to know anyway, indirectly, by pushing Woman around.

So what—if anything—is missing in Woman? Is it the penis? Only at that minimal level where the ghost of difference is a limit. Yet culture paradoxically crowns the male with the empty signifier of difference itself as standing in for limit or law. Still, this *einziger Zug* gives rise to myths—the essentialized imaginary—that base the mark of difference meaning itself on the serial ordering of identity around signifiers and things which are never identical to themselves. For Lacan difference has a "meaning" whose economy embraces the perpetuation of the social link, then, an answer he found in the clinic in the structure of psychosis. If a mother takes her child to be her (all), then the economy of psychosis waits in the wings. If the child becomes her fetish object, a mammocratic state of totalitarian horror rules. Such fetishization unveils another idealizing harmony, implying that a child can make up for what is missing. She "enjoys" by refusing identity to the child *qua* different from her desire. The child is, consequently, not nameable, not signifiable, not other. Fetishized as the phallus—cherished object meant to supplement whatever the mother lacks—such a child identifies with the real rather than the imaginarized symbolic which is not pushed away to the liveable distance that constitutes most people as subjects of the symbolic and imaginary orders.

In Lacan's teaching, what is missing for most people is *das Ding:* the real effects that remain unassimilated into the imaginary and symbolic. One trauma that most people undergo is learning an identity through the Oedipal straits of a given culture's myths about gender. But something is always amiss on this voyage where desire, gender and identity are forced into awkward, unnatural cohesions. Yet the gift of being (as a viable narcissism) supported by a differentiated name (social link), is bestowed on most people. Still no one wins, neither most people who lack or psychotics who do not. Because the "gift" of lack robs us of certainty and takes a bite out of ego and body— the masculine and feminine delineating different positions taken in regard to lack—the feminine masquerade automatically poses a question, while masculine identification with law, logos, or authority tries to stop the question. Yet, paradoxically, *his* effort at mastery shows a lack—a lie as the basis of the symbolic—while *her* lack of position is unbearable in the real.

As we said earlier, the impasse Lacan places at the heart of analysis is the impasse between the sexes that spurs humans to speak and desire at all. In *Television* Lacan said:

> "We'll go on, then, starting off from the Other, the radical Other, evoked by the nonrelation embodied by sex—for anyone who can perceive that One occurs, perhaps, only through the experience of the (*a*) sexed. Rather, she is a party to the perversion which is, I maintain, Man's. Which leads her into the familiar masquerade that is not just the lie of which some ingrates, themselves clinging to the role of Man, accuse her. Rather, she prepares herself on-the-off chance, so that her inner fantasy of Man will find its hour of truth. That's not excessive, since truth is already Woman insofar as it's not-all, unable, in any case, to be wholly spoken. But that is why truth is more often than not standoffish, demanding of love, sexual pretenses that it can't fulfill, misfiring—sure as clockwork. Thus, it follows that in love it is not the meaning that counts, but rather the sign as in everything else" (*Television*, 44–45).

Lacan does not mean the semiotic sign, but the sign of love, not always easy to ascertain since it is organized within and against the field of the gaze where judgmental truths that resonate beyond what the eye sees assign value. Meanwhile the eye or voice try inadequately to encompass, explain, unify. Lacan considered the body an imaginary signifier, lived on the side of the real, thus, a fragmented body that falsely believes itself to be whole. The feminine masquerade drama- tizes the *human* lie, materializing language around the someThing missing in the masculine and in the social. Scents, intimate details, and resonances surround female bodily orifices with a supposed es- sence of the feminine, quickly mythologized into gender fictions. The masculine, on the other hand, signifies a search for knowledge, author- ity, or prestige. When either sex subverts these normative myths, society seeks to reinstate the illusions of the sexual masquerade. Yet if each of us really addresses the Other (sex), how can one hope to theorize correct problems arising from sexual difference by descrip- tive theories? If indeed, unconscious desire drives us to identify with others and with words that are intermittently splintered by the real, of what value is this knowledge? If, like the fish skeleton or cuttle bone in the center of Holbein's painting of *The Ambassadors*, the object *a* rises up to become a death's head once one changes position, if by linking the void to the gaze as it bears on anxiety where loss *qua* loss appears at the center of being and knowing, it is logical that Lacan refer to Holbein's death's head as the naked gaze that reveals a void behind apparently stable images (*Seminar* XI "Anamorphosis," 78–90). At least we begin to know that our enemies are structural, "whats" before they are embodied in "whos."

This differs from the Heideggerean picture of Lacan's gaze Ned Lukacher paints in "Anamorphic Stuff." For Lukacher, anamorphosis seizes human vanity and itself "constitutes the subject as a subject that gives itself to be seen and to be seized by an other's gaze, which is to say ultimately seized by the power of death as a kind of being for death" (873). Lacan portrayed a truth of the body that speaks the real as a language of loss, resonant of a death drive *in* in the body whose *jouissance* is the stopper or limit to the desire(s) that delineate a subject as his own cause in the aims and goals of the drive. While *jouissance* is the joker that starts and stops the game, the subject—not one with itself—is always represented by language or by *jouissance*. But we deny this strange masquerade where we dance around each other, accommodating ourselves to others through monumental farces, the strangest of bedfellows, subject to intense contradictions, outrageous comedies, keeping the Other at arm's distance and blaming others instead.

Whether we see Mae West caricaturing masculine images of feminine sexuality—"This is what you want honey, so you've got it. But Ha! ha!, have I got you?!"—or Freud depicting the varied plights of widows in *Totem and Taboo* (53–54), we see that images of women and "talk" about women is an industry in its own right. Not only do I refer to the academic and political concern with feminist issues, but also to soap operas whose appeal to women daytime viewers rests, in part, on the presentation of men who are really talking women. Let's face it Men do not talk about abortions, divorce and feelings, about who ran away with whom in life, as they do in the soaps. But women talk, housewives and career women alike, while men control its flow lest they be engulfed by the Other. Lacan shows us that even if Woman is not represented by one unconscious symbol, she is, nonetheless, not deconstructable or readily decoded. Embodying the real and the enigmatic, she speaks because she is not-all, because she knows, even if she denies this knowledge, that something is missing in knowledge *qua* knowledge. She knows there is no totality, not even of the feminine or masculine. She speaks on and through her body, in a voice irreducible to grammar, and from a body that never ceases to pose questions about desire, whether she is nubile, pregnant, a sex bomb, or old and withered.

Woman gives the lie to what Robert de Beaugrande thinks *should* be: "An essential part of the needed innovations in the practice of discourse is to deconstruct all appeals to 'truth' " (265). In Lacan's teaching no such relativistic pluralism is thought to lead to freedom, change or hope. Indeed, I would call pluralism today's neo-conservative ideology that enjoins searchers for causes to look no further, to embrace Everything as the Answer, rather than to question the Gap between their theories and their lives. Lacan learned in the clinic of sufferers that by addressing the "truth" in language, by treating the real with which each person identifies, an analysand can find a source of possible change and freeing up of energy that turns to creation rather than destruction.

Finally, if the primordial layers of knowing *cum* desiring are joins between the imaginary and real, given specific meaning by a symbolic, then we see that the male gaze and female gaze will always intersect. Feminine sexuality is not only a mystery regarding a missing symbol impossible to interpret within a binary opposition. Feminine sexuality makes epistemological and ontological issues political ones as well. Why, for example, would the literal exposure of female genitalia as a painting hung on a living room wall be thought of as pornographic, rather than as portraying the aesthetics of feminine beauty? What would one want to hide from public viewing? What masquerade goes on here? Does this taboo express the structure of taboo itself: a yes and a no?

Is the Mona Lisa a terrifying painting because it too represents the structure of taboo? A smile that only seems to tame the gaze, hiding the Freudian "truth" that the meaning of the feminine is not to be unveiled through the nakedness beneath her clothes, but through masculine fetishising and essentializing of Woman in order to deny his own death and contingency. The feminine becomes a covering that reveals and conceals at the same time. Just as masks and moral posturing both point to something more, something invisible, the Freudo-Lacanian "Thing" reveals *jouissance* as the cement of ego constancy, a poison that seeps into all fantasies and illusions to disunify them, especially into fantasies of what Woman is or is not. At some universalized level of *jouissens*, the feminine coincides with limit itself, even as it evades limits, revealing language as a tool of desire materializing the body, there where the slip of language is itself only one more masquerade.

Works Cited

Andrès, Mireille. *Lacan et la Question du Métalangage.* Paris: Point Hors Ligne, 1987.

Beaugrande, Robert, de. "In Search of Feminist Discourse: The 'Difficult' Case of Luce Irigaray." *College English* 50, no. 3 (1988): 253–72.

Bouquier, Jean-Jacques, Nathalie Charraud, Geneviève Morel. "Ella Sharpe, 1875–1947: L'Esprit de la lettre." *Ornicar?* 38 (1986): 129–39.

Brousse, Marie-Hélène. Reference to her paper on feminine sexuality at the conference "Lacan, Discourse, and Politics. Kent State University (May 1989)," *Newsletter of the Freudian Field* 2, no. 2 (Fall 1988): 64–5.

Fenichel, Otto. "The Symbolic Equation: Girl = Phallus." *The Psychoanalytic Quarterly* 20, no. 3 (1949): 303–24.

Fink, Bruce. "Notes on Temporal Tension." *Newsletter of the Freudian Field* 2, no. 2 (Fall 1988): 23–8.

Freud, Sigmund. "Analysis Terminable and Interminable" (1937). *The Standard Edition of the Complete Works of Sigmund Freud.* Trans. James Strachey in collaboration with Anna Freud. London: Hogarth Press, 1953.

———. "Der Untergang des Ödipus Komplexes" (1924). Trans. as "The Dissolution of the Oedipus Complex." *S.E.* 19.

———. *Totem and Taboo: Some Points of Agreement between the Mental Lives of Savages and Neurotics* (1913). Trans. and authorized by James Strachey. *S.E.* 13. New York: W. W. Norton & Co., 1952.

Gallop, Jane. *Reading Lacan.* Ithaca, NY: Cornell University Press, 1985.

Jardine, Alice. *Gynesis: Configurations of Woman and Modernity.* Ithaca, NY: Cornell University Press, 1985.

Lacan, Jacques. "The agency of the letter in the unconscious or reason since Freud." *Ecrits: A Selection.* Trans. Alan Sheridan. New York: W. W. Norton & Co., 1977.

———. "Desire and the Interpretation of Desire in *Hamlet.*" *Yale French Studies.* 55 (1977): 11–52.

———. "A Love Letter (une Lettre D'Amour)." Eds. Juliet Mitchell and Jacqueline Rose. Trans. Jacqueline Rose. *Feminine Sexuality.* New York: W.W. Norton & Co., 1982. See *Séminaire* XX: *Encore.* Text established by Jacques-Alain Miller. Paris: Seuil, 1975.

———. "Ste. Anne." *Polysexuality: Semiotexte(e)* 4, no. 1 (1981): 208–18.

———. *Le Séminaire, Livre* V: *Les Formations de l'Inconscient,* unpublished text.

———. *Séminaire* XI: *The Four Fundamental Concepts.* Ed. Jacques-Alain Miller. Trans. Alan Sheridan. New York: W.W. Norton & Co., 1977.

———. "Of Structure as an Inmixing of an Otherness Prerequisite to Any Subject Whatever." Eds. Richard Macksey and Eugenio Donato. *The Structuralist Controversy: The Languages of Criticism and the Sciences of Man.* Baltimore: Johns Hopkins University Press, 1970.

———. "The subversion of the subject and the dialect of desire in the Freudian unconscious." *Ecrits: A Selection.* Trans. Alan Sheridan. New York: W.W. Norton & Co., 1977.

———. *Television.* Trans. Denis Hollier, Rosalind Krauss, and Annette Michelson. Special Ed. Joan Copjec. *October* 40 (1987): 5–50. See *Television.* Paris: Seuil, 1974.

Lukacher, Ned. "Anamorphic Stuff." Ed. Leigh A. De Neff. *South Atlantic Quarterly* 22, no. 4 (Fall 1989): 863–98.

Macey, David. *Lacan in Contexts*. London: Verso, 1988.

Meese, Elizabeth. *Crossing the Double-Cross. The Practice of Feminist Criticism*. Chapel Hill: The Univ. of North Carolina Press, 1986.

Miller, Gérard. Director of the Collective. "Clinique des psychoses: Approches et repères dans la clinique psychanalytique des psychoses." *Ornicar?* 34 (1985): 79–89.

Miller, Jacques-Alain. "Another Lacan." Ed. Helena Schulz-Keil. *Lacan Study Notes* 1, no. 3 (1984): 1–3.

Miller, John. "Jacques Lacan's *Television*." *Artscribe International* (Nov/Dec 1987): 40–41.

Mulvey, Laura. "Visual Pleasure and Narrative Cinema." Ed. Philip Rosen. *Narrative Apparatus, Ideology: A Film Theory Reader*. New York: Columbia Univ. Press, 1986. 198–209. Reprinted from *Screen* 16, no. 3 (1975).

Rivière, Joan. "Womanliness as Masquerade." Ed. Victor Bugin, James Donald, and Cora Kaplan. *International Journal of Psychoanalysis* 10 (1929). Reprinted in *Formations of Fantasy*. London: Routledge, Kegan & Paul, 1986.

Rose, Jacqueline. "Feminine Sexuality—Jacques Lacan and the *école freudienne*." *Sexuality in the Field of Vision*. London: Verso, 1986. 49–81.

Žižek, Slavoj. "Why Lacan Is Not a 'Post-Structuralist.' " *Newsletter of the Freudian Field* 1 (1987): 31–39.

———. *The Sublime Object of Ideology*. London: Verso, 1989.

II

Lacan and the Subject of Psychoanalysis

4

The Analytic Experience: Means, Ends, and Results

Jacques-Alain Miller

"The Analytic Experience: Means, Ends, and Results." The analytic experience—and I stop. I wonder: am I right to presuppose the unity or the typicality of analytic experience? Would the plural, analytic experiences, not be more attuned to my position, to the position I am here to present and re-present: that is, of another way of conceiving and practicing Freudian psychoanalysis, another way than the usual way in the United States of America?

Psychoanalysis is nothing new for you. Psychoanalysis was brought to the United States from Europe some years ago. Its audience, the audience for psychoanalysis, has already peaked, and it is already said to be declining. It is said not only by adversaries of psychoanalysis, but by American psychoanalysts themselves. So psychoanalysis is already part of American culture, is already a monument—perhaps already a memorial, a memory—in American culture. And a very large psycho-analytic community, perhaps the largest in the world, has already developed in this country, with its new societies, its very precise standards, and its well-established complex. That is not to say that this community is very largely represented here tonight. As a matter of fact, I believe that this very large community is, generally speaking, keeping its distance.

So, psychoanalysis has already been here for a long time. And here I come and I say, you are mistaken: psychoanalysis is not what you think it is. It is something else. You are mistaken as to its means, you are mistaken concerning its ends, and you are mistaken perhaps even concerning its results. You ought to rethink what you are doing, you ought to leave what you have been aiming at, and you must even renounce what you have already been producing. Here I come in front of this monument of psychoanalysis, saying this. I am sure you will agree with me that there is clearly what we could call a credibility gap. I have experienced that already, no doubt about it. I am the underdog. Or, to use another popular expression, it is a very uphill battle. I believe that to me and to you also, American psychoanalysis with its ensconced bureaucracy, must seem unmovable. And perhaps the decline of American psychoanalysis must also seem to you unstoppable.

Still, I am here. Why? First, for friends—to answer the call of friends, to support the effort of friends, whom I dearly thank. Second, to give a testimony of another way of conceiving and practicing Freudian analysis which is Lacan's way, Lacan's school, and in effect, to bring, after thirty-three years, this first seminar done in Paris to the American public this very year.

Third, I say the analytic experience in the singular, not because I would deem our path to be the only one deserving the name of psychoanalysis. I say the analytic experience because I believe that the analytic process as conducted by America psychoanalysts, in spite of what I have to say against them, *is* effectively analytic. That is to say, *it* is analytic, but *they* do not have the notion of the means and ends of analysis, of the inner logic of their practice. And that being so, they are unable to drive the experience to its radical consequences. So, I have not written off the idea of appealing to a community of experience with American analysts, of addressing what, from my point of view, the best among them feel are the dead ends of current American thinking on the subject.

But fourth, if I am here, it is because, after coming regularly to the United States for the last four years, I have arrived at a conclusion concerning the future of psychoanalysis in this country. I have arrived at the conclusion that the future of psychoanalysis in this country, if any, does not lie with the medical establishment, which has, I would say, appropriated the discovery of Freud, in spite of Freud's most explicit position. And they say they are orthodox Freudians. There is clearly a mistake which is just now, I believe, being exposed in the United States, not through analytic debate, but through litigations. That proves something: that fraud on Freud is being exposed after many years of concealing itself.

So, I believe that the future of analysis in this country does not lie with the medical establishment. It lies with the people of the universities, with you ladies and gentlemen; especially, I would say, with young people not yet established in a career and who are now keen on putting Lacan's teaching to use for literary criticism, as they call it. In so far as some among them, at least, will in the long run have sufficient belief in what they themselves think concerning psychoanalysis to enter analytic experience proper and perhaps (for some of them at least) to practice it, it is they, the new analysts stemming from the universities (and some, I hope, from the medical profession) who could in time change the course of American psychoanalysis. It is chiefly to them, here and elsewhere, that tonight I would like to be able to give a notion of what the analytic experience is according to Freud, at least according to Lacan.

Let me begin by saying that the word "experience" takes a very definite value concerning you in a negative way. When you, the participant in this conference, use Freud and Lacan to read or to re-read the works of an author, you know very well that you do not experience analysis. You experience literary criticism. "I use Lacan." How many times have I heard that sentence being said to me by one of you! And if it is not you, it is your colleague. I enjoy this sentence! I enjoy this way of saying things for, I would say, its flavor of pragmatism. Why would anyone be interested in anything if not for its usefulness? Is not usefulness the very criterion of being, the modern name of being? Is not this usefulness the law of the modern world, of the world as a market, of the market as a world where everything there is is there to be a means, a means toward something else, and not an end in itself? And this goes up to the point that the something else in relation to which everything is a means is itself not an end, but also a means, the means *par excellence:* money, value, "more value for the dollar." And up to the point where we could ask, "Is the useful useful or is the useful useless?"

"I use Lacan." Every time I hear that phrase, I am reminded that Freud's discovery stems from the useless, as you know, from the unusable, from the left-over of our conscious and purposeful activities; stems from the stumbling of parapraxis, the lapse of words, the escape in fantasy, the turning away from reality in fantasies and dreams— in dreams, which biologists now find secretly useful to mental, neural functioning. Did not Freud himself try again and again to demonstrate the usefulness of the useless, the purposefulness of the purposeless? What he called the unconscious—and that is a word erased from American psychoanalysis—was just that: the use hidden in the useless. The purpose hidden in the accident, fulfilled in the accident. The satisfaction realized in symptoms, the satisfaction realized in the very sufferings of the symptom. Certainly you are not satisfied by your symptom; you may even go to a doctor to cure it. But if you go to an analyst instead of going to a doctor, it is because you pre-interpret your own symptom. It is because you may think that in spite of suffering from your symptom, in spite of not being satisfied by your symptom, you may well be satisfied by it without knowing it. And if you lend yourself to interpretation, it is because you already suspect that this satisfaction can be known, deciphered. This secret satisfaction hidden in unsatisfaction, in displeasure, is what Lacan has called *jouissance* as distinct from pleasure, distinct from pleasure because it may be realized as displeasure.

I go back to this phrase, "I use Lacan," which could be the motto of this conference. "I use Lacan" is already enough to distinguish between Lacan and the unconscious, because the unconscious is such that no one can truly say, "I use the unconscious." The unconscious uses you. That is what one has learned from analysis, that one is nothing more than the means of one's unconscious. We could thus say truthfully that in the Freudian field, man is means.

"No one uses the unconscious." Is that true, when there is nowadays a cooperation of the analysts who, on the contrary, *use* the unconscious, use the unconscious of others to make a living, for instance, and occasionally to speak about it in conferences and articles and books? I would not be prone to reproach the analysts for that. I would rather be prone to reproach them for not making the most of it—I mean of using the unconscious. Lacan did not hide the fact—he boasted on TV—that he was a self-made man who had made a fortune from psychoanalysis.

But in spite of the cynicism that can go with the practice of psychoanalysis and of which the analyst is rather a victim, the analyst is no master of the unconscious. There is, nonetheless, an analytic knowhow of the unconscious—for instance, a know-how in the analytic experience of eliciting transference, of introducing a suffering person to the analytic experience—that is, to the directed experience of the unconscious. But this know-how provides no mastery of the unconscious; on the contrary, it is the knowledge that all know-how is derailed, foiled, thwarted by the unconscious. In the Freudian field, repetition does not preclude surprise, but breeds it. The unconscious repeats, but is nevertheless unforeseeable in its manifestations.

You may very well imagine yourself an analyst when you use Lacan to read a text. Language is language. That is to say, the structure of language is the same, be it spoken or written. And so, yes, you are interpreters as analysts are. But just think of this: you as literary academics are supposed to master the finite totality of your corpus. In France, national university regulations forbid any thesis to be received by the faculty concerning a living author. That is to say, the coffin must be nailed shut before the French as interpreters can begin their work of interpretation. Still, every corpus is supported by a corpse. Your practice of interpretation begins *par excellence* when it will not change anything for the author. You may certainly change the meaning of what he wrote; but you will not change the *jouissance* that he had in doing his work.

This is in contradistinction with analysis, where meaning is nothing more than a means, where change of meaning through speech and interpretation is the means of changing, displacing *jouissance*—what Freud called the libidinal investment. That's why Lacan made a pun with *jouissance*, blending meaning and *jouissance* and speaking of *jouis-sens*, enjoyed meaning. As literary critics, you are the ones who enjoy meaning; but, concerning your author, you will not separate him from his *jouissance*, and you will not clarify for him what his *jouissance* was.

That is not to say that there is not an effect of the unconscious in the academic world. For instance, when the corpse shows some signs of unrest. For instance, when a missing piece of the corpus sheds a new light on well-known works. We have at that moment something which looks like an effect of the unconscious. As a rule, the surprise is quickly tamed by the pouring forth of readings and re-readings. But in the scramble so produced, in the outpouring of speeches and writing, you may get an idea of what happens in an analytic experience when the repressed which, as Freud says, always returns, returns in a new light, is recognized, admitted, taken into account.

So, I correct myself. You do have, as literary critics, some experience of the unconscious. Your work takes place in the space, in the distance, in the cleavage, in the splitting between what an author wrote and what we know of what he meant. And that is enough to justify the use of the word *interpretation*. And in the momentum of your work, you may even come to ask yourself if he, the author, knew what he meant. I believe you can go up to this point; you may even go up to the point where you are not sure yourself that he knew what he meant. Certainly he did not know what he meant for you, even if a James Joyce knew that for the following centuries academics would be trying to make out what he meant. But you will never know. Never. You will never know for sure if your author knew or not. To be already where you are going means you would not look for it if he, the author, had not already found it.

And that is true also in the relationship between Lacan and Freud. We know that Lacan as reader, as critic of Freud, displaces the explicit center of Freud's works, when Lacan maintains that the unconscious is structured as a language. And we'll never know for sure if Freud knew that or not, in spite of the fact that the scholars of today who are using the works of Freud see references to language everywhere, which enables them to write a thesis without even mentioning the name of Lacan. There is a kind of assumption that Freud knew that already. So the equivocation of interpretation is also present for us, and it is a factor in the perpetuation of our transference to Freud. And interpretation of written texts is never free of this supposition of knowing ascribed to the author. Interpretation cannot desist from it. I would say that the most perspicacious readers of texts always look like perpetual analysands. And take it as a compliment.

So, "I use Lacan," when I hear it said to me by an academic, usually to establish a common, friendly connection to me, itself leads to an interpretation. It usually means, "I use Lacan instead of using an analyst." "I use Lacan to read X" means "I am the analyst of a dead analysand," or equivalently, "I am the analysand of a dead analyst." Dead analyst or dead analysand, I know in advance that my dead author will not answer me. I choose him instead of an analyst because I am sure that he will not answer me; and if he wants to answer me, I will reduce him to silence. Perhaps something like that happened between Sartre and Genet.

What is the result of literary criticism? For you, it is books, it is tenure. It is a chair endowed by one or another accumulator of money seeking to immortalize his name through your work and fame. And for your author, what are the results of literary criticism? It may be fame, it may be shame. And what are the results of analytic experience? For you, as an analyst, it may be books also. Frequently, analysts put the same case to use more than once. It may be tenure or titular membership in your society. And for your patient? As for an author, it could be fame. It is not so frequent, but Dora, the Wolf-Man, and the Rat Man are as famous as Moby Dick or Batman.

The result which is proper to analytic experience is something else. Let's say that it is a cure, a therapeutic effect. In analysis, there is someone to answer. There is you, as analyst, to answer through interpretation, and there is him to answer as patient. And it is hoped that he answers; that he gets better, that the symptom disappears, that he is no longer satisfied by these sufferings. That means that he is seeking his satisfaction through other means, through other more pleasurable means. That doesn't mean that his *jouissance* as such has changed, but only that it is realized through more pleasurable means. Thus the result that could speak for analytic experience is the disappearance of symptoms. That's what analysis can say for itself and be understood by the public, because concerning its ends as distinct from its results, it is not easy to make it understandable for the public.

The disappearance of symptoms then, may be deemed the desired result of analysis as cure. Of course, the symptoms could well disappear no matter what, that is to say, without analysis. You know that phobias in young children can disappear by themselves. And, actually, it is not through analytic experience that you cure the phobic symptom of a young child. I saw a young child seven years old who was so afraid of ghosts that he had nervous twitches in his face when he spoke about them, or nervous twitches that he *had* to make to keep the ghosts away. I saw him for three months. But I cannot say that it was this experience that caused him not to fear ghosts anymore. It was rather through an interview with his unmarried mother, who had conceived him during a "one-night stand," and who had wanted very much to keep this child. Living alone with him, she had the habit, so she said to me, of taking him into her bed at night. After I said to her, "Stop this immediately," and said it again in front of the child, the boy continued for three months to draw ghosts, with less and less enthusiasm. I showed him some books that I had on ghosts, we discussed the matter, and after the third month, he gave me a drawing saying, "That's the last one—there are no more." Can we say that this was an analytic experience which led to the disappearance of the symptom? Let us say that the child and his mother had an encounter, a meeting with an analyst.

With hysterical symptoms, especially when they concern the body, the results may be more spectacular, the answer more evident, than with other patients. I recall a young woman coming to see me on crutches. For five years she had been seeing one doctor after another. Her legs were slowly becoming paralyzed, and some believed that she had multiple sclerosis. One doctor, perhaps more perceptive than some, had advised her to seek analysis. As a matter of fact, it was clear that this symptom, so painful for her, which made her life so difficult, was also present as a means for her to master her surroundings, including the academic world around her. It took two years, and a serious worsening of her symptoms, for her to say that she did not enjoy being paralyzed anymore. And then to come on crutches to my office, but to leave them in the corridor when she walked from the waiting room to my consulting room. And then, without my saying anything about it, to come one day without crutches.

That is what I call an answer from a patient, an answer to a question I never asked. And an answer that she never formulated, but an answer, nevertheless, of someone who had in actuality been transforming herself into a corpse. Psychiatrists may call that simulation. Analysts do not, because there is no question that she had no mastery of what was taking place in her own body. That is not the answer of a jury. That is not the answer of a board of regents to which the works of academics are directed. That is the answer of a body that makes a visible and material change, like a raising of the dead. In spite of all you might say concerning authors or texts, in spite of all your interpretation, the statues of Shakespeare, Dickens, and Henry James will not stir and get animated because of what you have said. That is what we see in analysis. It is like saying, "Arise and walk," and she walked. Of course, I never said, "Arise and walk." I could have, because sometimes direct suggestion to an hysterical subject has a direct effect, but she was too brilliant an academic to be helped by pure suggestion.

You may see that this symptom was itself a crutch; and she used, in order to conceal this fact, a symptom of her mother: vertigo. Why not believe her, why not follow her when she confessed one day that her mental energy was devoted to keeping her sphincters tight and that she did not have any left to move her legs? She was speaking of what Freud called displacement of libido. And, as a matter of fact, the mystery of psychoanalysis, if there is one, is: how do you effect displacement of libido through what you use, that is, speech? Hysterical symptoms make some spectacular presentations that obsession does not have. It is, we could say, thought paralyzed, shut up. We still see hysterical cases in which a corporal intruder is at work. There are also mental intrusions. And in analytic experience you can see a lifting up of obsessions that is just as spectacular as this lifting up of a paralysis of the legs.

These examples, the lifting up of inhibitions concerning motor functions or mental functions, give evidence of cure. Hysteria, or at least the symptoms of hysteria, is curable. Obsessive neuroses are also curable in general. Phobias also lend themselves to analytic results. Psychosis, as distinct from neurosis, does not. When you read about the cure of psychosis, be careful that it is not confused with hysteria, and do not confuse cure with the stabilizing effect that analysis may have on psychotic patients. For perversion, or let us say for true perverts, psychoanalysis does not cure as a rule, but sometimes it enables the subject to tame the symptom or to live with it.

Let us not forget that other result of psychoanalysis, which is to produce a transference neurosis, a new illness substituted for the original neurosis. We have to give it an important place in our list of results, because we know that it is also a result of analysis. Not only does analysis bring about the disappearance of symptoms, but sometimes a new illness appears: being in analysis, enjoying analysis as such, and lengthening the treatment, which is a modern phenomenon of analysis. At the same time, this "way" enables us to discover in what sense all neuroses are transference neuroses—i.e., are established in relation to an other, a transferential other. You know that

Freud discovered transference as love meddling in the analytic work. For Freud, analysis was interpretation, serious, intellectual work; and the emergence of the affective component of the experience was for him at first not a means to cure, but an obstacle, and he had to turn the obstacle into a means. But do not believe that the knot between transference as a means and as an obstacle can be unknotted once and for all. And, more than that, the matter of how to make transference disappear is a problem for analytic practice—to make it disappear or transform it. Lacan believed that the best you could do when a certain point was already behind you was to transform transference to the analyst into a transference to psychoanalysis. Hysterics give us the example that we would rather love than know, and that is the value of transference as obstacle: love, instead of knowledge. And it is in this point that Lacan differs from Freud. There is no desire to know. It is love, not the desire to know, that is directed toward knowledge.

As results of analysis, then, I have alluded to the lifting of inhibitions, the disappearance of symptoms, the increasing of pleasure, and I could even say the increasing of adaptive behavior. And I have also mentioned the lengthening of analysis. I take these to be results about which analysts can concur even when their clinical categories differ. But results are not the same thing as ends: it was not Lacan, but rather Freud, who deemed the cure to be only a by-product of analysis, not an end in itself. And Freud always kept at a distance the desire to cure as such.

That remains the chief problem for analytic practice: to know what could be its ends as distinct from its results. But this cannot be elucidated without knowing what the proper means of analysis are. And it is strange, it really indicates a wish not to know, a denial of the obvious, not to recognize that both for Lacanians, as they are called, and for orthodox Freudians of Fifth Avenue, as Lacan called them, the legitimate means of analysis is speech. Failure to acknowledge this fact constitutes a denial of the obvious on the part of the analyst. The acknowledgment constitutes a dividing line which distinguishes the pupils of Lacan from others.

I have observed for some years now that this obvious position of analytic practice is slowly gaining ground—even if in the academic milieu, some literary analysts call it narration. The concept of narration captures something of what Lacan said: it is a reordering of the meaning of one's life, a transformation of the meaningless into the meaningful. And speech is the sole legitimate means: that is to say, speech that cannot be verified and cannot be satisfied by any material evidence, that cannot be verified or falsified by correspondence. Because verification is internal to the kind of speech that is the means of analysis, and internal verification occurs through gauging the coherence and inconsistency of the speech.

Why has it been so difficult for analysts to admit language as the obvious, sole, legitimate means of analysis? Perhaps because they thought language to be only an expression, a surface phenomenon. And perhaps because they thought that in analysis language functioned as it does in medicine, where you ask the patient, "Where does it hurt?" but where objectivity is obtained by using, for instance, a scanner. That is to say, a sclerosis exists: it can be seen objectively in a simulation. And of course language is also a scanner. But in analysis, the reality that is scanned is language too. That is to say, the analytic symptom is constituted in speech itself. And the proof is that, as a rule, entering analysis results in a worsening of symptoms. Language was also neglected, perhaps, because analysts have set up a dichotomy between language and affects (like the distinction between intellect and affects), forgetting that for Freud affects are fundamentally displaced and thus do not provide testimony of any final truth—that repression is a *separation* of the idea and the quantum of affect, with only anxiety standing apart as the affect that does not mislead. Perhaps the inattention to language derives from Freud himself, because he established the analytic process on the basis of physical science, the science of nature, and not on the basis of interpretation.

Perhaps at this point I could give you a quotation, an early quotation by Lacan, which distinguishes between means, range, and operation in analysis. "The means of analysis," he said, "are those of speech, as endowing a meaning to the function of the individual. The range is a range of concrete discourses filled with the transindividual reality of the subject. Operations are those of history as constituting the emergence of truth in the real." I understand this to mean the following. First, that the means is the meaning. That is, speech is the function that gives meaning to other functions—for instance, to the bodily functions in the different stages (what Freud called the stages of development), giving meaning and especially erotic meaning to excretion, to nutrition, and also to seeing and to speaking. That is *jouissance*, enjoyed meaning, as I said before.

Second, transindividualization relates meaning to otherness. When we say transindividualization, it refers to primary connection to another, which appears in logical analysis for instance, as the presence of a community of speech (the problematic of convention), which in analytic experience is reduced to two. Third, operation reduces to the truth the operation of analysis. What is radical in analysis, and which I believe literary academics could admit, is that truth in analytic experience is at the level of meaning and not at the level of reference. You know that Freud began by looking for the reference, and I would say confusing analytic truth with the idea of cured-ness. This was true when he looked for the facts of seduction and also when, in the case of the Wolf-Man, he tried to ascertain the materiality of the facts. On the contrary, in analytic experience proper, truth is not anything outside language but rather an effect of words. That's why we speak of truth-effect and acknowledge that one signifier more may change the meaning of a sign. That is to say, in logical analysis, we can distinguish between the theory of meaning and the theory of communication. In logical analysis, for instance, as practiced by Donald Davidson, it is perfectly correct to distinguish between literal meaning and contextual meaning. But in analytic experience—and in this lies the radicality of this experience—we do not distinguish. That is to say, communication absorbs meaning, contextuality absorbs literality.

This is crucial to the Lacanian concept of the Other. It is a complex concept: the place of language, but also the place of conventions, the place of the lexical and the syntactical. And the analyst is supposed to speak from this place. That is to say that for the time of the session he may be said to be the master of truth. He embodies whatever you want that can be attributed to otherness. You could say he embodies God, or society, or family, or language; that it is where truth is decided, sanctioned, guaranteed: so many heterogeneous contents which justify our considering the Other as a place, a place of otherness which endows the elements which come to occupy this space with the same property of otherness. That is why this complex concept is a powerful simplification. It is, as capital *A*, a signifier with various signifieds according to context. I would like to think of this capital *A* of Lacan's as a formalization, for instance, like the Fregean quantors.

When Lacan says the unconscious is the discourse of the Other, he goes to the point of accepting analytic experience in its radicality. That is, the patient as subject of speech is effectively, concerning the truth of what is said, at the mercy of the analyst. And that's why analysis has always created safeguards, railings, parapets. I want to conceive analytic experience as a pact, a compact: there is a compact between the analyst and the analysand. But who wishes for the compact if not the analyst himself? You might think that society would wish it for him, or the law, or standards and regulations, but such a view is only an effort to deplete the function of the Other in its radicality. Everybody knows that privacy is a fundamental condition of the analytic experience. And privacy and confidentiality are also a *sine qua non* of the transindividuality of that experience. I have heard many exclaim that it is antisocial to attribute this radical power over truth to the place of the Other, where literality is reduced to contextuality. It is certainly antisocial. And that is what was said of psychoanalysis at the beginning. Hence analysts have put all their effort into trying to guarantee to the established social order that they are not menacing its value, but on the contrary condoning its value.

Our position, the Lacanian one, is different. It is that analysis is a social link of a new kind. That is what Lacan called analytic discourse: a social link of a new kind unheard of before, which functions between the stitches of the net knitted by the state. And certainly a high level of individual freedom, a high level of uncontrolled liberty of speech and association, is necessary for analysis in this orientation to be able to function.

The time issue is also a distinguishing mark, because the issue of speech leads directly to the issue of time—the issue of speech as speech to the Other, the issue of speech as speech of the Other, that is, the unconscious. This implies that for analysis to function, an initial surrender to the Other is necessary. The time issue means that when it is standardized it has to be the same for everyone, that the course of analysis as such is predetermined, and that you yourself feel in the analytic process the weight of the institution and the continuity with a society where time is money. And what you say makes no difference in this timing.

The analytic experience, according to Lacan, and what we know of Freud, goes in the direction of an intensification of the analytic phenomena. It establishes analytic experience in a strange dimension, foreign to all we practice in our quotidian life, in our daily routine. It establishes analysis in a dimension of *Unheimlichkeit*. And it is because the analytic process as invented by Freud gives some power to the analyst that analysts have in the past retreated from confronting the coherence of the process, from confronting the tremendous personal responsibility it gives them in analysis, and so they have kept very far away from the point where it could lead. That is why Lacan called the IPA a society of neutral assistants against psychoanalysis— that is, against its internal logic—to protect the analyst from the responsibility which is his. The consequence of this responsibility is that no one authorizes an analyst; an analyst can only authorize himself in terms of using the responsibility he has. This Lacanian principle is one that could destroy analytic bureaucracy. As a matter of fact, it is already in the United States slowly doing just that.

Discussion

Q: James Strachey did not run away from the power that was conferred on the analyst. He said that it should be used by the analyst to instill values that the subject should have into the subject through using the position of the superego. Do you agree with that?

A: There is power. If I stop at that point, it looks rather menacing. The question of precisely what the superego is, is a complicated matter in analytic theory. When Strachey speaks of the superego, he believes that the superego is the agency which represents the best demands of reality. That is, since we all ensconce ourselves in the pleasure principle, since we dream rather than act, we need the analyst as a representative of the demands of reality: we need the analyst as an auxiliary superego. And, I must say, that is a prevalent conception of analysis in the United States. This is in the line of Hartmann, who conceived the end of analysis to be adaptation and synthesis.

That concerns the question of reality. Reality for Freud is nothing other than the continuation of the pleasure principle by other means. Reality itself, what we call reality, which substitutes itself for the domination of pleasure, is nevertheless, for Freud himself, in the service of seeking satisfaction. So, there is something true in this figure of a superego which propels the subject from the reign of one principle to another. The superego embodies nothing other than the very demand of *jouissance,* the most profound demands of satisfaction. This is the way Lacan translates the superego imperative: not as forbidding, but, on the contrary, as enjoying. You have this imperative at the beginning of analysis, as the imperative of free association: speak as you want. You can translate this: enjoy, enjoy with speech. Or even: enjoy your unconscious. The question is why? To enjoy one's unconscious in the analytic experience changes something in your mode, our modality, of enjoying your unconscious.

So I stressed the power of the analyst, because not doing so is what Lacan deemed to be neurotic cowardice. In the history of psychoanalysis, analysts are particularly notable for this neurotic cowardice. That is why Lacan stands out. They feel that their practice entitles them to this cowardice. In contrast, I am advocating tonight a position which implies taking risks. For the moment, as an example of people taking risks in this direction, I can mention Stuart Schneiderman, who is the only American to have traveled to Paris to be analyzed by Lacan. Now he will be forever the sole one. This kind of risk, this kind of courage, is rare.

Q: What is the range of the length of the Lacanian analytic hour, and what is the theory behind the Lacanian practice of having sessions of variable length?

A: I will not resist answering this question which I have in some way elicited, and which is always something very difficult to explain. As a matter of fact, the three-minute session, the one-minute session, is not the rule. It is true that Lacan, in the last years of his practice, gave very short sessions. He explained his concept of variable-time sessions and regularly shorter-time sessions starting in the 1950s, but he never gave it as a standard. He stressed very much the individual component of practice. He reminded us that Freud himself invented the couch because he could not tolerate being face to face with people for long.

In addition, the sheer weight of transference is a component of the session.

That is to say, Lacan could do things in the last years of his practice which he would not have done before and which younger clinicians would be stupid to do. So it is not standard, and Lacan never really advocated anything other than variable-time sessions. The common practice of Lacanian analysis is, certainly, shorter sessions. And I would say that in France there is a general shortening of sessions, whether the analysts be IPA or not, because of the influence of Lacan. But IPA analysts cannot admit that they use shorter sessions, so it is a hypocritical, disguised practice.

For my own analysis, I do not know how long a single session lasted during those years. And when I began to practice, I had no prejudice. I began with listening as long as I believed it was useful: useful to me to understand and useful to the patient to get to a point. As a matter of fact, I have observed that I have rather shortened my sessions from my first years of practicing analysis, to now. And I would say that there is a limit to the variability, which everyone can understand: you give appointments to people. You give appointments, and the variability is limited. But it is difficult for me to ascertain, when you come to my waiting room, if you are going to enter the consulting room immediately or wait half an hour. That places a large demand on the patient, which means that the rest of his life must be organized very differently. But I believe that to establish a very demanding situation in analysis can cure. I do not mean making a patient wait for pleasure or for intervention or interpretation. But sometimes for a period, and for certain types of patients, short sessions can be technically the right thing to do. There are patients you must not receive at rush hours, certainly. There are patients that you have to listen to every day for half an hour, let us say, which is, I would say, the covert, standard practice of French IPA analysts.

You try to maintain this kind of open agenda. Sometimes I regret not having had the audacity of cutting a session very short, and sometimes I am obliged, after having waited for ten or fifteen minutes—twenty minutes, perhaps—to dismiss the patient, remind the patient what was said in the very first phrase or the second one, which I could have intensified by cutting the session at that time. Sometimes, more frequently, I reproach myself with having let him lose himself in rambling, in what Lacan called vacuous talk, rather than giving a punctuation which could have produced an effect of truth. Of course, it could be said it is better to err on the side of prudence. And there are patients that you can never cut so short. I believe that certainly in Paris and in our school, some would give different answers than I give, and we maintain, perhaps without speaking about it sufficiently openly, a certain non-standardization, a certain freedom of practice in spite of the homogenization which comes from working together.

Q: You have spoken tonight about differences between analytic practice and its application in other disciplines, for example, literary theory. One of the comments you made about literary theory involved the function of death in literary theory as, I think, some sort of defining margin for an imaginary relationship that the reader constructs when she imagines herself to be an analyst or an analysand of a text. Could you address the difference between the position of death in that kind of relationship and the position of death in analytic treatment?

A: In some way, we might say that the subject of the signifier, as such, is dead. When Lacan writes a capital S and a bar—$—this subject has no other definition than being represented by the signifier. It does not matter if he is dead or if he is alive. And if you admit the radical definition of the subject as represented by the signifier 1 (S_1), it does not make a difference even if he is not yet born as a living being. I would say that the subject—not as speaking subject, but as spoken subject, the subject which is spoken about—is spoken by the Other before he begins to live. He is conceived is speech before being born as a subject, as a result of the combinations and constellations of family, society, and universal concrete discourse. That could be deemed paradoxical. It is not if you admit the subject as *hypokeimenon*—i.e., as what is talked about and not as an active speaking subject. What gives the impression of this subject's being alive is that there is a change of meaning because of the signifier 2 (S_2), which *nachträglich* (retroactively) changes the meaning of the signifier 1—i.e., changes the effect of truth effecting the subject, which gives the appearance of life. It is like the father in one of the dreams recalled by Freud, the father who is alive only because he does not know that he is already dead. Now, the problem is that concerning *jouissance*, concerning enjoyment, no enjoyment is conceivable except that of a living body; and when Lacan writes the formula of the phantasm, like this, $ \$ \lozenge a $, connecting the subject and the famous object small *a*, he connects two distinct elements, one which embodies death and the other which is unthinkable without the living. The formula of the phantasm is a rather horrendous couple where, as we say in French, "*le mort saisit le vif*"—the dead captures the living. That is why there is a problem when people die if they continue to enjoy in some way. That is the most terrifying of thoughts. There are a lot of practices in a lot of cultures which take their satisfaction from giving satisfaction to the dead. What is the part we have to take from the living, then, to give to the dead for satisfying their drive, which perhaps continues despite their death? Sometimes when you see what certain authors have left behind them, you wonder if they did not have the idea of enjoying the situation from their grave at the expense of their good friends!

Q: Wittgenstein remarked near the end of the *Tractatus* that death is not an event in life because we do not experience death, we do not live to experience death. And in speaking about uselessness and usefulness, which I think gets to the point he was making, how is it that we can use in analytic practice to inform that practice something that we do not live to experience; and, furthermore, if something that we do not live to experience can indeed be useful, what does that say about the status of phenomenology, the science of experience?

A: Wittgenstein had a very deep relationship with psychoanalysis, a very deep relationship of turning away from analysis in spite of the fact that his sister, I believe, was in analysis. He was in Vienna at the time when no intellectual could have remained apart from it. There are various factors in Wittgenstein's life which we know through various memories and memoirs of his friends, be they in Vienna or in Cambridge, and even some personal anecdotes.

Certain personal anecdotes of former pupils of his which I heard—George

Kreisel, for instance—suggst that it would be very interesting to try a literary criticism of Wittgenstein inspired by psychoanalysis. After all, Lacan did not hesitate to say that Socrates was an hysteric. We know that Kafka was a copraphagic psychotic, so why not try once, as an exercise, to have an idea of the position of Wittgenstein? You say that death is something which we do not live to experience. I wonder about that. There are testimonies from various subjects about what they deem to be deaths in their own life. For the obsessive patient, Lacan used to say, the question is, "am I alive or dead?"—a doubt about being alive or dead. As for the hysterics, there is a doubt, a nagging doubt, about whether they are a man or a woman, in spite of all the material evidence which could give a testimony. So, when you hear, year after year, the suffering of an obsessional patient who is not alive enough for himself, who believes that he, in his sufferings in life, is in a living death—well, you might modify or qualify the idea of death as something which you do live to experience.

But second, I do not mind my argument being contradictory, I do not mind it anymore than Wittgenstein. You cannot say that an analysis would be an experience of death; you might say that it is rather an awakening. For Lacan, the question is, what would be a true awakening. He thought—and that is exactly what I said a few minutes ago concerning reality—he thought that when you stop dreaming and you stop sleeping and open your eyes, it is to continue to dream with your eyes open. That is to say, reality is continuous with the fantasized world, and the effort of analysis is to bring about what would be a true awakening to the structure of *your* world, you as a subject— the true awakening to the signification, the meaning, with which your world is structured, and to the signification by which you live your life. Let us say you live your way of enjoyment. Thus when we get too near some point of horror in dreams, we stop dreaming in order not to meet this real, and we open up our eyes in order not to face this point. Sometimes it can be observed that in analytic experience people begin to dream a bit longer. They begin to dream beyond a point where before they would have awakened in order not to see it.

Q: Since phenomenology is the science of experience, what becomes of phenomenology?

A: Concerning your final question, the word phenomenology is not enough to give me the contextual meaning of what you ask. The phenomenology of Hegel and that of Husserl are not the same. Let me answer like this: Lacan began as a phenomenologist. He did not begin as a structuralist at all. He began in the thirties as someone explicitly writing a phenomenology of the analytic experience. In the thirties, before structuralism and before post-structuralism, he began, through phenomenology, to pinpoint speech as the means of analysis, and to pinpoint speech to the Other as the operation proper to analysis. This is the function of the Other which is so difficult to incorporate into what is called analytic philosophy. The path of Lacan is from phenomenology to structuralism, from the thirties to the beginning of the fifties. In the sixties that was the path taken more quickly, but later, by various philosophers who were essentially my professors, such as Foucault and Derrida.

Works Cited

Lacan, Jacques. *The Seminar of Jacques Lacan, Book* I: *Freud's Papers on Technique* (1953–1954). Ed. Jacques-Alain Miller. Trans. with Notes by John Forrester. New York: W.W. Norton & Co., 1988.

Sartre, Jean Paul. *Saint Genet.* Paris: Librairie Gallimard, 1952.

5

Signifier, Object, and the Transference

Russell Grigg

I would like to talk about the function of both the signifier *and* the object in psychoanalytic treatment ("la cure") and think that the best way to introduce this topic is to center my remarks on the transference.

We know that in Freud the transference is described variously as suggestion, repetition, resistance, love, and, finally, as a combination of all of these. He did however reject the term "suggestion" very early on, preferring to speak of "transference." He did this for two reasons: first, whatever the force behind hypnosis, Freud wanted to distinguish it from the forces at work in psychoanalysis; second and more importantly, the catch-all phrase, "suggestion," appealed to as explanation of *all* phenomena of influence, including not just psychoanalysis but hypnosis as well, was far too vague a term and served no real explanatory power.

The term "transference," "*Übertragung*," appears for the first time in *The Interpretation of Dreams*—where for some reason it is here translated as "transcript." Freud describes how dreams are constructed out of the day's residues, that is, the insignificant and trivial memories that remain from the day preceding the dream itself. The dream strips these memories of their original meaning and reinvests them with new meaning. This is "transference," and transference of sense or meaning, in accordance with unconscious desire which thus disguises itself in otherwise innocent representations. Desire expresses itself through the medium of those representations which are acceptable by virtue of their very banality. It seizes forms that have little value in themselves and that function in the dream separated from their initial meaning. Functioning like words or letters, they can be called signifiers.

The first appearance of the transference in Freud is therefore bound up with the general process of the formations of the unconscious—dreams, slips of the tongue and pen, the forgetting of names, and bungled actions, as well as symptoms.

Freud later gave "transference" a more narrow meaning, applying it to a phenomenon that arises only within the analytic discourse, where desire becomes attached to something quite specific—namely, the person of the analyst. But the connection with the early use is not merely verbal, for desire attaches less to the person than to the signifier of the analyst. The signifier of the analyst is a position within the analytic discourse occupied by the analyst as person, but with which he should neither be identified nor, as we shall see, identify himself.

There are further grounds for drawing this distinction between the analyst as person, in flesh and blood, and the analyst as signifier, as place within the transference relation. For one thing, if as Freud says the transference bears all the hallmarks of being in love we need to ask why it occurs more or less automatically, when falling in love requires such specific conditions. Lacan put it this way in his first Seminar:

> How can a transference be so easily generated in neurotics, when they are so fettered when it comes to love? The production of a transference has an absolutely universal character, truly automatic, whereas the demands of love are, on the contrary, as everyone knows, so specific. (142)

Thus the transference is the point at which the analyst as signifier becomes the object of the analysand's desire. There are two observations I would like to draw to your attention at this point.

The first, which I take from Jacques-Alain Miller, is that the analyst is not external to the unconscious but internal to it. I believe we ultimately need to appeal to this observation to explain a number of readily observable phenomena, anyway. It explains, for instance, the fact that the analysand dreams for the analyst, as well as the fact that, as Freud observed, "the symptoms join in the conversation." The analyst's implication in the unconscious means that there is no vantage point lying outside the transference, accessible to the analyst, from which it would be possible to observe the analysand. The analyst is called into question just as much as the analysand. As in most of these things, Freud gives the clearest illustration of this in his own case studies; we can learn as much about Freud from the case studies as from *The Interpretation of Dreams*.

What these observations on the transference point to is an acknowledgment that there is a place in the subject's "inner world" that the analyst comes to occupy. Most and probably all psychoanalytic theories recognize this, for in acknowledging that the transference is the driving force of an analysis, there is an implicit recognition that the analyst's position is a formation of the unconscious. The differences of opinion on this subject tend to be over what this place is that the analyst comes, or should come, to occupy.

The second point is this. Freud had discovered that formations of the unconscious could be deciphered and that symptoms could sometimes be lifted by this deciphering. But the transference came as a surprise, and an uncomfortable one at that. It came as a surprise to discover that the analyst appears to hold a special interest for the analysand, to occupy his thoughts, and perhaps even become his love object. In its early days the psychoanalytic method could have been regarded as applied hermeneutics, since symptoms were shown to have a hidden meaning which when deciphered and conveyed to the subject would cause a symptom to disappear. This was the truly golden age of psychoanalysis, when a walk with Professor Freud in the garden after lunch was enough to conjure away a troublesome symptom.

The age soon passed, of course, and Freud was led to the analysis of the resistance, that is, of the subject's *refusal* to admit the hidden meaning of his symptom. This difficulty in getting the analysand to acknowledge the meaning, or even existence, of symptoms also led to the belief that a force has to be overcome before symptoms could be removed. It was as if the unconscious had made itself less accessible to analysis. Indeed, the various modifications in technique Freud introduced were made necessary by an evolution in the nature of the unconscious itself.

There is something charmingly innocent nowadays in many of the symptoms described in the early *Studies on Hysteria* and a guilelessness in their interpretation—for instance, the hysteric's shortness of breath as a symptom associated with overhearing the mounting excitement of a couple making love. Now, in following up Freud's discovery that because the transference, far from making the analysand a willing collaborator in the task of deciphering his own text, is actually a form of *resistance*, the post-Freudians came to the conclusion, in one way or another, that what mattered *above all* was to regard analysis as an interpersonal relationship, an intersubjectivity that was only incidentally, and not essentially, mediated by language. This is, I believe, the fundamental point shared by those techniques that aim at analyzing the resistance, at the development of empathy, or at the countertransference. Lacan, on the other hand, is widely regarded as holding the exact opposite of this view, namely that it is language, or the signifier, that is paramount in analysis. One can see why Lacan was read, in the English-speaking world particularly, as promoting the function of the signifier in psychoanalysis—not least because for a long time Lacan himself emphasized this very aspect. There is however something else Lacan emphasizes equally strongly, even more strongly in his later work, namely the object. And we need to discuss *both* aspects.

To return to the point I was making before, which was that Freud introduced modifications in technique because of an evolution in the nature of the unconscious, it can I believe be argued that both the unconscious and symptoms have a history. This is difficult to reconcile with the claim that the unconscious is an instinctual reservoir, but quite simple to understand if it is essentially linguistic in nature.

Further, it can be argued that the unconscious is essentially a discourse, and not merely structured like a language, and that with changes in the nature of this *discourse*, the nature of *interpretation itself* was also forced to undergo modifications.

Now, symptoms undergo not only historical change, but when an analysand enters analysis, their symptoms will all take on a new meaning. Freud observed this phenomenon under the name of transference meaning, *Übertragungsbedeutung*. However, if symptoms do in fact take on a new meaning in analysis, then it follows that a symptom is not something fixed and frozen, but changes according to the person to whom it is addressed. Lacan has expressed this by saying that the symptom is addressed to the Other. The Other is not so much a person as a place, a "locus," required by the structure of discourse.

We can now give an indication of the analyst's position in analysis by saying that he is situated in the place of the Other, the place to which the message is addressed, and thus becomes its receiver. As Lacan states in "La psychanalyse et son enseignement": "It is only from the place of the Other that the analyst is able to receive the investiture of the transference which entitles him to play his legitimate role in the subject's unconscious" (454).

Freud saw that the locus of the Other is also capable of provoking love—*real* love—in the analysand, and the erotic component of this love is often unmistakable. His remarks on the obligation of the analyst in this context are worth noting in "Observations on Transference—Love." Of course, professional ethics require that the analyst refrain from entering any sort of liaison in the circumstances; but more fundamentally, to form a liaison would, he says, run counter to the intention of the analytic treatment. The reason for this is that the transference is a repetition of unconscious desires mainly formed in childhood; in the transference these desires are transferred onto the analyst, making him their object—and so the woman fell in love with Freud. But the aim of analysis is to get the analysand to remember, and thereby to bring their unconscious desires within the range of things over which the subject has the ability to make a choice. But the aim of remembering can only be achieved where the analyst refuses to allow the repetition actually to take place, since remembering can only occur in place of repetition. And so to form a liaison is to allow the patient's unconscious the desired repetition, which thereby frustrates the capacity to remember, and the aim of the treatment.

Although Freud suggests that transference love differs from real love by its intensity, he is more impressed by their similarities—both transference love and real love are repetitions of behavior stereotyped by conditions registered within the subject, ready to emerge under favorable external circumstances.

Lacan introduced a new concept for the place in analysis to which the analysand's message is addressed, *le sujet supposé savoir*. The usual, rather awkward translation is the "subject supposed to know," however I prefer Stuart Schneiderman's suggestion, "the supposed subject of knowledge," taking his point that what is supposed is not that a particular subject should know, but that there should be a subject of knowledge at all.

The supposed subject of knowledge is introduced by Lacan in order to unify the diverse forms under which the transference expresses itself in Freudian theory, where it appears as resistance, repetition, love, and suggestion. It is not a question of deciding that the transference is one of these things and not the others. All are forms in which the transference can appear. As Jacques-Alain Miller has observed, the supposed subject of knowledge is the constitutive principle of the transference, from which these various forms of the transference follow.

Lacan is not alone in arguing that the emergence of the transference is the direct consequence of following the "fundamental rule" of analysis, which requires the subject to say everything that occurs to him, without being prevented by considerations of decency, displeasure, or irrelevance. He thus regards the supposed subject of knowledge as purely the consequence of a very particular type of discourse, the analytic discourse.

The role of the analyst in this context in which the analysand is invited to say anything and everything, is to act as a guarantee. His presence is the guarantee that this work of speaking to no end into the void actually means something, even well before he is able to know *what* it means. It is this very special and delicate arrangement that Lacan sees as the foundation of the phenomena that will ultimately produce the transference in analysis.

The structure of the analytic situation places the analyst in the position of being the listener of a discourse he has solicited from the analysand, requiring the analysand to omit nothing, according to the process of "free association."

The position of listener—the analyst's position—is not passive. Although the analysand is the active member, Lacan insisted that the listener's response, his uptake, or his interpretation, decides not just the sense of what is said but also the identity of the speaker. Though it is true of all communication that the interlocutor has the power to decide the sense of the speaker's words, outside analysis this power is shared round a bit since we occupy both locutory and interlocutory positions. But in psychoanalysis the very structure of the relation is asymmetric since one of the subjects delivers the material and the other listens to it; he receives, evaluates, and, sometimes, even interprets it.

In analysis there is a question of the truth about oneself. The contract to follow the fundamental rule is undertaken in view of a commitment to this position of looking for the truth about oneself and one's desire. The analysand does not however seek this truth within himself but within the analyst in his role as Other, as the fundamental listener who decides on the meaning of the subject's discourse. This is why silence is so important, since it must leave enough space for truth to unfold within speech.

Otto Fenichel observed a long time ago, that while a person may enter analysis with a demand for help in coping with this symptom or that neurotic condition, during analysis this demand will be transformed. It will eventually become the question: What is my desire? but also: What does *he* (the analyst, the Other) want from me? But Lacan argues that the analyst's silence is important here, too, and that he should not hasten to reply to this demand.

While the supposed subject of knowledge is a necessary requirement for psychoanalytic treatment, its emergence also constitutes a risk and a temptation. Michel Silvestre wrote that while it is only with the emergence of the supposed subject of knowledge that it is possible to avoid an imaginary, dual relationship and deflate the effects of the imaginary, at the same time, such a leverage point confers on the analyst an authority able to lend considerable weight to these same imaginary effects.

We find here, according to Silvestre, a reason to be circumspect with respect to the technique of interpreting the transference. By means of the transference repetition will implicate the analyst, who is thereby invited to interpret and expose the "false connections" made with his person.

However, the subject's resolution of the transference is not a *primary* but a *secondary* effect of its interpretation. After all, the analysand knows all along that the analyst only *reminds* him of his father or mother. However, Silvestre argues, detaching the signifier from the analyst will only serve to reinforce its strength and increase its weight. The effect of separating the signifier from its imaginary accompaniments in the transference may well end up having the effect of purifying and solidifying the subject's submission to the signifier. While the identification of the signifier with the analyst is thus avoided, it is at the cost of consolidating the analysand's subjection to the major signifiers (or "master signifier") of his history (64–66).

I have said that there is a need to distinguish the person of the analyst from the analyst as a place or locus within the unconscious, from the analyst as supposed subject of knowledge, which is a symbolic position that arises from the fundamental imperative of analysis. I should like now to explore a bit further why in Freud's view the analyst should never personally assume this position of the supposed subject of knowledge within analysis.

In the 1970s Lacan elaborated the four discourses: the master's discourse, the discourse of the university, the hysteric's discourse, and the analyst's discourse. There is a close connection between the master's and the analyst's discourse, due to the fact that the position of Other is a position of mastery. And over the short history of analysis there has been, despite Freud's explicit warnings, a temptation for analysts to fill this position and to exploit it in the interests of the patient.

This tendency sees analysis as a process of re-education that is to be brought about by virtue of the fact that the analyst is located as the analysand's superego. Note that the theory underlying this approach also amounts to assigning a position to the analyst in the unconscious. It holds that the analyst must occupy the place of the superego; and that the cure is the process of the analysand's identification with the analyst as superego. The belief here is that the analyst, from his position of superego, will be able to inject positive values into the subject's ego.

The cure appears, then, as above all a form of re-education, of educating the analysand by suggestion, and the analyst offers himself as the measure of reality who will, by virtue of his authority, lead the subject to a superior conception of reality and a better adaptation to it; the catch is, as Lacan was always quick to point out, that the judge of the superiority of conceptions of reality can ultimately only be the analyst himself.

The consequence of this, in any case, is that the cure becomes an enterprise of indoctrination. It becomes an attempt to crush a fundamentally ineducable desire; the analysand becomes engaged in a constant struggle against the analyst's effort of indoctrination, against the analyst as a person who is full, as we all are, of his own prejudices.

A paper by James Strachey is one of the major influences, in the English-speaking world at least, on the question of the position of the analyst, in large measure setting the terms of subsequent debate. Strachey argues explicitly for the view that the analyst should operate from the position of superego:

> Thus there are two convergent lines of argument which point to the patient's superego as occupying a key position in analytic therapy: it is a part of the patient's mind in which a favourable alteration would be likely to lead to general improvement, and it is a part of the patient's mind which is especially subject to the analyst's influence. (149)

Strachey indicates that he draws this conclusion about the suitability of the superego to psychoanalytic intervention from Chapter 8 of *Group Psychology and the Analysis of the Ego.* But Freud, in the passage Strachey is referring to, is attempting to give an account of the power of "suggestion" in hypnosis. Freud's reason for attempting this, in this uncannily prophetic work on group psychology written in 1921, was to grasp how it is that the members of a group can all come to identify with the group's leader, and how their egos and their behavior become "standardized." Yet this particular type of ego-identification with a leader is what Strachey appeals to as the source of the analyst's power in analysis. A theory developed to account for hypnosis and for the power of a leader over the group is being used to give an explanation of the power of psychoanalysis itself!

It is odd, then, that Strachey should use precisely this part of Freud to attempt to articulate in his own way that the analyst is located in the place of the Other. However, the important objection against Strachey bears upon his conclusion that the analyst must identify himself with that position, and that the analysand must identify himself with the analyst.

Here we have a clear example of the way in which the original sense of Freud's discovery has come to be distorted and lost. While the superego may preserve in the subject an adaptation to reality, it is an adaptation completely unadapted to the current situation, for in no way is it an agency in contact with *present* reality.

The Freudian superego is a legal code, yes of course, but an archaic one. It performs its function automatically, blindly, as a reflex, being linked with the compulsion to repeat and the death drive. Its demands are incoherent. It is a law, an injunction, that it is impossible for the subject to obey. Lacan mentions what he calls the "obscene and ferocious figure of the superego" (*L'Ethique* 15). Insatiable, it lies *beyond* the pleasure principle, which, essentially a biological function, subsides once satisfaction is achieved.

All of this is already in Freud when, in an inversion of Kant's wonder and awe at the starry skies above and the moral law within, he writes:

> Conscience (or more correctly, the anxiety which later becomes conscience) is indeed the cause of drive renunciation to begin with, but . . . later the relationship is reversed. Every renunciation of drive now becomes a dynamic source of conscience and every fresh renunciation increases the latter's severity and intolerance. (*Group*, 128)

There is one further issue I would like to mention here with respect to Strachey's views on the position of the analyst. This is the issue of the shift towards the ego.

Underlying Strachey's appeal to the power of the superego (and determining the entire orientation of his approach) is a view that has been dominant in analysis since Freud, and that involves a deep and significant shift in the orientation of the entire framework of psychoanalysis. It is against this shift that in the 1950s Lacan was arguing, in his appeal to a "return to Freud."

It is in fact closer to the truth to say that this shift actually took place during Freud's own life time, because the 1930s became for him a period of increasing doctrinal isolation. His views on sexuality and the Oedipus complex, on the death drive, on the splitting of the ego, found fewer and fewer adherents within the psychoanalytic movement.

What orientates Strachey's view, that the analyst should use the position of superego in the interests of the analysand's re-education, is that therapeutic progress is to be assessed from the perspective of the ego—in other words, that the modification of the ego is the measure of therapeutic success. Now, I believe that Ernest Jones was quite right in saying (in a paper with the wonderful title "The Concept of a Normal Mind") that if we view an analytic cure from the perspective of ego modification, then the therapeutic aim has to be conceived in one of two general forms: *either* that of a better adaptation of the ego, person, or personality to reality, both internal and external; *or* that of an increase in the ego's capacity for attaining happiness or well-being (204).

Various views about the means of achieving these ends essentially come down to increasing the freedom of the ego, whether by reinforcing it, by making the unconscious conscious, or by replacing the unconscious superego with a harmonious conscience: 1) The ego has expanded at the expense of the id and superego. 2) The energy of the id is discharged towards the outer world *via* the ego and not independently of it. All these statements are merely different ways of saying the same thing.

Not only does Freud's "Copernican Revolution," however, signal a radical move away from the perspective of the ego, but further, the whole ethic of psychoanalysis runs counter to the view that treatment in analysis consists in the subject's identifying himself with the analyst. Treatment consists in what Lacan has called the "original pact" of analysis; psychoanalysis is based on the free consent and liberty of the patient. The difficulties Freud encountered in his analysis of the young homosexual girl arose from the fact that it was her family that forced her into analysis against her own wishes. The necessary pact between analyst and analysand was not possible under these conditions. But to conceive of analysis as a *further* alienation of the subject in the form of an *identification* of the subject with the analyst completely flouts this *sine qua non* of the consent of the analysand.

These terms, "subject," "Other," "signifier," are all terms of the symbolic order. And affect? Affect does not have the sort of epistemic privilege often attributed to it—and I think this point undercuts much of the criticism made of Lacan's "interpretation via the signifier."

But there is another point that should also be made. Affect is *also* an expression of transference love, and *this*, transference love, is *all important* in the treatment. Why is this so? Because it results from the presence of the analyst as something *other* than a signifier; it results from the presence of the analyst as *object* in the treatment. It is to this second, the object, no less important than the signifier, I should now like to turn.

It is not true that for Lacan everything in the transference operates at the level of the signifier. It is true however that as formations of the unconscious, symptoms are fully analyzable; they are, as Freud saw, nothing but symbolic structures. What, then, lies *beyond* the signifier?

That something *beyond* the signifier is at work in the transference is grasped by Freud in the concept of the drive, the death drive in particular. But there are some other remarks to which I should like to draw your attention. There is, first of all, Freud's admittedly rather enigmatic remark in "The Dynamics of Transference" in reference to the transference that nothing is destroyed *in absentia* or *in effigie* (108). But if the symptom is *just* a *symbolic* structure, it ought to be fully displaceable from object to object and there thus seems no reason to suppose that the analyst should not simply be a substitute, a place marker, in an endless play of signifiers circulating from one person to another. If the symptom is purely a formation of the unconscious— and, therefore, a function of the signifier—it would appear to be *par excellence* that which *can* be destroyed *in effigie*. The second indication that Freud is looking beyond the signifier is that the transference is not *just* repetition, for which an explanation in terms of a pure signifying chain could be exhaustively given—repetition as a function of the signifying chain is precisely the sort of explanation Lacan was formulating in the seminars of the fifties. But in recognizing that the transference is also love we are obliged to acknowledge the sometimes massive, sometimes subtle presence of the analyst qua object as something other than pure symbolic place marker.

Let me briefly elaborate on this function of the object, by first referring to some of the developments in Lacan's own work on the question of desire.

Desire was for Lacan initially modeled on intersubjectivity. At the outset (i.e. in the "Function and field of speech and language in psychoanalysis" [1953]) he characterized desire as the desire for recognition, and the end of analysis as the recognition of desire. There are however two difficulties with this view which soon became apparent. First, there is, as Freud points out at the end of *The Interpretation of Dreams*, the indestructibility of desire. How is it possible that desire is indestructible if desire is desire for recognition? Second, if desire is desire for recognition, why does it express itself in such obscure terms? To be sure, these are not insurmountable difficulties, but overcoming them became irrelevant once Lacan had developed the theory of metaphor and metonymy as fundamental structures of the signifier. This development led to the articulation of a second position which ascribes the cause of desire to the signifier. This is the view, put forward, though not unambiguously, in *The Agency of the Letter in the Unconscious* (1957), concerning the metonymy of desire: the object of desire is always a metonymy for the cause of desire; desire is always desire for something else, related metonymically to the cause of desire. Whereas the cause of desire is here regarded as symbolic, in a third phase dating from the 1959/60 seminar on *L'Ethique de la psychanalyse*, the seventh seminar, the cause of desire came to be regarded as the real, in the form of the *objet petit a*. Moreover, the development of the concept of *objet a* we must regard as of no small moment, given that Lacan regularly referred to it as his most important contribution to psychoanalysis.

In order to appreciate properly this category of the object and its function in the real, we need to return to Freud who is, as always, the major source for Lacan's own conceptualization.

On certain of the sociological readings of psychoanalysis, which have emerged particularly in this country, it is thought that for psychoanalysis the only reason sexuality plays a role in the aetiology of the neuroses is that there are social forces opposing its free expression. Whether or not these forces are necessary is of course another question, but the argument is that it is *social forces* that cause sexuality to be repressed and hence traumatic.

However, this view ignores Freud's repeated contention that the *very encounter* with sexuality is itself traumatic—a contention that begins with the so-called "seduction" theory and persists to this observation in *Civilization and Its Discontents:* "Sometimes one seems to perceive that it is . . . something in the nature of the [sexual] function itself which denies us full satisfaction and urges us along other paths" (105). Is this anything different from Lacan's aphorism, "there is no sexual rapport"? (*Encore*, 35).

The second observation, which is related to the first, is that after prevaricating for some time over Otto Rank's theory of birth trauma, according to which birth is the prototype of all later traumatic experiences, Freud came to a categorical opinion: the ultimate source of trauma is castration.

Though of course they need further discussion, these brief indications nevertheless indicate Freud's view that sexuality *itself* is traumatic; and Lacan's contribution has been to theorize how it is that trauma is related to a lack, ultimately a lack in the Other; and how it is that the *object a* is the stop-gap located in the place of this lack.

There is a second point. The *objet a* plays an important role in the formation of fantasy in the psychic life of the subject. (See the matheme: $ \$ \lozenge a $.) Though, as I say, the theorization of *objet a* was repeatedly described by Lacan as his major contribution to psychoanalysis, it is already implicit in Freud that in fantasy there is something that lies *beyond* the symbolic.

Not until 1919, with the crucial paper "A Child Is Being Beaten," did fantasy take on a special significance in Freud's work. This interest in fantasy followed closely on a period in which a practice based exclusively on formations of the unconscious and directed towards the treatment of symptoms began to encounter real and disturbing difficulties. Freud points out that whereas it is *obvious* that the unconscious is implicated in the treatment, because of the manner in which interpretation interacts with symptoms, there is a particularly striking "inertia" associated with fantasy—particularly surprising in comparison with the responsiveness to analysis of the symbolic formations of the unconscious. He is struck by the apparent isolation of a fundamental fantasy from any symbolic network, as is indicated, e.g., by the difficulty analysands have in talking about their fundamental fantasy, in associating to it, as well as in its permanence and resistance to treatment.

It seems that this attention to the nature of fantasy was one of the reasons that led Freud in the 1920s to his second theory of the psychical apparatus (ego, superego, id) and to the new drive dualism (libido, death drive).

From the mid-seventies Lacan came to consider that conducting or directing the treatment must ultimately center on constructing the analysand's fantasy. This work of construction cannot, as I'm suggesting Freud saw, be reduced solely to interpreting formations of the unconscious. The reason is that the subject's position in relation to the *objet a*, to what *causes* his or her desire, is not modified by working upon symbolic identifications and other unconscious formations. The symbolic operations are valid for working upon symptoms, but fantasy is *not* subject to these laws of interpretation. Fantasy is *not* interpretable. Marie-Hélène Brousse points out that it nevertheless remains the fixed point, the hub, around which interpretation revolves because of the role that transference *love* gives to the analyst. The analyst retains a quality of an enigma—"What does he want?"—through which the lack in the Other is brought to life again. (This is the "hysterization" of the analysand.) As Lacan says: "Fantasy effectively holds the key to the place that the analyst occupies for the subject, which is the place of the real" (*Ornicar?* 29:10).

The *objet a*, the thing, is for Lacan the object as such, the object in the real. Though present in language, as a result or product of the signifier, it nevertheless evades the signifier, appearing as what is ineffable or unsayable, as falling outside signification. The *objet a*, which is not specular and therefore not imaginary, not symbolizable and thus not a signifier, is the lost object.

It is this lost object, caught up in the drive, that is the cause of the division of the subject. It is therefore essential to the subject's entry into analysis, where this division must be inscribed in the transference in what Lacan has called the subject's "hysterization."

Freud described psychoanalysis as the third impossible profession—alongside governing and educating. Impossible or not, the aim of analysis is neither to govern nor to educate. Freud became increasingly preoccupied towards the end of his life with the tendency to view the analyst's role as that of fulfilling the superego functions of oral educator and spiritual adviser. In the final months of his life, Freud raised the question whether the position the analyst is placed in by the analysand gives him the opportunity for a sort of after-education of his patient. But he warns against this in "An Outline of Psychoanalysis" on the grounds that it runs counter to the ethics of psychoanalysis:

> But at this point a warning must be given against misusing this new influence. However much the analyst may be tempted to become a teacher, model analyst and ideal for other people and to create men in his own image, he should not forget that that is not his task in the analytic relationship, and indeed that he will be disloyal to his task if he allows himself to be led on by his inclinations. (175)

It is this ethic that the analyst's assumption of the position of superego runs counter to.

The analyst has the function of guaranteeing the analytic experience, that is, he intervenes legitimately in his role as Other, as master, when the framework of the analytic relation has to be maintained, while within this framework it is the subject that does the work.

The end of an analysis, which is the discovery that there is no real supposed subject of knowledge, constitutes the desire of the analyst; a very singular desire that Freud placed at a certain moment in history, the analyst's desire not to identify with the Other, to respect what Freud calls the patient's individuality, not to be his ideal, model, or educator, but to leave the way open to the subject's own desire. Here there is something ascetic, and Lacan believed that analysts had often worked against the analytic discourse. Through installing the analyst in the position of superego, many had taken exactly the opposite path, that of offering themselves as ideals and models.

Lacan is closer to Melanie Klein, in whose theory the end of an analysis has a depressive character which shows that it must be brought into connection with object loss. Object loss, the mourning of an object of love, is symbolized in analysis by the rejection or abandonment of the psychoanalyst. The psychoanalyst therefore represents the residue, the detritus of the psychoanalytic operation. And it was Lacan who developed the theory that makes the analyst the reject of the operation, but at the same time the cause that all along animated the patient's desire. The end of analysis is the rejection, the refusal of the analyst as master signifier, as master of the sense of the subject's speech. This renunciation of the master in the psychoanalyst is something quite paradoxical and enigmatic. Never before Freud has such a theory for non-mastery been developed, and Jacques-Alain Miller suggests that it is perhaps because this desire is so completely novel that some psychoanalysts have renounced it. However, for others, including Lacan, the greatness of Freud was to have committed himself to this place of reject.

It is tempting for the analyst to become his patient's therapist and act, since his integrity is not in doubt, according to the patient's best interests—evaluated, and here is the rub, according to his own lights.

I have however been trying to present a rather different view, one that holds not only that the superego is an agent of repression and cannot be used to undo repression, but more importantly that therapy as re-education contradicts the ethics of psychoanalysis which are premised upon the absence of control and direction, premised upon what Freud calls the dignity of the person.

Works Cited

Brousse, Marie-Hélène, "La formule du fantasme? $ ◊ a" in *Lacan*. Ed. Gérard Miller. Paris: Bordas, 1987.

Freud, Sigmund. *Civilization and Its Discontents* (1930). *S.E.* 21. Ed. James Strachey. New York: W.W. Norton & Co., 1961.

———. "The Dynamics of Transference" (1912). *S.E.* 12. Ed. James Strachey. London: The Hogarth Press, 1958.

———. *Group Psychology and the Analysis of the Ego* (1921). *S.E.* 12. Ed. James Strachey. London: The Hogarth Press, 1958.

———. *The Interpretation of Dreams* 1901). *S.E.* 4–5. Ed. James Strachey. London and New York: Hogarth and W.W. Norton, 1955.

———. "Observations on Transference-Love" (1915). *S.E.* 12. Ed. James Strachey. London: The Hogarth Press, 1958.

———. "An Outline of Psychoanalysis" (1940). *S.E.* 23. Ed. James Strachey. London and New York: Hogarth and W.W. Norton and Co., 1949.

Jones, Ernest. "The Concept of a Normal Mind." *International Journal of Psychoanalysis* 12 (1931).

Lacan, Jacques. "Comptes rendus d'enseignements." Notes from the *Séminaire Problèmes cruciaux pour la psychanalyse. Ornicar?* 29 (Summer 1984).

———. "La psychanalyse et son enseignement," *Ecrits*. Paris: Seuil, 1966.

———. *Le Séminaire. Livre VII: L'éthique de la psychanalyse*. Texte établi par Jacques-Alain Miller. Paris: Seuil, 1986.

———. *Le Séminaire. Livre XX: Encore*. Texte établi par Jacques-Alain Miller. Paris: Editions de Seuil, 1975.

———. *The Seminar. Book I: Freud's Papers on Technique (1953–54)*. Ed. Jacques-Alain Miller. Notes and translation by John Forrester. Cambridge: Cambridge University Press, 1988.

Miller, Jacques-Alain. *Cinco Conferencias Caraqueñas sobre Lacan*. Caracas: Editorial Ateneo de Caracas, 1980. Cf. his remark, p. 85, that the case of Dora is also the case of Freud. For this paper I have derived much inspiration from Miller's lectures.

Silvestre, Michel. "Le Transfert" in *Demain la Psychoanalyse*. Paris: Navarin, 1987.

Strachey, James. "The Nature of the therapeutic Action of Psychoanalysis." *International Journal of Psychoanalysis* 15 (1934).

6

Theory and Practice in the Psychoanalytic Treatment of Psychosis

Willy Apollon

I have been asked to speak about the theory of psychosis and the setting of the psychoanalytic treatment of psychotics. As a psychoanalyst, referring to Lacan's theory of transference, I can't help but consider that demand as a declaration of love, insofar as love has to do with transference. That demand, as a matter of fact, supposes me to know about the *jouissance* of the Great Other to which the psychotic is subjected as an object. So I do not know what our meeting tonight is going to be! Maybe—let us hope—something in the field of psychoanalysis, rather than an ingenious discourse about Lacanian theories of psychoanalysis and psychosis. Anyway, I am here tonight with a desire, which I cannot give up. It has to do in some unconscious way with the analyst's desire. Instead of answering the demand for knowledge about the Other's *jouissance*, I shall be attempting to break up the prejudice of the predominant thinking in North America according to which analysis has nothing to offer concerning the treatment of psychosis.

We would have to agree, if we shared the assumption operating in that assertion that psychosis has a biological ground. Unfortunately, we find that theoretical position to be a futile defense against the horror and the anguish caused by the link between the unbearable foolishness that limits the psyche and what is at stake in psychosis today.

Let us try to identify that link as a starting point for understanding psychosis. In doing so, I do not want to distance myself from the point of view of the practitioner. I want to remain at the place of the analyst who has to conduct the treatment of the psychotic in a Psychoanalytic Treatment Center, where the whole life and all the activities of the subject are involved in the treatment. It cannot be the point of view of an external observer who is not necessarily preoccupied all day long with the challenge of digging a way out of the psychotic phenomenon with the psychotic subject.

What is that madness that designates the frontier of the human experience of the psyche? We can approach that point by a first level theoretical discussion. For anyone, male or female, there is a first experience of a limit of madness in the psyche which is conditioned by the sexual division that language operates in speaking beings. When speaking one to another, man and woman rapidly meet with a decision which is a risk concerning the position of the other. She or he would prefer to deal with logical or practical issues easy to verify in terms of facts, as a search for truth or mutual agreement. In speaking as a means of negotiating satisfaction in coexistence, one has to face words from the other, which have no visual or perceptual reality that might be used as a guarantee of truth or good faith from the other. Even if we could deal with words with obvious references in reality, we would stumble upon those empty words—"portmanteau words," we say in French—words that you can fill up with any content, and for which there are no common references between the speakers, even if there is no cultural ambiguity between them. Such words with which anyone tries to be clever with the other—suggesting and using stratagems to surround and approach the other's aim without risking a refusal from the other—such words could be considered as inside jokes if language were to be reduced to a human tool for translating reality. The fact is that language is language for human being, because words and things are not linked together. And even if they were, the mental reality which is the ground of sex and meaning could never be represented in such a language.

Facing the fact that man has to put faith in the other only on the basis of his words, without any confirmation of facts or perceptual proofs, creates a specific relation between speaking beings. In such a situation the subject has to let himself into the other's word. And it is a veritable limit for the subject of knowledge or the subject of discourse, because he is obliged to decide on the ground of his lack of certainty and guarantee. We are then on the borderline where folly and psyche cannot be well distinguished, one being perhaps the limit of the other. What can be indeed the support and the ground of a full and confident relationship between the speakers, if there are not any guarantees of credence or good faith? For any one at this point, the experience of limit can be translated into the question which leads to an ethical but very hazardous issue: "To what degree of uncertainty can I go without either speculating in horror or toppling over the edge?" A question whose answer is in some way a matter of mental health, and which supposes that other question which is more specific to the adolescent, who faces the fact that there is not any ultimate truth to guarantee the hierarchy of social values: "Why this rather than that?"

I. The sexual division that language introduces in speaking beings

What is at stake in madness is supported by those questions which no speaking being can escape, whatever the biochemical conditions of his social integration. Such questions represent the very limit of the psyche—i.e., the way the human body, as letter and traces of the other's *jouissance* (the so-called death drive in Freudian terminology), is articulated or linked to language, on which are dependent social ties, which are a condition of the subject's satisfaction. And the reason that the subject has to face such a limit in his relation with the other is that sexual division in speaking beings is introduced by language, which links one's satisfaction to the other. The position of the other becomes a determinant element in the subject's strategy for attaining satisfaction. Once again, this has nothing to do with the specific biochemical conditions of his insertion in the world. It's the same for everyone. And when scientists succeed in providing us with drugs capable of getting rid of the biochemical sources of mental illness, the problem will remain the same, exactly the same, with all its acuteness. That is in fact a consequence of the sexual division of speaking beings by language. Language divides humans into subject and object, subject of a demand addressed to the other, object as an answer coming from the other. There is no division such as male and female language; either males or females have to be subject of the desire in the speech or object, as bearer of the object in the answer. That is the question at stake in psychoanalysis, but also psychosis. The sexual division in speaking beings introduces an enjoyment into sex which depends on the object of desire in the other, and not on the good functioning of some biochemical components of sexual activity. That enjoyment is satisfaction insofar as the other provides the correct answer to the demand, or anything else he has to do, for and with the same enjoyment. And the question is how, using only words, to carry the other to do what he has to do—just enough, not too much—for the enjoyment of the subject. The answer to that question leads to the site of specific strategy and tactics in dealing with the other's subjective involvement.

Such a division introduced by language is thus a commitment to the power of the other. It establishes power relationships between speaking beings as strategy in the field of language—i.e., as rhetorical slyness rather than physical violence grounded on biochemical or neurological conditions. It brings the subject into demand as a maneuvering to decipher what the other is able to give up, hiding what he wants behind what he can drag out of the other, losing in the process even the consciousness of what he might desire. Dealing with the other in that field where language is playing tricks rather than signifying things supposes one can achieve mastery over metaphor. That is what I shall designate here as aesthetics. Aesthetics is that site opened up by the signifier in language when language, in distributing things, looks toward something else, but nothing in particular, forging an area for the investment of desire. Thus the sexual division of speaking beings by language brings to ruin the very possibility of sexual relations or congruity between them. Language can therefore be perceived as including a failure, or achieving a trickery of man. The trickery of language, or of the Other, as Descartes suggests, is mastered by the ability to take advantage of metaphor in dealing with the area of aesthetics. This is the case in neurosis. Psychosis, in contrast, chooses to consider the default in language as a failure or an evil of the human condition, a fundamental lack that must be corrected by changing the myths and beliefs which sustain meaning in language as a link between the speakers in a given society.

II. What is psychosis?

We shall therefore not consider that the psychotic has loosened any relationship with reality; that is not the way we interpret Freud's position on psychosis. Following Lacan, we shall state instead that the psychotic has loosened the social tie to the Other. For must of us—neurotics and perverts—the lack of foundation or guarantee in language does not impress us as an evil in the human universe. We hardly even acknowledge that this lack concerns the very foundation of our world of meaning, the absence of any final evidence, the want of any instance of undoubtable truth as a guarantee of adequacy between speech acts, ideals, and events. On the contrary, for most of us, the lack in language is neutralized by myths and beliefs of all kinds, on which are grounded the values of our social relationships. What can the neurotic establish to counteract that lack of the One at the site of the Great Other? This will stand for what Lacan proposes as the Name-of-the-Father.

In face of this lack in language, the psychotic is destitute and empty-handed. The foreclosure of the Name-of-the-Father refers us to the absence of the signifier of the Father, when the psychotic has to answer to that want in the great Other, in order to maintain a social tie with others. Lacan identifies that moment as the period when the crisis arises in psychosis, the release mechanism of that process. During this period, the subject in search of an object from the Other confronts the lack of any guarantee in dealing with the other's answer, and has to counterbalance that lack, supporting in some way the whole language of his One, forging and handling the metaphor in that aesthetic field of uncertainty.

The collapsing of the universe of the subject is the answer of the drive in that situation where the subject is incompetent, deprived of the signifier or of a keen use of metaphor to mastermind the area of aesthetics where he could have built a fictitious ground in his relation to the Other. In the sampling of one hundred and twenty-two patients that we have treated during the last six years at our clinic in Quebec City, it is amazing to observe that most of them had their first crisis when they were between twelve and nineteen years old. Why does adolescence seem to be a preferred time for collapsing? That question is significant in relation to our notion that psychosis is determined by language instead of being mainly an effect of biological or biochemical substrates. Let us define the child as one who believes the mythical foundation of things—i.e., the social values and laws embodied in the parental discourses. Even if he were questioned by the foreclosure of the signifier of the Father, he might relate to some "homemade" belief which would keep the whole of language from jeopardy. The adolescent, on the other hand, is one who is aware of the want in the Other as a lack of foundation for the justification of the law and for the status of social values. The adolescent questions the foundations, and confronts their wanting in a hysterical contest. Even if he suffers from that lack of the signifier of the Father, he won't accept the myths and social beliefs that sustain the social ties. Thus in our experience, at least, the time of adolescence has been for most psychotics a period of great philosophical questioning—as is true for anyone, of course, but with that specific anxiety that is related to the inability to deal with the want in the Great Other, without any fictitious basis to master metaphor in the aesthetic field of the signifier.

Thus the psychotic arises from the collapse of the world, constructing a delusional foundation for a new and incipient world of his own. His attempt to repair the world of language rotted by that absolute evil—that wanting which corrupts language—has the structure of a narrative in which he is identified as the hero who dedicates himself to his mission. He tries in the same manner to commit himself to the titanic work of repairing the loss of a credible ground in the symbolic order of language, to decipher the problem of his own identification and to establish the foundation of his social ties to others. That feature can have the appearance of the evolution of a paranoid structure, where the psychosis grows specifically on the ground and in the field of language. But in terms of the treatment (insofar as it is necessary to achieve an end), in schizophrenia, where the psychotic structure digs its way out to a solution by exposing his being and dedicating his body to mending the default in the symbolic order, we find out that psychosis always presupposes the presence or the undiscernible action of voices.

During his childhood, he may seem quite "normal," just like other children except for some peculiarities that later appear as elementary phenomena connected with the latent structure of psychosis. Thus Esthel, a patient treated for schizophrenia, when emerging from the phenomena of her illness, said some months ago: "As far as I remember, in my childhood, even when I was a girl of only three or four, until those last months of my psychoanalysis, I always had to struggle against voices, in order to keep my distance. They always speak into my ear, murmuring to me what to do, and uttering orders against which I had to fight my way." It is as if the schizophrenic subject, preoccupied for so long with her numerous physiological symptoms—the seizure of her body in the Other's *jouissance*—could not be aware enough of the significance of the voices to confess their presence in the back of her mind.

Psychosis is characterized by the unchaining and disenthralling of the voices, which function as detached from language. And insofar as language must be conceived as the support of the symbolic order which structures the social link, the unchaining of the voices in psychosis, as a parasite in the speech of the subject, testifies to a crack in the way the unconscious subject relates himself to the Other in the symbolic. Facing the fact of the want in the Other leads the psychotic subject to the lack of foundation in the symbolic order, the absence of a truth, in the final instance, as a guarantee for the human search for happiness in social ties. And that very situation musters the unattached signifiers of the voices into a disruption of the order of language, in the form of disturbing the investment of the drives.

One can observe that such an approach is not aware of the biological sources of psychosis, which is the American psychiatric way. The question is quite a large one. But our position is to continue to wait for progress in biochemical approaches to treating psychosis. It is sure that it will come some day. And it will be the best for psychotics. We assume that any important change and improvement in the biochemical conditions of the subject in psychosis will involve a reshaping of his whole life, bringing a state of relief and alleviation of his sufferings. But the point is not only the physiological distress in psychosis; it is first the psychic inability which causes anguish and sufferings. Suppressing the one without even acknowledging the other is a way to reduce one, the psychic level of the psychotic dilemma, to an effect of the other, the biochemical conditions related to psychosis. In any case, it is of some importance to recognize that the relief biochemical progress can bring to the psychotic patient is not a solution to the problem of the relation of the subject to the want of the Other and the lack in the symbolic order, or to the absence of a foundation in the agency of the Law. Psychosis does not imply only a physiological default in the organism where a subjective position is at stake; it also hints at an encounter by the psychotic subject of a want or a *jouissance* in the Other as a substitute for a default in the symbolic order. The biological approach supposes that the structure of psychosis does not imply any external correlation, as if it were a pure physiological or biochemical abnormality, ignoring the crucial problem of a "supposed normality" in such a field for the very complex human being.

Do we have to think that an improvement in the biochemical conditions of living in the subject will provide him with a capacity to deal with the want in the Other? Or produce negotiable fictions to sustain the lack that injures the symbolic order? As a matter of fact, in his relation to the Other, the psychotic as a subject has to face an object of *jouissance* as an answer from the other. The demand of the subject does not encounter desire as want in the Other; he confronts a demand for *jouissance*. Taking some account of the position of the psychotic subject facing the lack of foundation and guarantee in the symbolic order and language, we must admit that all his efforts and his strengths are directed toward correcting that shortage which he considers as a calamity and a disaster for the world. Building his delusion, he is in search of a foundation, a final truth to provide an ultimate support for mankind, a guarantee for the social ties between speaking beings.

It is precisely that aspect of the delusion that psychoanalysis has to bring to an end. Our practice of the treatment of psychotics reveals to us that the delusion provides a path to the signifiers where voices expel the subject out of the symbolic order of language and its aesthetic effects. We do have to take specific account of those signifiers in the delusion in order to build with the subject a way out of the effects of the psychosis. But this can be done only if we do not enter the process of the delusion, looking around for a ground or a physical basis for establishing a foundation for the symbolic order—i.e., for some certainty that might stand for that final truth, that guarantee that there is no longer any lack in the Other. Now the most we can say about the biological approach to psychosis and its therapeutic practices is that they strengthen the delusion, while correcting the subject's physiological effects, fortifying the subject in the certainty of a physical cause and verifiable ground for his psychosis. As some patients say to us concerning their drugs, they alleviate their pain and suffering, but they don't put an end to the action of the voices, which continue whispering and murmuring in the background. We might add to that complaint that after the relief provided by the drugs, the subject is still in the same position regarding the Other's *jouissance*. Of course, this fact is no argument for neglecting or showing a disregard for the necessity of lightening the distress of the subject with appropriate drugs. Looking to modify the subject's answer to the foundation of the psychotic production does not justify any disrespect for his pain. And it is precisely that which is the purpose and justification of biochemical therapy, insofar as the analyst is concerned.

Concerning the Lacanian concept of the Other's *jouissance*, let us give a hint of its relevance to the clinic. We have pointed out that what is at stake in psychosis is the unchaining of signifiers, removed from any bondage in the subject's speech. That "auto-enjoyment" of signifiers in psychosis, if I might propose that expression, is the very *jouissance* of the Other, following Lacan's position that the Other is the site of signifiers. Moreover, that enjoyment of signifiers, the power of the voices, enrolls the subject's drives and answers in the same self-regulated and enfranchised autarchy of language and social ties. It seems to the patient that she is cut across by strangers and things going their own way, without any regard for her, controlled and constrained in her most intimate thoughts, constantly instructed about what she has to do, or what she has to say. Describing that psychic position of the subject in the structure of psychosis, Lacan points out that he or she is in the position of the object of the Other's *jouissance*, where Freud refers to the uncontrolled action of the death drive in psychosis.

Is it possible to modify such a position of the subject in regard to the *jouissance* in the structure? That is the issue at stake in the treatment of psychosis, whether the approach be biological or psychoanalytic.

III. What can psychoanalysis do to achieve such an aim with psychotics?

Before pursuing the logical steps of the process of psychoanalytic treatment, I would like, on the basis of the theoretical approach I have outlined, to bring into focus some prerequisites of my position. Speaking of the theoretical approach to psychosis and proposing to-

night for the first time in the United States a comprehensive understanding of the logic of our approach to the treatment of psychosis, I
want to emphasize that the basis, the very foundation, of this presentation is first and foremost the practice we have had in Quebec City
since 1974. Thus it may appear at first glance that this paper accords
rather little place to the writings of Lacan or Freud. In fact, it is
significant that Freud did not believe that psychoanalysis would be
of more help in treating psychosis than to offer an interpretive explanation of the psychosis. Did Lacan go further? Without a doubt. Rereading the position of Freud, Lacan stressed that the question of the
father as a symbolic agency is fundamental in the issue of psychosis,
as it is for psychoanalysis itself. Moreover, Lacan entered the psychoanalytic field via psychosis, as a psychiatrist. And at three periods of
his teaching, besides the case presentations at Ste. Anne's Hospital, he
returned more specifically to the discussion of psychosis, enlightening
and expanding Freud's views and theories with his own. With "Le cas
Aimée," "Le président Schreber," and "Joyce, le sinthôme," he put
forward the main concepts that have guided our psychoanalytic experience and clinical practice with psychotics. But is it fair to say that
Lacan gave us a clear theory of what the treatment of psychosis must
be? As far as I know from Lacan's published writings, the answer is
no. We have had to discover the logic of the treatment of psychotics
by using the conceptual approach of Freud and Lacan for guidance,
but without any precise indications concerning that process.

There is another critical point to mention, which is a basic requisite
to the logical process in the treatment of psychosis. Most of the psychoanalytic writings on psychosis are essays, treatises, and explanations
dealing with knowledge. Psychoanalysts in their writings demonstrate that psychoanalysis has an acute comprehension of what psychosis is. One might wonder if such an acuteness and understanding
are not the only contribution that psychoanalysis can bring to psychosis, in view of the distance analysts usually keep concerning their
commitment in the treatment itself. On the other hand, for many
psychoanalysts the analytic work still consists in working through to
consciousness those repressed thoughts and representations from the
unconscious: unconscious knowledge is the model in the direction of
the treatment. Such a position is still largely bound to scientism,
which endorses the mirage that science will get rid of human problems. From that point of view, knowledge, or access to unconscious
representations, would overcome the symptoms. Such a position is
not too far from the position of the biological approach to the psyche,
which is a scientific one, with the presumption that a specifically
human problem can be mastered by the logical process of scientific

means, which entails observation, hypothesis, verification by experiment, setting up of laws, and field or domain of application. Focusing analysis on the power of the symbolic order and its consequences in desire, Lacan opens the way out of such an illusion, pointing out how language divides the human senses, disconnecting desire from need, through the signifiers of demand, and repudiating sexual relations between speaking beings.

Our starting point in the theory of our practice derives from that opening made by Jacques Lacan, to an analysis oriented by the encounter of desire as an effect of language, rather than by self-knowledge in access to the unconscious, which achieves scientific knowledge—biological or any other ones—as rational ways to elucidate human problems. On the basis of our clinical experience and its outcome, we think that psychoanalysis has the most to bring to the treatment of psychosis by changing the perspective of that treatment from a standpoint in human knowledge to a focus on desire. As psychoanalysts, we do not have much to offer in the field of human knowledge that has not been (or cannot be) elucidated by poets, artists, saints, scientists, and others impassioned by desire. More specifically, in the field of therapy as the search for improvement, in the use of scientific and experimental knowledge, we cannot match the other approaches, because our tool is transference and not scientific or theoretical knowledge; interpretation and not application of a set of theories in a certain domain; maneuver and not correction of behavior or of physiological dysfunction. Our action thus stands on the aesthetic site created by the signifiers that excluded *jouissance* in language, and the basic conviction that we must not give up on desire, which is excluded from any scientific purpose. The specific field of analytic action is the only site where analysis can bring some rupture and alternative to the destiny of the psychotic, and that field is the aesthetic site where the analysand's demand encounters the analyst's desire. These remarks describe quite accurately the boundary of our action in the treatment of psychotics.

Within such a limit, the psychotic engaged in transference will encounter a boundary that limits the certainty of his delusion, so that the signifier, supported by the analyst's desire, will be able to discover its trace through the writing of the symptom, to connect the unbound drives to an object in fantasy. That will be the outcome that the analyst will require for the desire of the psychotic subject. In what follows, I will elucidate the four logical steps of that process. This logical process of the analytic cure of psychosis should not be taken as a theoretical revelation of our knowledge of what could be the direction of the cure with the psychotic. We are quite opposed to such a theoretical position, which remains in the field of scientific delusion. We do not have at our disposal any magisterial or authoritative texts or manuscripts as clinical references for treating psychotics, when doing our work in Quebec City. Even if we did, I do not think we would proceed in any other way. Freud's and Lacan's writings, as theories of their own practices, were our only guide, particularly the way they maneuver in the transference in order not to give up on the desire for knowledge when confronted with the demands of patients who supposed them to know. Thus our references in presenting the logical process of the treatment of psychotics are mainly those treatments themselves, including the psychotic transference as opened up by a specific demand, the writing in the symptom of that "thing" foreclosed from the site of the signifier, and our maneuvering to bring it to the analysand's speech, so that it might carve out its route as an object in fantasy. At the beginning of our venture with over one hundred and twenty psychotics in "388," a large and beautiful house in Quebec City, there was no evidence that such a logical way was possible, nor was it attainable. But now—having gathered and computed data from six years of clinical practice and research, and having surveyed some external but established facts about the evolution of these patients, such as their mastering of social ties, correlated to the treatment process as it unrolled—we are now on the way to identifying the process of treatment and its logic, insofar as a remodeling of the psychotic's social tie is concerned.

IV.   The logic of the process in the psychoanalytic treatment of psychosis

The psychosis engages spontaneously in the task of constructing its solution as an answer to the Other's want. Captured by the *jouissance* of the Other, possessed by its voices, the psychotic assumes the task of repairing the world of language, and of constructing his identification and place in that new world. How can we, analysts, introduce a cutoff point and a doubt in that work, in order to remodel it for a negotiable social tie? At "388" and at the Psychoanalytic Center for Psychotic Treatment in Quebec City, we use the four logical steps previously mentioned. Let us now focus on the study of twenty-five cases who followed our path of treatment for six consecutive years, and of thirty others who are still following it with some profit. Those steps are:

First, the signifier: the production of a subjective position that involves a renewing of the identification of the psychotic subject in his speech, regarding the *jouissance* of the Other. This is the time of a rebuilding of the subjective story as a foundation for the assumption of speech.

Second, the writing in the symptom: the restoration of the body image, the time of the symptom, where the subject inhabits his body ultimately, as a referential point, a limit in the writing and the return of *jouissance*, to correlate and manage his time and space.

Third, the object of fantasy: the production of a substitute in the fantasy, the time of the object around which are constituted the issues of the Other's *jouissance* for the subject.

Fourth, desire in the social tie: the exploration of the aesthetic foundations for an ethics of the social tie, where the subject of desire confronts the lack in a society that refuses the tragic scope of human life. The exigency still remains for the psychotic to recover a social tie, a way to rebuild his relations with others and with the Other from the ground of the signifiers of his desire.

V. The identification of the subjective unconscious position, from the signifier

At the beginning of the treatment of the psychotic subject, the analyst faces the specific problem that the process must be inaugurated by a demand from the subject, which constitutes the subject's position as analysand in the structure of the treatment process. Most of those who think that psychoanalysis is impossible with psychotics argue that a psychotic has no ability to sustain a personal demand—i.e., to take the floor and to speak on her own, rather than under the dictation of the voices or the will of the Other. Clinical experiences seem to confirm such a position. Expecting the psychotic to speak on her own may provoke an upsurge of the crisis, which is perceived as a worsening of the psychosis. Consequently, the initiation of the process of transference can be jeopardized by the subject's position with regard to the *jouissance* of the Other.

Nevertheless, at the Psychoanalytic Treatment Center for Psychotics in Quebec City, it is a fact that psychotics do address their demand to us. Our rule is that any patient must address a personal demand in order to be admitted to the Center. It was obvious to us that any process of treatment has to be founded on the basis of a self-commitment of the patient. So the patient has to phone the Center and obtain an appointment with the "admissions committee."

What, then, can the demand for an analysis be in psychosis? Psychotics come to us with all sorts of demands. One could say that they are not necessarily demands for analysis. One comes and demands to become a priest; another wants to be an Olympic champion in order to deliver his message to the world after receiving the gold medal. But what specifically constitutes a demand for analysis in what a psychotic subject might submit to our committee? We often have to refuse admission to patients because they have been sent by their psychiatrist, or their parents, or someone else, and so are not asking for anything. Most of the time such patients do not think they are sick, nor do they think they have any need for help. But for a number of psychotics, those we have accepted for a treatment in the Center, we may have noticed a break or failure in their certainty and a collapse in the delusive system they have built to palliate the lack which wounds the universe of language. That failure in what they have constructed as a solution and an answer to the Other's *jouissance* is what leads them to make a demand to the Center. From then on the position assumed by the subject when he asks for analysis is a challenge to the position he had assumed concerning the *jouissance* in which he is captured, and his failure to answer the demand or injunction of the Other.

In such an instance, the demand of the psychotic is for help in mending his delusive system of certainty. He wants to fill the break in his demented construction, in order to set up an obstacle to the Other's aggression. The scientific position—for example, that of the psychiatrist—is to answer that call for help as a need for physical relief. In Lacanian psychoanalysis, such a demand encounters the analyst's desire, but not an answer. That confrontation of the psychotic's demand with the analyst's desire opens the way to the transference and inaugurates the process of analysis.

The analyst's desire is to not give up on the want in the Other—that is, in the case of the psychotic, to maintain the absence of a final truth as the foundation of language, which introduces and keeps in reserve for awhile that space of uncertainty and doubt that weakens the delusion. The opposition between the analyst's desire and the psychotic's demand can be an obstacle throughout the process of psychoanalytic treatment. Its result, then, is first a worsening of the crisis, and a strengthening the position of the subject as an object for the Other's *jouissance*. In that moment, it is obvious that the psychotic would confuse the analyst's desire with the Other's *jouissance*. This direct effect of the analytic process on the psychotic subject has often been put forward as an argument for discarding analysis in the treatment of psychosis. But the maneuver of the analyst in installing the transference can prevent such a confusion.

As a matter of fact, at the same time, the analyst's desire has to evoke the subject in the process. For the first time, the psychotic is conscious of being listened to as a subject, and not observed and surveyed or scrutinized as an object. Someone is paying great attention to what he has to say. Moreover, one is asking him to tell more about his illness instead of reducing his peculiarity to a catalogue of classified cases. The psychotic is aware that the analyst's position is one of a listener, with the desire of knowing from him something about *his* psychosis, and not about psychosis in general. He is no longer confronted with a scientific position looking for the objective or physical causes of his troubles and anguishes, with the specific aim only of lessening the effects of those causes. The psychotic is certainly very interested in going as far as possible with the scientist in search of a physical basis for what is destroying his life and ruining large parts of the language from inside him. Such searches confirm his certainty and comfort his delusion. But the analyst's desire to know opens a way to the remodeling of the subject's position in regard to the Other's exigency in psychosis, instead of looking into his physiological conditions to find a basis for the evil in the world. If the analyst seems to have his interest aroused and stimulated by the fictional and elusive tale of the psychotic, it is for the purpose of holding out a place for the Other's wanting to appear. For the analyst, the point remains that he has to take the psychotic from a position of a demand of *jouissance* from the Other, to a position of relation to the lack in the Other.

Thus a place is granted for the crisis, where the subject is referred to his own speech as supported by the signifiers the analyst extracts. Of course, there is no chaining of the signifier at that stage of the process; neither can the patient produce a narrative as a whole. But fragments of a chain, as well as detached pieces of history related to them, can be pointed out by the analyst. In that first step of the process, such a maneuver of the analyst—relating fragments of chaining to pieces of subjective life—produces a boundary that limits the delusion and offers the patient some disjointed portions of his subjective history to refer to, instead of such and such a part or detail of his delusion. The patient is asked to tell the reason for his illness in his own words, so that he develops his theory for that first very special listener. But at the same time, the analyst maintains doubt and uncertainty by his inquiring into the psychotic's search for some fragment of chaining. As a result, both patient and psychoanalyst renew the relation to the Other on a new basis where a failure is opened in the certainty, when some signifiers begin to guide the analyst's desire in his search for a basis for the subject outside of the Other's *jouissance*. It is important to emphasize that the signifiers in the first steps of the treatment of the neurotic are related to the Other's desire. In the case of the psychotic, in contrast, those signifiers, related to the demand and injunctions of the Other, determine the place of the subject in the structure with regard to the Other's *jouissance.*

It is fair to notice here that during that period of psychoanalytic treatment in our Center, the patient organizes her treatment with a care team, where she is a member in good standing, under the guidance of a psychiatrist who is not her analyst, a social worker, and one intervener who will assist her during all the time she is in treatment in the Center. For all the members of the team, the relation of transference between the patient and her analyst is the key to the treatment, even if the analysts, although present in the weekly clinical meetings, never say anything or give any information about the progress of the treatment. The team assists the patient during crises. And we have developed an analytic approach to gain mastery over a crisis until the analysand can deal with it by herself. But all interventions by the team or by any member of the team are governed by the analytic perception of the case drawn out during the weekly clinical meeting for and by all the interveners, and during the weekly meeting of the team with the patient. That is to say, the objective is to consider the patient as a responsible subject confronting the want in language— indeed, the failure of the whole order of the symbolic—with her own theory of what is happening to mankind as well as to herself as a result of that weakness and lack of guarantee in the Other. That objective is never jeopardized by any intervener in the Center. People working in the Center have experienced in their own analyses, in their own lives, or in the course of clinical process in the last six years with over one hundred patients, the relevance of such a position for the treatment of psychosis.

Ultimately, that first step in the process positions the subject in the structure concerning the signifiers that offer a path for remolding such and such a fragment of his history as a referential substitute for the certainty of his position in his delusive construction. Thenceforth, we witness a progressive withdrawal of the delusion and sufficient control of the crisis by the patient for him to renew some social activities, including his former work, or his studies, or his friends, or looking for a place to live. This first stabilizing in the treatment may take from eighteen to thirty-six months, according to our data. It is an established fact that those patients who have left the center without any significant improvement—some twenty-five percent of our clients—left during the first thirty-six months of the treatment. All the others kept on their treatment until they arrived at significant changes in their lives, and in their subjective position in the structure, but, of course, without working out the end of the analysis. Nor did they overcome the phenomena of the psychosis. We stress the distinction between the phenomena through which the subject is referred to as being subjected to the *jouissance* of the Other, and his position in the structure, which defines what is uncommon in psychosis. In the process of treatment, we are trying to obtain a shift in the position of the subject in the structure in order to gain control and significant changes in dealing with the phenomena of the psychosis. Such a problematic is not one of a cure with the restorative and physiological meaning it includes in medical science, even if we use the concept of the cure in the Lacanian approach. Our concept of the psychoanalytic cure refers to the changes in the subject's position and life that occur through the transference on account of the analytic act.

VI. Rebuilding the body image through the symptom as a writing

The first step of the analysis identifies the signifiers of a structure which opens a subjective and historical position for the subject on the ground of the want in the Other that the analyst maintains as a substitute for the Other's *jouissance* to which the subject is submitted. Identifying such signifiers creates the structure of a limit and boundary to the Other's want. The second logical step in the treatment is largely involved in the resetting of a body image for the subject as a limit to "*das Ding,*" that sting from the Other's *jouissance*. That has to do with the schizophrenic dimension of psychosis, where the subject faces the action of the Other through the writings—letters and traces—of *jouissance* as constitutive of his body, whose parts, unattached to any image or fiction of unity, are tossed about by all sorts of events—those phenomena of the psychosis which the Other's signifiers determine.

Once the transference is well installed as a result of the gap of uncertainty that the analyst has opened up in the psychotic's delusional theory, at this time only the presence of the analyst compensates for the absence, and the hole, that the foreclosure of the Name-of-the-Father leaves the subject with. Through listening to the patient and helping him master his crises, the subject's position in the structure, in regard to *jouissance*, has been clarified. Now the analyst and other interveners have enough insight into the position of the subject to involve themselves in the next step. This is a very difficult one, because of the distinction one must maintain between the medical, scientific, or psychiatric concept of the organism and the Freudian or psychoanalytic concept of the body. On that point it is obvious that any decisive theoretical statement has important consequences in the clinical field, because the theory of psychoanalysis is the theory of a practicing and not an explanatory theory of a domain of reality. Moreover, our psychoanalytic theory of the body intends to clarify practices such as the working through of the letter, and the writing in the seizure of the subject in the Other's *jouissance*, at the level of the primary process of repression. At this level the body arises as an archaeological fragment. It is not what psychiatrists, or medical workers and other pro-scientific tenants of the origin of psychosis, are dealing with when they speak of the body of their patients. Thus our psychoanalytic concept of the symptom as a writing and a letter from the Other is not to be confounded with the medical or the psychiatric one.

We have stated that in the speaking being, the symbolic order links any satisfaction of needs to a relation with the Other, and to an object that appears as an answer from the Other. That symbolic link renders impossible the immediate and totally satisfactory *jouissance* of needs, as well as free access to their objects. Indeed, the objects of the needs cannot be reached for the sake of total and immediate satisfaction. And the human body is, so to speak, a direct effect of that insufficiency and that hollowing out of *jouissance* from the organism. That primary action of language or the symbolic order constitutes in mankind the primary repression of *jouissance*, which installs the human subject, as a result of that primary symbolization, as a fundamentally lost subject. The body retains traces of that primary traumatic seizure of the being in the symbolic field of that exclusion of *jouissance*. Those traces—erogenous zones, Freud called them—detach the body from the organism, relating it to that excluded *jouissance*, which stands therefore for an intimate exteriority, rejected but still present, haunting the being as an internal sting, a genuine and unbearable injury inflicted by the body upon the organism. That "thing" with and from which the hysterical subject contests and defies the authority of the master and the knowledge of the scientist—*"das Ding"* where Freud identified the ground of discontent in civilization—that *jouissance* is what invades and possesses the whole site of the psychotic subject, when he is requested to face the lack in the Other. It is also that "thing," the return of that excluded *jouissance*, which he is trying to contain as if to limit the want in the symbolic by opposing his being and his body to it.

In this second stage of the treatment, we have to face the return of the excluded *jouissance* in the symptom, with the means we extract from the first period in terms of signifiers of the Other's want, fragments of the subjective story, the release of the *jouissance* and the mastering of the crisis. The analyst rapidly encounters the limit of such means. The real coming back to the organism, through the action of the death drive, finds its way through the letters and scripts on the body. At this turning point of the treatment, in the same way that we used the signifiers from the delusion to drag out fragments of subjective history in order to position the unconscious subject when identifying structure, we now use the writings of the symptom to maneuver a way out of the rule of the other's signifiers. As a matter of fact, psychotics interpret that situation as if they were struggling against the exigencies of the Other. They are no longer in the position of giving up and sacrificing their own life or body in order to mend and repair the lack or evil in the world. What is new is that they want to live. They have experienced in the three years in the Center that they are not necessarily at a dead end. In addition, they can attest to the changes in the lives of a lot of their colleagues. That is a very important point for them in going through this difficult period, where the crises are profound and very painful, and where psychotics seem to go as far as they can in the destruction of the past and of anything related to it, even their own being. The symptoms are the means by which the unconscious subject tries at the same time to get rid of the Other and to erase all traces of *jouissance* in his or her past.

Esthel, a patient who is now beyond that step, writes: "In the deepest part of myself, I think that I wanted to be sick. Unconsciously, I believed that through my sickness I would become nothing and that would give a meaning to my life, and fill the void. . . . But now I want to live. I could not explain the change that happened. All I know is that now I want to live; I do not want to be sick. I have so much to do with my life."

Thenceforth, in relation to the Other's exigencies, the symptom is the investment of the letter, the script from the Other, by *"das Ding,"* the return of that *jouissance* that language excludes from the speaking being. As a letter, the script on the body is outside meaning; it is not related to the signifiers of the Other, of which the concatenation, even partial, supports meaning and therefore the injunctions from the Other. Here interpretation, dealing with the signifier, would have the effect of connecting the letter to the Other's injunctions and *jouissance*. So the analyst's maneuver will be different. Apart from interpretation, she will manage to relate the script in the symptom to writing in language. As a matter of fact, the psychoanalytic symptom is always connected in language to some nomination: it may be a scientific denomination in a diagnostic manual, or it may be an expression in language—an idiom, a proverb, or maxim, or a given formula in everyday speech. In fact, the wandering of the signifier as phonetic units in language has a limit: it is limited by writing in language—

i.e., by those units of cultural meaning such as proverbs, idioms, and metaphors, as well as insults, abuses, or slanders, rhetorical figures or stylistic devices, and so many turns of phrase in language that gather words and phrases in emergent meaning when conditioning logical relations, allowing the speaking subject to compute an answer from a listener in the language. Writing in language thus structures the trails for the wandering of the voices. They support symbolic rules of speaking and of producing meaning and social ties, while the voices arising from the lack and the want in the Other carry along the *jouissance* in language, by means of the law of writing. The letter on the body fastens the wandering of *das Ding* to the littoral of the being.

By connecting the script in the symptom to writing in language, the analyst offers a new trail to the death drive that is working through the symptom. The unconscious subject pointed out in the drive is thus referred to the law of writing in language and no longer to the law of the signifier in the Other. The symptom bears witness to that real *jouissance* that cannot be represented in the field of the signifier. The analyst's maneuver, correlating the script of the symptom to writing in language, symbolizes a part of that real as structuring the space and the time of the subject. In fact, that maneuver sets out to emphasize the way the body, as a writing, binds together subjective time and space. Thus if the first stage of the treatment can be called the time of the signifier, the second is the time of writing and the letter. The effort to make a minimum chaining in order to initiate a place for the subject outside of the *jouissance* of the Other leads the process to that real of the symptom, rejected from any representation according to the law of the signifier. Maneuvering the letter within the law of writing sustains for the unconscious subject a remodeling of his body outside of the Other's *jouissance*, reappropriating his time and space in a way that opens a road for him to the internal object.

We have proposed this concept of an internal object to refer to that specific moment where a multitude of symptoms seem to center around a point, identified as an internal organ or an internal object, that conveys a meaning to the whole life of the patient. At that time, one subject speaks, for instance, of a microphone placed under his tooth, another will appeal to his loosened spleen, and a third will invoke a needle introduced into his brain. At the end of the analysis of the symptom we face that remaining rock of *jouissance*, as the final part of the subject reduced to an object of the Other. It is a final knot of delusion that the analyst's desire will contest until it can be externalized, under the working through of what takes the place of an emerging fantasy. Thenceforth, it is not a matter of dismissing or removing that rock, but of shifting the subject in his position in the structure that is at stake in the psychosis.

In that step, the analyst's desire appeals to the analysand's desire at the place of *jouissance*. From that position, she maneuvers in order to separate the analysand from the signifier of the demand under the rule of the Other's *jouissance* in order to refer him to the law of writing in language, through the letter of the symptom. That shifting of the subject's position in regard to the Law (from the non-barred Other of the signifier to the Other of the Law) introduces the analytic process to the possibility and the field of desire.

VIII. The production of an object

The coming of that third time in the treatment of psychosis is signified to the analyst by the appearance of dreams. I mean psychoanalytic dreams—those that come as answers to a desire from (or imputed to) the analyst. By that time, as in the other stages of the treatment, the process is directed by the encounter of the analysand's demand with the analyst's desire. Most of the time, the analysand has discovered more about the life she is now able to live. She has another relationship to her body, and begins to fantasize the position of object of the Other's desire. Some patients begin new sexual relationships, where the point is not a search for satisfaction or pleasure, but rather an attempt to negotiate a desire arising in the words of a partner. Now she lives in her own apartment, she has renewed social works and commitments, and she has begun to face the problem of her position in the sexual division of speaking beings. Only at that moment is it possible for the analysand to no longer confuse the analyst's indefinite desire that has sustained the want in the other with his or her own delusive injunction for the Other's *jouissance*. The analysand must face the difficulty of identifying the Other's desire by means other than her own computation through the signifiers and the object of her fantasy, or through the Other's *jouissance*. This point offers the possibility for the psychotic subject to encounter the Other's desire without falling into the phenomena of psychosis.

Three years ago, we proposed the following hypothesis to the analysts who treat psychotics in our group in Quebec City. The construction of a fantasy in psychosis, when an object is proposed to the subject to support his sexual division from the Other as far as *jouissance* is concerned, is a time of great consequence for the kernel of *jouissance* remaining from the writing in the symptom. That internal object is a confluence of meaning, and holds together a lot of events in the life of the subject as though it were a surrogate for the Name-of-the-Father. But at this point in the transference the analyst elicits an object of desire, in place of the internal object of the symptom. The maneuver on the script which authorizes the substitution from kernel of *jouissance* in the symptom to an object produced by the fantasy, is possible only through the encounter of the patient's demands with the analyst's desire in the transference. In that transferential situation, the analysand meets with some indefinite object of desire at the site of the analyst. That object circumscribes the deficiency in the place of the Other where the analyst stands in. It is from the fact of that wanting upheld by the presence and the withdrawal of the analyst, that the kernel or remainder of *jouissance* that stands in for the lack in the Other can be subjected to a loss.

What is at stake for the subject at that moment in the process is the sexual division of speaking beings by language, which submits the want of the subject to the object as an answer of the other. As a matter of fact, the subject does not demand what he desires. On the contrary, he has to discover the want that causes his desire in the demand he addresses to the other. Insofar as his demand is only the computation of what the other is assumed to give away, what he can bring to light as his desire remains confusedly bound to the desire of the other. This ultimately does not satisfy his desire, nor does it answer his demand. The relation to the other's desire opposes an obstacle to the demand, disconnecting demand and desire, underlining the division between the subject and any other. This division *as a fact of language* can be situated now by the subject as deeper than any physiological division, and as the very obstacle to sexual relationships between speaking beings. But what can stand for the field of language for the psychotic subject?

Thenceforth, the psychotic subject himself represents that new aspect of the wanting. His wanting has to be related to the lack in the other so that he represents himself as the object of the other's desire. But the discovery of desire and its object is not discernible from the fantasy that gives a shape to them. The imaginary form of that exploration preserves the subject against the damage of reality that is the outcome of an answer from the other. Most of our patients go through that experience of the want in acting out the fantasy. It becomes an axis for the meaning of the patient's life, as a substitute for the symptom. But that meaning is based upon what arises as an impossible desire from the wanting of the Other, where the analyst stands, instead of upon the *jouissance* that was the concern of the symptom.

As an example, Carl, who two years ago related all his pains and sickness to a needle supposedly forgotten in his head by a doctor, began recently to dream about his father, after his analyst had referred that internal object of the other's *jouissance* to an idiomatic phrase. The needle, *aiguille* in French, had been related to a compass he got from his father, through the French expression, *"perdre la boussole,"* "to go out of one's head," after recalling that as a child he used to be furious when he heard his parents making love late at night, after midnight—the time when the hands on the clock are like the "needle" on a compass indicating North and South. Some sessions later the patient began to speak about something very new that was happening in his life. For the first time in many years he had succeeded in creating new relationships with his father. Every Friday evening they now went bowling—in French, *"jouer aux quilles."* The object appears to move from *aiguille* to *quilles*, and through the externalization of the object as a crystallization of the Other's *jouissance*, to provide a frame and a space of desire for the subject separated from the Other's *jouissance*.

Such a position in relation to desire is quite different than what is at stake in neurosis. The externalization of an internal object as a *sinthome* signifies the shifting in the position of the subject in the structure, as an enacting of what comes for, or at, the place of the fantasy in psychosis, to support the displacement of a part of *jouissance* from the real to the symbolic. In neurosis, the fantasy is linked to a *jouissance* hidden in the subject which must be brought to face the law in the analysand's speech. In psychosis, what comes from the fantasy in the transference is an access to meaning or to new social ties, as a momentary frame for the void left behind by the other's *jouissance*, for the enacting of a space for desire.

At the place where his life was signified in the symptom that remains under the power of the other, insofar as the internal object can be conceived as representing the whole subject, the analyst's desire and withdrawal elicits an object to support the desire for the subject. The analyst carries out that elicitation in the field of the letter—i.e., outside of meaning, outside the domain controlled by the signifiers of the Other's injunctions and demands for *jouissance*. The analyst carries out the entire process under the law of the letter and writing, which are trails of the symbolic in language. In doing so, instead of remaining in the field of interpretation, which occurs in the domain of the Other of the signifier, he substitutes writing in language as the Other of the Law. He no longer deals with meaning or knowledge; he calls for the act, entering the field where the logical equivalents he puts forth by soliciting alternative grammatical sequences in the fantasies of the patient, can carry the disconnected drives into desire.

Under such conditions, the object appears as the conjunction of all possible alternative sequences or logical equivalents of the fantasy as an axis of meaning for the subject. That operation in the so-called fantasy in the transference constructs the object as an equivalent and a surrogate for the lack of the signifier of the Father. The object arrives at the place where the analyst stood for the object *a*, solely by his presence, framing the void opened by the foreclosure of the signifier of the Father, and sustaining language as the structure of the relation of the subject to the object in the place of the Other.

We do not know how many times such changes will be profitable to the psychotic subject, nor do we know when and why the entire constructed substitute ego will be jeopardized by the return of the *jouissance* (the phenomena of psychosis always being related to the structure of psychosis). There is no definitive cure in the psychoanalytic treatment of psychosis. But through the transference the analyst's desire arises as a limit to the working through of the psychosis, maintaining an obstacle to the spontaneous productions of such a work. Through the guidance of the analyst's desire the spontaneous work of the psychosis goes, rather, into the building up of a surrogate for the lack and the failure of the signifier, and into building an object for framing the void where the voices come back to submit the subject to the exigencies of the Other's *jouissance*.

IX. The subject is the social tie

The object comes forth out of the manipulation of the script in the symptoms through the law of language. That object articulates the unattached drive to the law of the symbolic order. The object acts for the failing signifier in the Other. From that start, the subject begins to arrogate his own desire as the ground for a new social tie, instead of granting given social values and beliefs as the basis of his relation to others. Then, the process reaches the very point at stake in the psychoanalytic treatment of psychosis. Indeed, at that point of the process in the transference where the analyst's desire is still directing the process, that desire goes farther than the gain of subjectification of *jouissance* under the object of fantasy in neurosis. The analyst's desire elicits the subject's desire at the place where the myth of a Father is lacking, as a substitute for the failure of knowledge to found the symbolic order, and a support against the fundamental anguish of the absence of the Great Other, who is supposed to be the subject that enunciates the Law.

The analysis thus leads the psychotic subject precisely where he did not want to go: toward assuming a world disturbed and perverted from nature by language, in which there is no guarantee concerning the outcome of such an adulteration of things. But it is also what the society of neurotics cannot take for granted. The result of the process thus confronts the subject who has just come out of the phenomena of psychosis with a dead end, since his new position in the social tie contests the credibility of that tie.

Thenceforth, at the end of the process the psychotic subject finds herself at the starting point, facing the want in the Other, without the support of a still lacking signifier. But she is no longer in the position of looking for a final truth in the foundation of the world, bound by the necessity of sacrificing her life to such a chimera. She has experienced the division that language introduces into mankind as a structural one and not as an evil whose responsible party she has to identify. But she faces a society where the division is still repressed and supplanted by collective myths, ideologies, and beliefs. As a hysteric, she can look for shelter in an endless quarrel with the master, as a master of *jouissance*. A society that hides and enshrouds the tragedy of humans facing the emptiness of the world of the signifier with the defense of believing in the rightness of their choices and values has no available place for a subject coming out of the phenomena of psychosis. But the plurality and uncertainty of ways in this same society is, incidentally, a piece of good luck for such a subject.

At that point, the analyst waits. He longs only for a decision from the subject, who therefore has to go his own way, and with only the support of the surrogate but ephemeral object he has constructed in the transference as a substitute for the lack in the signifier. He knows by now that he will have to construct it again at the next emergence of psychosis, but he now also knows how and why. The process is reaching an end that cannot be inferred from the analyst's desire. Even if the psychotic subject has only the knowledge of that possible and momentary alternative, thenceforth anything can happen to hasten the conclusion for the best or the worst. The analyst's desire is moved out of the process by the emergence from the Other (that Other of the Law) of the object and the subject's evanescent desire at the place where the signifier of the Father was lacking. From the voices to the surrogate object through the writing in the symptom, a frame has been established for the void where the irreducible rock of *jouissance* returns in the structure. The phenomenon of psychosis as an effect of the Other's *jouissance* in the body is modified according to the shifting of the subject in the structure, but the subject does not escape the structure: he is still a psychotic. But now he can deal with the phenomenon, from his position in the structure and according to the object he ejects as the last remnant of the delusion.

Works Cited

Lacan, Jacques. *De la psychose paranoïaque dans ses rapports avec la personalité suivi de Premiers écrits sur la paranoïa.* Texte établi par Jacques-Alain Miller. Paris: Seuil, 1975.

————. *Le Séminaire de Jacques Lacan. Livre* III: *Les psychoses* (1955–1956). Texte établi, par Jacques-Alain Miller. Paris: Seuil, 1981.

————. *Le Séminaire de Jacques Lacan. Livre* XXIII: *Le Sinthome* (1975–1976). Unpublished text.

III

Lacan and the Subject
of Literature

7

Style is the
Man Himself

Judith Miller

Under the title, "Style is the Man Himself," I will propose a reading of the two pages that inaugurate the *Ecrits* with the heading "Opening of this Collection." Jacques Lacan starts with the definition of style by Buffon, "Style is the man himself," and then alters this definition on two occasions. The first time, he adds an extension: "Style is the man to whom one speaks" (9). The second time, at the end of this opening, he states, "The object—the object *a*—responds to the question of style." Lacan makes this object occupy the place of man in the definition of style.

I will proceed in three steps. After an analysis of Buffon's definition, I will try to show that it illustrates the first modification that Lacan imposes on it. From there, I will examine how Lacan's second definition covers Buffon's concern about his own style. In speaking about style, Buffon reveals (without knowing it, or consciously trying to formulate the cause of his desire) the object which holds him as a subject divided between knowledge and truth. Insofar as Buffon questions his own style, we have an encounter between psychoanalysis and literature. This example shows how this encounter does not in any way "apply" psychoanalysis to literature, but rather illustrates one by the other.

Let us then examine the formula of style given by Buffon and its context. It is on the occasion of his selection to the *Académie Française* in 1753, as the replacement for the Archbishop of Sens, that Buffon gives this formula in his acceptance speech. Buffon has to acknowledge the reception of the choice of which he is the object. He justifies this choice by expressing his gratitude to his colleagues. He is overjoyed to have been selected. Already a member of the Academy of Sciences since 1733, he now sees himself recognized, not so much as a great scientist, but rather as an author whose work deserves to be inscribed forever in the memory of mankind. By this selection, he is assigned to become an Immortal, since it is by this attribute that the members of the French Academy are designated. It is by recognizing their immortality in return that Buffon expresses gratitude to the Academicians who have elevated him to the rank of the Immortals. He says it clearly: he only returns to them what they have given him. "Gentlemen," he says, "I can only offer you your own good, that is, a few ideas on style." He was able to find those ideas in reading their works. Addressed back to them, these ideas reach their destination, to be transmitted to future generations.

By opposing true eloquence to mechanical eloquence, where "body speaks to body," Buffon states the components of true eloquence, which far from shaking the senses and passions by the tone, the gesture, and the sonority of words, only touches a small number of people sensitive to and concerned by "things, thoughts, and reasons."

What does style demand? An outline. First to put one's thoughts in order, so as to define one's subject and its scope, to pick out those thoughts that are fertile and those that are sterile, to determine the intervals which separate the main ideas, and to put in accessory ideas in order to indicate the unity of the subject, at the same time as articulating its complexity. This time of meditation should seize all the aspects of the subject, and the relations that constitute it, before the author proceeds to their explanation. Once this period of conception is over, the author will have overcome the real difficulties: expression follows directly from conception. Thus, the outline supports or holds up the style: it gives it orientation, submits it to its principles, and directs the pen in a way that restores to the subject at hand its wholeness and its unity.

In Buffon's eyes, the author should have to think in order to intervene in the moment of writing, so that he may see if the time prior to the conception has been well utilized. Let us note that this insistence regarding the determining function of the implementation of the outline indicates that Buffon is speaking of his own experience more than of the lessons he learns from his readings. It goes without saying, in his remarks, that style cannot measure up to themes other than that of his *Natural History*. Thus Buffon maintains a parallel between style and nature, correlating their processes and their production. Just as nature works on an eternal outline from which she never separates, and prepares in silence the seeds of her productions, so style consists first of patiently developing concepts and organizing ideas that are productive. From there the foundations of the "immortal monuments" on which style is able to build are assured. Monument here should be taken in the strong sense: it is that by which one keeps the memory of what has been.

The main task of style, then, is to reach a *point of view* that allows one to obtain ideas that are productive and gather the main threads of the subject at hand. All else follows from this position, the point of view that "ideas will flow and the style will be natural and easy." The author will then be blocked by nothing, he will have no more hesitation, will not face any embarrassment, and will only experience pleasure. He will be carried away by the heat born from this pleasure. His work will be animated by its flame and its light will reverberate. Through style, the author knows a *jouissance* that Buffon defines in terms proper to describing the relief of a woman when she gives birth, or *jouissance* as such. Buffon will never speak of his way of writing otherwise. When he is in dialogue with Hérault de Séchelles, he will not tell him that he has composed the Epoch of Nature, one of the pieces of his *Natural History* that he is the most satisfied with, by repeating a word one hundred times. He will only say that he has always tried not to load himself with his notes and rough drafts, documents and reports, which he ordered from craftsmen and specialists whom he considers as laborers of Natural History, of which he is an architect.

Buffon damns to obscurity those who do not reach the required *point of view*. Those authors of a short and narrow view who want to shine by their writings are condemned to remain obscure, in both senses of the word. On the one hand, they are unintelligible; on the other, they fall unavoidably into oblivion. Contrary to academicians, they will only have produced ephemeral flickers, "by shaking the words," falling short of reaching the lights of sublime ideas by the genius of meditation. "Nothing is more contrary to the light which gives body to the writing and which expands itself in a uniform way than the sparks produced by force by knocking the words against each other, which only dazzle us to leave us later in the darkness. These are only thoughts that shine by opposition; only one side of the object is presented, with all the other sides being left in the darkness."

The key to style, then, is to arrive at the point of view which allows one to see everything and, maybe, to say everything. It is the title "view" which Buffon will give to the most important chapters of *Natural History* where he presents the fundamental laws of the natural order and of its becoming. Once this place from which style is born is established, Buffon gives some indication of the attention that an author must pay in order to assure his style of complementary qualities: severeness, majesty, nobility, etc. To conclude, "to write well is at the same time to think well, to feel well, and to render well" and to remember that only well-written works will pass into posterity.

In saying, "Style is the man himself," Buffon is "saying" himself, his fantasy of being a great man—a "saying" that is irreducible to the knowledge he communicates. Does he himself not distinguish between knowledge and truth, at the time he produces his formula of style? "The quantity of knowledge, the singularity of facts, the novelty of discoveries are not sure guarantors of immortality. If the works that contain them run only on little objects, if they are written without taste, nobility and genius, they will perish, since knowledge, facts and discoveries are removed easily, are transported and can even be implemented by more skillful hands. These things are outside man; style is the man himself." This style is not altered, nor is it transferred. It does not belong to anybody other than the one who obtains it; it comes from a personal experience, non-transmittable, in which each one finds his unalterable identity. The academicians should be reassured. It is not by the durability of their discoveries in the field of knowledge that they are immortalized, since all discovery can be hit by obsolescence, or at least by anonymity. That they will be perpetuated in future centuries is guaranteed by Buffon—it is by their style. Why? precisely because style is the man himself. To man himself, to his essence, Buffon produced a treatise in his *Natural History* with the heading "Of Man," published in 1749.

The proper nature of mankind is defined by its difference. While all the other animals that crowd nature find their identity in the species they belong to, of which they can only reproduce the traits because of this belonging, each human being is defined by its aptitude to be different from all other human beings. While the order of the actions of all living beings is traced in the entire species and "does not belong at all to the individual," man has the privilege—this is what makes him the king of creation, of being different, of being individual—of not being submitted to the programming of his species and in particular of being able to speak differently from all the others who, like him, speak and think. The essence of man, man himself, is his difference by which he stands out from the common lot. And this difference resides in style. Everybody speaks, but only few accede to style, which assures them immortality. Immortality: that is to say, the *jouissance* that a man who would be creator of himself could know.

Lacan proposes an addition to Buffon's formula by writing, "Style is the man to whom one speaks." The first effect of this extension is to submit style to the common law of language, that to which every speaking being is subjected, according to which the sender depends on the receiver for his inverted message. This seems to go against the sense of Buffon's formula: far from being outside common law, style submits to it. Man is no longer the author of his difference, he is the subject of the law of language; it is in the discourse of the Other with a capital O that he finds that by which he exists. He is situated and designated by his relation to the Other, with a structure divided between knowledge and truth. Being subjected to common law does not mean, however, that style cannot keep the function that Buffon gives it—i.e., to assign someone his differential identity. On the contrary, the identity of the subject can be placed in his style, squeezed the closest to his division.

We still have to agree on this identity. There is no identity of man, as a whole or totality, even if he is a great man. The discovery of the unconscious by Freud has definitely shaken this unitary and totalizing notion of man, master of his thinking and his speech, integrating his different modalities during his development.

But I should be more precise. You will tell me that when Jacques Lacan completes Buffon's formula by writing, "Style is the man to whom one speaks," he does not eliminate the reference to man. Granted. But it is not the word that counts here. It is a notion that is at stake. From the moment that style refers to another, the one who is defined by his style is defined by his relation to the other. The substitution of the word "himself" by "to whom one speaks" indicates that identity is divided between what style represents and the one before whom it is represented. A subject, says Lacan, by the fact that it is inscribed in the order of language, is represented by a signifier for another signifier.

The man to whom one speaks is himself a subject who addresses another, who in turn addresses another, and so on. This other to whom one speaks is the Other, with a capital O, whose non-fulfillment is structural, but whose chain-like character requires of the subject to find a place to house it. This Other to whom one speaks lends itself to be as indefinite and non-countable as the pronoun "one" who is addressed to it. This indefinite character leads to the question formulated by the principle of communication, "our message comes to us from the Other in an inverted form." What is the use of addressing a message to the Other, if all it does is to return it? What good does it do to speak if speaking is only the game of recognition referred to by Buffon in his acceptance speech at the Academy? This game consists only of really recognizing the multiplied image of himself in each of those who have recognized themselves in him. Or again it consists of reflecting back to them an image of themselves in order better to assure himself of his own image: in you I see style, and by you I see better that I am man himself, the elite of the elite.

To this game of mirrors, where each party is reconfirmed in his image of himself, Buffon's final address gives the key, if we read it in light of Jacques Lacan's completed formula which transforms its sense. Among the members of the Academy, if some of them think on account of the others, the image that satisfies their respective ideals—if in this game of reflections they see the profile of their own immortality—their glory, says Buffon, depends only on the presence of the one who is their king, Louis XV, who does not belong to their assembly of fellows, but who makes of the assembly a body, a whole, precisely external to himself.

As Buffon explains clearly, from the place of the king, from his gaze over them, the Academicians receive their glory and the impetus to exercise their most beautiful talents in the best style. All their efforts, all their successes, only find their *raison d'être* in the one and only: the look (gaze) of the king. All the differences which make of each one a "man himself" only express the same thing: the glory of the king and his praise.

Working to maintain the immortality of the name of the king, they reap the glory that makes them immortals. Without the look (gaze) of the king, the Academicians would be simple mortals. They support each other under the look (gaze) which passes through them and which gives them glory at the same time, a glory which he would be lacking if they did not give it to him. We shall come back to the circuit described by Buffon, that of the object of his desire. It forms a loop.

Buffon, by declaring that "Style is the man himself," only illustrates the extension proposed by Jacques Lacan, in a perfectly suitable situation. Buffon receives the message, "We choose you from among mortals," and he responds to them, "You are style and thus immortal." And then he explains why they are immortals: because they are like him. He also receives the message, "One of us is dead; you are called in his place." He answers, "The place of the name of the immortal king, nobody can take." The final address of his discourse means nothing else to the Academicians than their common immortality. Where does the assurance of their immortality come from? From the discourse of Buffon whom they have selected, and who by defining style shows them how they will not disappear after death, and on what their glory depends that will make them survive.

One can make fun of this fantasy of glory; it calls for the impertinence that Lacan signals at the beginning of the Opening of the *Ecrits* in referring to the pamphlet, "Journey to Montbard," which contains interesting details on the character, the person, and the writings of Buffon. It is one of the first interviews with a famous person who has done everything to become famous, and who knows that he has become famous. The pamphlet is not a tribute to the greatness of Buffon's genius. Rather it was composed by a young lawyer of 25, Hérault de Séchelles, as a portrait of Buffon the man with all his faults, in particular his vanity, but also of the constancy, the firmness, and the perseverance that this vanity demanded in order to maintain it.

From the beginning, Hérault de Séchelles establishes a relation of exaggerated reverence. He responds to Buffon, "Whatever my avidity, my Count"—he knows that Buffon likes to be addressed that way—"I will respect your occupations"—Buffon is then 78 years old—"that is to say, a large part of your day. I know that all covered with glory"—this glory of which Buffon spoke to the Academicians in 1753—"you still work, that the genius of nature ascends with sunrise to the top of the tower of Montbard, and often descends only in the evening. It is only at this moment that I dare solicit the honor of consulting with you. I will look at this epoch as the most glorious of my life."

He borrows this term "epoch" from the author of *Natural History*, who uses it to refer to the great overviews of Natural History which the volume provides. Buffon desired a literal overview while working: he desired that the tower in which he had his office provide him with the panoramic view that his enterprise of interpreting nature required. It would assure him a panoramic view from which the order and the dynamic of creation could be understood. It provided him with "the point of view," almost in its touristic sense. From there, he could give a correct idea of the synchronic and diachronic layout of nature. From there, he could master the whole, see all the sides without any of them escaping him. This wide view (gaze) is of course no different from that of the king. Buffon appropriates it: if he cannot create anything in the proper sense of the word, at least he can produce the adequate image of Creation.

This all crystallizes the rock on which Buffon stumbled throughout his long work, his life, and his experience of writing. Language is constituted in such a way as to be inadequate to account for the reality of nature. While nature is deployed in at least three dimensions, its forces working along multidimensional axes, language is linear and the chains that it weaves are thus insufficient for grasping the texture of the world, its depth and its volume. Thus Buffon's perpetual concern was to overcome the structural inadequateness of language for rendering the density and multidimensionality of nature. To restore nature's flesh is the impossibility that Buffon did not cease to confront, despite the reductive character of the bi-dimensional concatenation in which language is quartered.

Hérault de Séchelles observes only that "it is of Natural History and style that Buffon likes to speak the most." He reports a remark of

Buffon's about style which illuminates the statement on style in Buffon's acceptance speech:

> There are two things which make up style, invention and expression. Invention depends on patience; you have to see, and watch your subject for a long time, so it is happening and developing little by little. You feel as though a little electric shock has hit your head, and at the same time has grabbed your heart. This is the moment of genius. It is only then that one experiences pleasure in work, pleasure so great, that I spent 12 hours, 14 hours studying. It was completely pleasurable; I really gave myself more to it than to going after glory. Glory comes afterwards if it can, and it almost always comes. . . . When you have to treat a subject, do not open any book: draw everything from your head; consult writers only when you feel that you cannot produce anything anymore yourself. This is how I have always done. One really enjoys like this. When one reads the authors, one finds oneself at their level, or above them, and one judges them. . . .

Buffon was a living expression of his speech on style. Not only did the kings of France—Louis XV, then Louis XVI—give him glory and benefit from the shining of his work, but many other kings (he kept their letters) recognized their debt to him, and admired him without limit. What Buffon always desired was this glory—it comes by itself, he said, to whoever has been able to accede to style. Buffon did not say any more on that which maintained him and concerned him during his entire life, and which never left him. (He instilled it in his son, who, Hérault de Séchelles says, erected a column in the courtyard of his chateau with the inscription: "To the high tower, the humble column, to his Father, Buffon Junior, 1785.") Nevertheless, it was to defining the object of his desire that Buffon devoted his work—this object that comes in addition, but that only the Other can give him, at the same time as expecting it from him: glory. Buffon's conviction was that it is only obtained by style. Knowing how to say was the impossible path chosen by Buffon. He defined a real constituent of the proper space of writing and language where his faith and their faith will be played out. This real bases the possibility of discourse on an initial lack, and devotes it to the impossible task of dealing with this lack, short of style. Style is the form that discourse should take, if it can, in order to take up its paradoxical function: to erase what makes it possible.

This necessary and impossible task is defined as man himself. It is a challenge, the challenge of writing that which does not stop not being written. By the path of style, man is thus made the cause of himself. How not to drop this object by virtue of which man is structurally incomplete and from which he is suspended as desiring? Style revealed itself to Buffon as the object of his desire, and he declared this in his acceptance speech at the Academy: "Style is the man himself." The king, in this speech, is as much the consecrated as the inspirer. To his glory, this speech consecrates that of its subject, who, swept by the royal gaze, is also supported by it. In this speech, Buffon by his own admission, seems only to be giving what he receives: Buffon wants to fill a hole, wants to occupy the place left empty by the death of the Archibishop of Sens. How to fill this hole? For the king himself who marks out the Academy as a whole, the whole of this body, which is formed from an element that decompletes it, fails.

My aim is not to take up the function of a plug, but to surround this place, and to keep open the question that it asks. I hope to have indicated that on this point—that of the object *a* in relation to the question of style—Jacques Lacan has pointed out a possible encounter between style and psychoanalysis.

Works Cited

Buffon, George-Louis Leclerc, comte de. *Discours sur le style* (1753). Paris: Hachette, 1843.

————. *Histoire naturelle.* Paris: L'Imprimerie royale, 1750–1804.

Lacan, Jacques, *Ecrits.* Paris: Seuil, 1966.

Séchelles, Hérault de. *Voyage à Montbard.* Paris: Solvet, 1785.

8

Fictions

Stuart Schneiderman

In formulating a commentary on Poe's account of the purloined letter, Lacan was led to invent a fiction. His intention was to allow the truth to speak to you, to address you from a written text through veils of critical inquiry. If Lacan succeeded in allowing something to speak to you through the gaps in a written text, the subsequent issue must be how and whether it was heard and by whom?

Lacan's fiction concerns the point at which Dupin prepares to purloin the letter from the Minister D—. The act that finally accomplishes this will lead eventually to the removal of the letter from its deviant circulation, return it to the Queen, and thus to its true destination, obliteration. This final return will put an end to the seemingly endless cycle of repeated purloinings. Only the narration will remain to torment the faithful.

Lacan's fiction focuses on the crucial moment of the story when Dupin sees and identifies the purloined letter; it describes a scene that is other than the actual scene. The fiction makes sense of Dupin's identification of the letter and also of his act. His act appears to be an *acte manqué*, a parapraxis, but it is thoroughly intentional. The action takes place in the offices of the famous Minister D—, and Dupin's act is an act of intelligence. It is Dupin's act, not that of his unconscious, and it is not his last act.

Here is the story. Having been apprised of the theft of a letter from the royal apartments by the Minister D—, and having heard the Prefect of Police explain in detail his futile efforts to find said missive, C. Auguste Dupin decides to pay a visit to the Minister. His eyes covered by green sunglasses, Dupin enters the office of the Minister. His concealed look scans the room until it lights upon the purloined letter. He continues his conversation, and, upon leaving, forgets his snuff box, thereby having a reason to return to abscond with the letter.

He has devised a strategy, roughly as the Minister had in purloining the letter in the first place. His act is part of his own strategy.

Lacan's version of the story introduces what we will call a fictitious entity. Again Dupin enters the room wearing green sunglasses. But now spread out before him is an immense female body, waiting to be undressed. Lacan avers that Dupin did not need to listen at Dr. Freud's door to know where to look for the object this body is made to conceal. It is there, between the legs of the fireplace, within reach, waiting to be ravished. But Dupin restrains himself, recognizing that if the Minister knows that the letter has been ravished and that the ravisher is under his control, Dupin will not leave the house alive. Thus Dupin prepares an act that fictionally will be the ravishing of a female body, one where the subject of that body will not know immediately that the body has been ravished or by whom.

Dupin knew that he could not take possession of this signifier, of an inscribed signifier, a localized signifier (not all signifiers are inscribed), without leaving in its place a fac-simile, a substitute, an object, a worthless piece of paper whose destiny will be to be rolled up into a ball and tossed out with the trash.

As you know, Dupin did not believe that his fac-simile was worthless, but Lacan emphasized the unlikelihood of this substitute producing the effect Dupin expected. There, of course, Dupin did commit a lapse of judgment; due, as Lacan said, to the fact that those who take possession of the letter are possessed by it. Dupin repeated the scene in which the Minister purloined the letter in the first place, because when the Minister substituted a worthless piece of paper for the precious letter, there was, Lacan said, a remainder whose importance no analyst will fail to recognize.

So we have two letters of which only one is a signifier and which are certainly not doubles. The second letter, the fac-simile, is the object *a* and its connection with the letter as barred signifier constitutes the structure of a phantasy. Lacan's fiction was generated out of the phantasy he read in the text.

Such is, with variations, Lacan's telling of the story of Dupin's theft of the purloined letter. The female body in question is properly a fiction and it is because Dupin knows this and disregards the real space that he engages his desire and succeeds in taking the letter. His desire leads him to modify the real. The truth found in the fiction concerns desire and Lacan consistently made the point that to turn away from this truth was not just a function of an excessive fascination with facts, to say nothing of texts, but was also a symptom of an overestimation of the importance and usefulness of working with the ego. This is not to say that facts are not significant or relevant, nor that they do not have a place. Desire is not the facts, but to translate your desire into reality, you had best know the facts. As Wittgenstein said, it is one thing to know whether the window is open or shut, quite another to know whether you want it open or shut.

Lacan saw Dupin as having revealed the naked truth of a fictitious entity. The sight of the nakedness of truth has led Jacques Derrida to essay to cover it up, all of it, to cover its entire surface. Whether he wrote out of compassion or prudishness, I will not venture to guess. "That the inscription [or scription] in its entirety—the fiction named 'The Purloined Letter'—is covered, over its entire surface, by a narration by a narrator who says 'I' does not let us confuse the fiction with the narration" (Muller and Richardson, 180).

Basing his approach on the phenomenon of the script, of the activity of writing, Derrida inadvertently and with passion engages himself in a massive cover-up. Many, if not most, of his errors have been revealed by Barbara Johnson in her excellent article "The Frame of Reference: Poe, Lacan, Derrida" (See Muller and Richardson). However accomplished his writing, Derrida's criticism of Lacan has a familiar ring. To refute Lacan Derrida falls back on the points Lacan has always been criticized for: the failure to give sufficient weight to the imaginary, to the ego, to narcissism, to the horrors of corporeal fragmentation. In a sense one might rightly say that Lacan could have given more weight to these points, though one should in the interest of fairness note that Lacan did devote considerable theoretical effort to them. The point is that Lacan asserted the primacy of the symbolic over the imaginary, and that Derrida sees the imaginary as swallowing the symbolic.

And so we find Derrida accusing Lacan of everything his psychoanalytic adversaries have criticized him for: the overvaluation of the Oedipus complex, the overestimation of the phallus, overintellectualizing, being too interested in philosophy, failing to take into account the pre-oedipal fears of corporal fragmentation, failing to give place and importance to the ego; there is even a sense that Lacan is being accused of giving insufficient place to affects.

To empower the narrating ego, the psychic censor leads first to the glorification of the imaginary problematic of narcissism, aggressiveness, and the fragmented body (a problematic analyzed first by Lacan, incidentally), but it leads more ominously to the collapse of an imaginary identification into the real. Instead of having to deal with the ego and its counterpart you are faced with the phenomenon of the double, a phenomenon which is properly delusional.

To say that the narration, commanded by the narrator's I, covers the fiction entirely supports a tendency to avoid seeing, but more especially to avoid hearing the truth when it speaks. As though the unconscious, i.e. the letter, could be entirely censored by the ego, irrevocably blocked, so that its message may perhaps not reach its destination, which is of course to be spoken. To be brief, Derrida's argument rationalizes disinterest in the unconscious, by asserting that if you never stop writing or if the writing never stops, you will not have to hear its message. At the same time this argument pretends to express great interest in the unconscious, in the play of writings, but the unconscious thus in play is collective, not personal.

What is Derrida's scriptural strategy and to what is he opposed? This is not a very difficult question. Certainly, "Le Facteur de la Vérité" is an overwritten and overwrought text that reads like an indictment. It constantly repeats the same charges, piling up evidence of tendencies that appear to be worthy of condemnation. The tone is moral, and the text is animated throughout by the mostly seemingly indubitably correct moral passion. Ultimately, that is the secret appeal of deconstruction.

Derrida's condemnation of Lacan's discourse is based on the fact that Lacan emphasized the division of the sexes. Nothing else. The opening attack on Lacan's use of the concept of truth in its connection with femininity will eventually yield to another attack on the importance Lacan accorded to the phallus and speech, especially as these are linked to the structure of masculinity. As I have pointed out in my book *An Angel Passes*, there is nothing new or radically subversive in such a strategy.

Was Derrida then denouncing Lacan's theory of sexual difference, or Freud's, or was he denouncing sexual difference as originally defined by pagan writers like Plato and Aristotle? Presumably, the answer is the latter. I have said that in his zeal Derrida is led to make many mistakes in reading Lacan. One basic misreading should however be underscored; I am not certain that it has been remarked before.

Derrida insists that Lacan's reading is about the castration of the mother, a topic not unworthy of a psychoanalyst. He sees Lacan as saying that the proper place of the letter is between the mother's legs (*La Carte Postale*, 489). Thus he declares that Lacan is saying the same thing that Marie Bonaparte had already argued, namely that the destination of the letter is the place of the Queen (480). However, Lacan said clearly that the destination of the letter is the place previously occupied by the Law, thus the King. According to Lacan this place comports blindness, and the point is that blindness not only prevents one from reading, it also assures that the letter will be spoken, that what is to be spoken will eventually be spoken.

What did Lacan mean? Quite simply that the final destination of the purloined letter, as of all letters, is to be destroyed, thus that the physical presence of the letter will necessarily yield to speech. This point is well understood by Derrida and he understands it clearly as a significant threat to his enterprise. Thus the importance Lacan placed on the remainder left by the Minister in the royal apartments, left to be rolled up in a ball and thrown away. Similarly for the fate of the fac-simile Dupin left in the Minister's apartment. It is only when the letter embarks on its detour through the agency of the Minister and Dupin that its place is between the legs of "an immense female body."

Let us, in any case, begin to evaluate the argument for the central importance of the narrating ego. In everyday practice if you have a case where you have a patient who, for the sake of the argument, has an ego that covers entirely all fictions, then the thing to do is to disregard the communication, or in other words, to refuse to respond to the demand to take the productions of that ego as a road to the unconscious. We have nothing against telling a story; after all, Dupin does just that after he has exchanged the letter for a considerable financial payment. But he tells of an act in which he was engaged while the narrator tells a story of an act in which he was not engaged. In the first case the narrating is part of an engagement of desire while in the second the narrating represents a way to continue to avoid acting upon any desire.

If you are listening to what the ego would like you to believe, you will miss the message, a message which in these cases is spoken only in a lapse, or better, unintentionally. If the message is not heard, it has effectively not been spoken, and if it is not spoken, what happens to it is that it becomes inscribed and not on paper. At that point the analyst suffers it, just as the patient's symptom, represented by his own suffering, is the inscription of an unaccomplished speech act. Once the letter is inscribed as a symptom, efforts to write oneself out of it will simply double the inscription and confuse the issue.

Why does the narrator do such a thing? To avoid anxiety, you might say, and this failure is repeated in the writer who takes his writing to be a repetition of what the narrator has done. There is anxiety that something might be spoken, then it might be addressed to the subject and that the subject might have to do something about it. To ward off this anxiety, to make sure that nothing is spoken, all you have to do is to keep writing.

One of Derrida's accusations against Lacan is that he fails to consider the importance of anxiety over bodily fragmentation. In effect, there is some truth to this since Lacan's Freudian view sees the structure of anxiety in the context of castration. To understand this we refer to a point Lacan made in a discussion of Little Hans. In his (unpublished) seminar on anxiety Lacan stated that the boy's anxiety was not produced by castration threats. Rather, he suggested, it was when the boy saw his own genitals in his mother's hands, thus, in a place he knew to be lacking a phallic attribute of its own, that he experienced anxiety.

He does not experience anxiety because it looks like his mother has a phallus, but rather because the boy knows that she does not have one, thus that the existence of something that looks like male genitals on her body can only be uncanny—especially when he recognizes them as his own. Anxiety, Lacan said, is not without an object. This object, cause of anxiety in this case, is not a new phallus for mother, but rather something that designates a lack.

The structure in question here involves on the one side of the object *a* in his mother's hands, the cause of the subject's desire, and on the other, the cut of the subject's body that has separated him from a most precious object. In my view this cut is produced by the proper name and the function of naming thus will become crucial.

To say that the cut corresponds to the purloined letter is to say that it is the barred signifier, the signifier that undergoes a detour by being inscribed in the unconscious.

This does not tell us the meaning of the letter or the meaning in the letter. Of course Lacan was not and never claimed to be a hermeneut. Names do not have meanings and they do not say anything about the person named. Their function has everything to do with the structure of the signifier. It is only in the absence of a functioning proper name that the problematic of hermeneutics opens up. Where the proper name does not function to hook language into speaking subjects, the search after the meaning of words becomes of critical importance.

Proper names identify the subject and place him within a symbolic structure. The impulse to deconstruct the "proper," often indulged by Derrida, would normally have a bearing on the function of proper names. If we are no longer to use proper names to identify people, what is left but descriptions of personality traits and activities. And however much these descriptions appear to identify a person uniquely, there is no way of knowing whether the person so identified is the person or his double. Thus the deconstruction of the proper, thus of proper naming, creates the problematic of the double.

To return to Dupin and the narrator, we ask what differentiates them, and even why Lacan privileges the place of Dupin? Here the pertinent fact is that Dupin is the only character in the story with a proper name. By contrast the narrator is unnamed, thus anonymous. This anonymity seems to provide the advantage of making him identical to whatever is written about him in the text, but it also obliges us to identify him only in relation to his narrating activity, through a nominalized verb.

It is almost as though Lacan is advising that one ought not listen to someone who presents himself as nameless. Either you speak in your name or you are not speaking. Other characters are designated by letters, as though their names had been censored, or by titles or even epithets. C. Auguste Dupin is the only character whose name has not been censored, and clearly the story is his story. He is the subject. He is the only character who truly speaks as an I. While the narrator's I is a substitute for a proper name, Dupin's is the only I that is in apposition to a proper name. Within the context of the story the purloined letter will become the referent of the proper name of Dupin. The object he lost in receiving this cut is the fac-simile he leaves in the Minister's apartment. And there is no doubt that Dupin leaves something of himself in the place left vacant by his purloining of the purloined letter.

So, Dupin speaks in his own name and acts in his own name. He transports himself into a space of desire and his successful act is in accord with a desire that he assumes as his own—at a price to his person. He is the one who confronts the fiction of the immense female body, just as the Minister had confronted it before him. Such a confrontation is in no way a part of the activity of the narrator, as Derrida correctly states, because the narrator is attempting to cover over the fiction, to cover up the action, and to lead the reader astray. You may feel compassion for the narrator; and you may wish to assert that his acting to retrieve the purloined letter was never in question. He was never called upon to act. This is true enough, but the narrator makes no suggestions, has no ideas about what to do. He is content enough to allow his friend to act. He never sees himself as acting, but rather he sees himself as serving his friend.

Dupin's act is effective and its effect is not diminished fundamentally by the vengeful message he leaves behind. But note that when Dupin becomes impassioned and leaves a vengeful message in the fac-simile he does not sign his name. He expects that he will be identified by his distinctive handwriting—well known to the Minister. This does not prevent Dupin from narrating the events that transpired in the Minister's apartment, if only to demonstrate that he, as we, have nothing against narrators or narrating in general. This is in stark contrast to the position of the narrator, to say nothing of the writer.

The narrator does not act, he does not tell his story, and one might even say that it matters little to the narrator that Dupin succeed or fail; a good narrator can narrate either with equal skill. It is interesting to note a literary parallel here. The problematic of making someone else's story your own when you have failed to perform a prescribed act is precisely what happens in *Hamlet.*

If Derrida's text "illustrates" anything, it shows the false sense of superiority gained by those who fail to act, for whom acting in accord with their desire is never in question. The ability to find a flaw in the acts of others gives a conviction of the moral virtue of their own position—that of compassionate and ultimately innocent bystanders.

The narrator is a fictional device, a pretense, an invention of the author. It places a buffer between Dupin and the reader. Dupin does not address the reader, does not write his story for public consumption, and if we know the story it is because the narrator and writer have taken it from him to present it to us. This appears to many readers to be parallel to the other acts of purloining recounted in the story. It is not. It represents a gaining of ego mastery, understanding, awareness, and insight into acts that one is not capable of performing.

The position of the narrator seems to provide for the reader an entry into the story, but this entry is a ruse. It is not because the reader identifies with the narrator, or takes the narrator to be his double, that he is interested in or by the story. To the extent that he identifies with the narrator he avoids being interested in the story, he avoids seeing his desire in a fiction.

The narrator's I does not designate him, does not identify him, but is an indexical which in fact could be used by anyone engaged in the activity of telling the story or writing the text. An indexical does not designate a subject, but rather an activity, speaking or writing, or else, if it is something like "here" and "now," it establishes a place or a scene.

Not only will the reader be identified, but he will have to have an interest in what happens in the story. The reader's interest in the fiction derives first from the fact that something of his, an object, is to be found therein. Roughly as Little Hans might have seen something of his in his mother's hand. As Lacan elaborated in his discussion of art in *The Four Fundamental Concepts of Psychoanalysis* the viewer of a work of art finds his own look dissimulated in the painting. It is only through this structure that the work of art can be said to regard the viewer or audience.

But ought we not say that Dupin himself is a fiction, an invention of the author? There are many theories of fiction which begin with just such a premise. My response is that if the proper name is, as

Kripke said, a rigid designator, then it designates rigidly even where the reader does not know whether a person has ever received that designation. My hypothesis is that a fictional proper name seeks a person to designate, and that the reader, while he is reading the story, allows himself to be identified by that name. You read the story as if you were Dupin, as if the story were about you, not as if you were the narrator.

To pay attention to the nameless narrator is to eliminate the function of proper naming as designating the same referent rigidly in all possible worlds, even in fictional worlds. It is also to place oneself on the side of the almighty Verb, loved especially for its capacity to avoid reference. This is done with the greatest clarity in the privilege accorded to an activity like writing, or better the scene of the writing.

The privilege of the scene of the writing annuls the subject, referent of the proper name, and throws things entirely on to the side of the verb and its predicates. In the absence of a reference the scene of the writing harkens to another scene of writing and yet another; each text is joined to another text in a multiplication of meanings or even a multiplication of unmeaning, each of which is superceded as soon as it is established. The process, as you can experience while reading texts produced according to such principles, continues ad nauseam.

So the Writer writes that it is all an affair of writing, of writing about writing about writing, leading to some ultimate fall into the abyss of non-referentiality. What you have here is a contemporary translation of a form of mystical ecstasy, of an enjoyment that responds to the demand of a superego who prescribes that the command *"Jouis"* or "Enjoy" is best satisfied by writing. Compulsively writing or compulsively seeing everything as a function of writing responds to that Law. And it is that Law that is satisfied by this approach.

Let us elaborate what we have said about proper names. As far as the name Dupin is concerned, it was the real name of a real detective, though the real detective had a different first name. And it happens often enough that a fiction will concern a real person, a point noted by Aristotle in relation to tragedies and repeated recently by Thomas Pavel in *Fictional Worlds*. A play about Julius Caesar may well be a fiction but the Julius Caesar in the play is not a fictional Caesar, a counterpart of the real Caesar. Whether or not the author is telling the truth about Caesar, the play is still about the historical Caesar. But the referent, being the same, may certainly, like the purloined letter, be moved to different places, to be detained by different people. Thereby the reader can identify or be identified by the name of an historical character by appropriating the mark or cut that is the referent of that name.

The fiction is in the telling or in the saying, even the predication, and this is not the same as the naming. While it appears that a character in a fiction is simply the cluster of characteristics and actions that are said to be his in the fiction, I would argue that these characteristics and actions are no more determinate of a reference than they are for a real person. It is just that in a fiction you are allowed to believe that they are.

This does not resolve the difficulty of proper naming of fictional characters; rather it defines it. It leads quite naturally to fictional characters with proper names who are not real. In other words, what about Sherlock Holmes? And here I think that the same applies. If a fictional character has a proper name, then that name designates rigidly, except that you do not know whom it designates. Here the act of naming is not public, but is private, known perhaps only to the author. My supposition is that the character of Sherlock Holmes was based on a model, someone with another name, who was given the name Sherlock Holmes for the purposes of fiction. One of those purposes is that since the reader is not supposed to know who the model is, the author is not obliged to accord what he says about his character with what is known about the model. If the reader is not called upon to know whether the statements made are true or false in relation to a person, he is more likely to be drawn into the story. The reader's ignorance of the identity of the model functions in this case to open the path for the reader to allow himself to be identified by the name of Sherlock Holmes. This would sueprsede any identification by resemblance.

So long as you do not know who the person in question is, then your usual tendency to judge the truth of the statements about a person in relation to your knowledge of the real person is subverted. You cannot when reading a fiction map the fictional predicates onto a real person, even when the character's name is that of a real person. The person designated or identified by the name is not the cluster of recognizable or verifiable characteristics we see in the person. The name designates no matter what you say about the person.

How then do we determine the truth value of statements made about someone about whom you effectively know nothing, about whom there is no history? How do you determine truth value when the saying or the telling is radically non-referential, but where the naming is? Obviously we are not talking about something being true to the facts, because there are no facts, nor are we talking about the theoretical situation described by David Lewis where the events of a fiction are facts for the characters in the fiction. How, in other words, do you know what your desire is? Assuming that desire does not correspond to the facts and that it is not something that you feel in your gut, how do you know what it is? And even if you arrive at grasping a desire, how do you know that it is yours and not that of someone else? Or else, how do you verify a statement of that desire? What is the truth value of a fiction?

A relevant question here is why should you take yourself to be designated by the name of Sherlock Holmes and not that of Dr. Watson or of Prof. Moriarty? It may well be that your own personality corresponds more closely to that of Watson or of Moriarty. As someone who has no talent for detection and strong impulses to write you may find yourself more in sympathy with the position of Watson. You may even attempt to rationalize that choice by writing a study of the Sherlock Holmes stories demonstrating that Watson is really the central character, the hero of the affair. If you tend toward the character of Moriarty, of course, you would be less likely to be sitting at home at your desk writing down your exploits.

Intuitively we would like to say that the reason lies in the fact that Sherlock Holmes is more intriguing, more interesting, more sympathetic, more engaging; he is the agent, the one who acts in the world after engaging in a series of more or less complex mental acts. Sherlock Holmes is the hero of the fiction, the one who is most fully engaged in the world of the fiction. He is always the subject. All of this to say that it is Holmes's desire that is in play in the fictional reality described by the stories. Or better, that the desire manifest in the stories is one that the character named Sherlock Holmes takes to be his own. To refuse to be identified by that name reveals a failure on the part of the reader.

The author's act is a renaming, a repetition of the first act of naming, and this renaming is essential to the formation of an unconscious. The new name, which I have called an improper name, is considered to be meaningful in a way that the proper name is not, to define a being rather than a lack of being, to be adequate to descriptions of the person, to be in a direct relation with whatever can be said about the child. As philosophers like to say about fictional characters, they are whatever their authors say that they are. Finally, of course, this is not the case; the new name, as a signifying structure, is no more meaningful than the proper name. It is just that the reader is allowed to believe that it is, thus the appeal of fictional characters. The reader is allowed to believe that within this new world of fiction, not only will he be renamed, thus, be permitted to break out of the symbolic constraints imposed by his proper name, but that this new name, received by the grace of the author of the fiction, will absolve him of the obligation to act and to speak in his own name. This is the lure of the literariness of some fictions; it provides a disinterested aesthetic enjoyment. The question is whether this is all that it provides.

We will return here to Lacan's fiction of Dupin's encounter with the immense female body waiting to be undressed. In fact, what Dupin encounters upon entering the room is the Minister in a room. To say that he encounters a female body is counterfactual. So Dupin surveys the room as if it were a female body, and it is only by shifting himself into this "as if" perspective that he can identify the placement of the letter.

The "as if" construction translates well into a counterfactual conditional: If this were a female body, the letter would be in such and such a place. And in fact the letter is in precisely that place, which does not mean that the room is a female body. So you have a reality that can be exactly measured and on another level you have another world which is a fictional body.

But the truth in the fiction is not to be confused with the facts, even with what the characters take to be the facts. And I would add the following conjecture, which I derive more or less from the theorization of Thomas Pavel in *Fictional Worlds*.

The idea of undressing and ravishing a female body, while it may certainly be part of a fiction, has, when compared to the events of the story, a quality that is closer to myth. Pavel argues in his book that fictions are the residues of myths that have failed, that have ceased to function socially, to be part of a discourse as a social link. Or you might say that a myth is a particular kind of fiction that has a social function. As Pavel states: "When a mythological system gradually loses its grip on a society, the ancient gods and heroes start to be perceived as fictional characters" (41).

Pavel asserts that the function of myth is to provide the truth of whatever happens in everyday situations. If a person living in a culture where myths are functional has a certain experience and if he compares it to the story of Diana and Acteon, that story serves as providing the truth of the experience. The myth is the truth of the desire in play, and if desire should be taken literally, it does not admit of interpretation.

Fictional entities exist at a remove from real ones, they are in relation with real ones, and perhaps this is true of characters in fiction. Perhaps the truth of the fiction or even the coherence of the fiction will only function if the fiction is at a certain remove from the real entity. The question is what is the kind of relation in play here? We could say simply enough that there is a resemblance between character and model, that something like a form has migrated from the one to the other. This is simple, it suggests mirroring, but it is not consistent with what we have been saying up to now.

My assertion is that a fictional character is always based on a model, a real person, who has been renamed. Needless to say, whatever story is told about the character does not necessarily have to be accurate about the model. If the reader does not know who the model is, the question will often not even arise. This leads to the question of whether anything of the model makes its way into the fiction, not as an identifying characteristic, but as a remainder of the process of renaming.

A more radical argument is that an object is cut off from the model to find its way into the fiction, roughly as Little Hans sees his severed genitals in his mother's hands. Another example Lacan offered was a fiction of his invention in which the eyes of Oedipus, torn from their sockets are now lying on the ground looking back at Oedipus. Or else, in Holbein's *The Ambassadors* the death's head in the foreground has a look that is the place from which the painting is looking back at the spectator while the spectator does not see the look. We should mention that the object in question here has other than uncanny manifestations. Little Hans might be horrified to see his genitals in his mother's hands, but later on, after his psychoanalysis, he might find a pair of diamond earrings hanging from a woman's ears to be extremely attractive.

Of course, if we are talking about a literary fiction, it is not sufficient that something from the model is in the fiction; for if the fiction is to interest an audience, then the object must function as a severed part of the body of each spectator. This is hardly a simple task. Certainly, it would preclude making a mirror identification of spectator and character the rationale for the spectator's interest in the fiction.

You may consider this to be an impossible object, one that is not within the realm of the possibilities of possible worlds, one that even is in contradiction with the rest of the world, whether it is the look in the death's head in the Holbein or the figurines, the *agalmata*, that Alcibiades glimpses one day in Socrates. On the one hand this object comes from the model, and on the other hand it is to the spectator something of his own that he now sees or hears in the work of art.

How do you find out what your desire is? Freud responded to this question by saying that a dream always contains a realization of one's desire. The problem is that in most cases the desire is inscribed in code; it is available only after it has been deciphered. The deciphering is an intellectual act; whatever desire is encoded in a dream is necessarily one that the dreamer has avoided recognizing. But if the desire is grasped intellectually only at the cost of suspending sentiment, how does one know that the deciphering has been performed correctly?

And if, for example, you should decipher a desire, how do you know that the desire in play is yours and not that of a parent or friend? How do you know that the desire and its truth are yours? And how does the speech act which articulates the desire function in relation to the desire and in relation to the ethical obligation to act upon the desire? Is desire something that cannot be grasped outside of spoken dialogue?

Such are the questions at issue here. To attempt to offer responses to all of them in a short paper would be to diminish their seriousness. My position is that the scene of desire cannot be grasped outside of a spoken dialogue and that the judgment of the correct performance of the intellectual act of deciphering will lie in the response of the person to whom it is spoken. Thus a written "proof" of the correctness of the reasoning will never suffice to establish the desire as the one deciphered in the dream. Not only must it be spoken by the speaking subject in his own name but it must also be addressed to the listener in his own name. Finally, I propose that the subject knows that it is his because there is within that scene a lost part of his body.

Works Cited

Averroes. *Averroes' Middle Commentaries on Aristotle's Categories and De Interpretatione.* Princeton: Princeton University Press, 1983.

Bentham, Jeremy. *The Works of Jeremy Bentham.* Vol. 8. New York: Russell and Russell, 1962.

Derrida, Jacques. *La Carte Postale.* Paris: Flammarion, 1980. See also *The Post Card.* Trans. Alan Bass: Chicago: University of Chicago Press, 1987.

Knuuttila, Simo and Jaakko Hintikka, Eds. *The Logic of Being.* Dordrecht, Holland: Academic Publishers, 1968.

Kripke, Saul. *Naming and Necessity.* Cambridge, Mass: Harvard University Press, 1980.

Lacan, Jacques. *Ecrits.* Paris: Seuil, 1986.

Lacan, Jacques. *Le Séminaire, Livre 2: Le moi dans la théorie de Freud et dans la technique de la psychanalyse.* Texte établi par Jacques-Alain Miller. Paris: Seuil, 1978. [See especially the chapters on "The Purloined Letter."] See also *The Seminar of Jacques Lacan, Book* II: *The Ego in Freud's Theory and in the Technique of Psychoanalysis* (1954–1955). Ed. Jacques-Alain Miller. Trans. Sylvana Tomaselli. Notes by John Forrester. New York: W.W. Norton, 1988.

Lewis, David. "Truth in fiction," *Philosophical Papers.* Vol. 1 New York: Oxford University Press, 1983.

Loux, Michael, "*Significatio* and *Suppositio*: Reflections on Ockham's Semantics." *The New Scholasticism*, 51. (Autumn 1979), 407–427.

Muller, John and William Richardson, Eds. *The Purloined Poe: Lacan, Derrida, and Psychoanalytic Reading.* Baltimore: The Johns Hopkins University Press, 1988.

Ogden, C.K. *Bentham's Theory of Fictions*. London: AMS Press, 1932.

Pavel, Thomas. *Fictional Worlds*. Cambridge, Mass: Harvard University Press, 1986.

Schneiderman, Stuart. *An Angel passes: How the Sexes Became Undivided*. New York University Press, 1988.

Walton, Kendall. "Fearing Fictions." *The Journal of Philosophy*, 75 (January, 1978), 5–27.

Wittgenstein, Ludwig. *Philosophical Investigations*. Trans. G.E.M. Anscombe. New York: Macmillan, 1958.

9

Where is Thy Sting?
Some Reflections on the Wolf-Man
Lila J. Kalinich

I can think of few fates worse than having one's life and psychology reviewed and re-interpreted by countless generations of psychoanalysts. To me, this is a vision of Hell that rivals both Dante and Steven Spielberg, a prison of mindless pretensions encasing a life. Yet such was the destiny of the Wolf-Man, Freud's famous case. Since the inception of his analysis in 1910, his pimples, bowels, sexual preferences, and dreams haves preoccupied scores of Freudian friends and foes. It was the price that late Sergei Pankiev, the Wolf-Man, had to pay for his place in psychoanalytic history. And today I will number among his jailers.

The literature on the Wolf-Man is abundant. In addition to Freud's "From the History of an Infantile Neurosis" which appears in Volume XVII of the Standard Edition, he finds his way into the Freudian *œuvre* in "The Uncanny" (1919), "Fetishism" (1927), *New Introductory Lectures to Psychoanalysis* (1932), "Analysis Terminable and Interminable" (1937), and "The Splitting of the Ego in the Process of Defense" (1938). Patrick Mahony, in his 1981 book *Cries of the Wolf Man*, chronicles the efforts of subsequent analysts, among them Kurt Eissler, to grapple with his case and to provide additional assistance and treatment. Most notable of these efforts was that of the analyst Muriel Gardiner. She had been a medical student in Vienna at the Anschluss, herself in analysis with Ruth Mack Brunswick, the woman to whom the ailing Freud referred Pankiev in 1926. Over a period of thirty years, Gardiner assisted him, befriended him, corresponded with him, and, finally, encouraged him to write his own *Memoirs*, a task which fortunately he undertook during the late sixties. Pankiev therefore provided a piece, unique in psychoanalytic history: a portrayal of Freud's patient's view of his life in his own words. To quote Anna Freud:

> The Wolf-Man stands out among his fellow figures by virtue of the fact that he is the only one able and willing to cooperate actively in the reconstruction and follow-up of his own case. He is not shrouded in mystery like Katharina, nor estranged and inimical toward his former therapy like Anna O., nor reticent and shy of publicity like the adult Little Hans. His grateful respect for and ready understanding of analytic thinking lifted him, according to his own testimony, already during his initial treatment from the status of a patient to that of a younger colleague of his analyst, a collaboration with an experienced explorer setting out to study a new, recently discovered land. (Gardiner, xi)

And Pankiev's portrayal is of great interest. First identifying himself as a Russian emigré of 83 years, he next states that he is the Wolf-Man, one of Freud's early patients. He continues: "I was born on Christmas Eve, 1886, according to the Julian calendar in use in Russia at that time, on my father's estate on the banks of the Dnieper, north of the provincial city of Kherson" (4). In a prose style which is so simple and straightforward that it verges on the arid, he describes from childhood his life as a Russian aristocrat, first in Czarist Russia, then Vienna, then in the Russia of the Bolsheviks, and finally in the poverty-stricken Vienna of the Nazi and post-Nazi occupation. His narrative is filled with tales of family, nurses, governesses, tutors, events on the estates, moves, school and job difficulties, and finally romance. He tells us of his tumultuous courtship of the woman Teresa, who was to be his wife. He mentions wolves but once, only telling us they inhabited the vicinity of one of his father's estates when he was a small child. He provides the history of his efforts to obtain psychiatric and later psychoanalytic help for a condition which had been diagnosed as "Neurasthenia," emphasizing descriptions of his physicians, asylums, and fellow patients, rather than taking us into his inner life.

Apparently disappointed in the ordinariness of this man's life, despite the embellishments of money, nobility, and psychoanalytic notoriety, commentators such as Nicolas Abraham and Maria Torok, who wrote the *Wolf Man's Magic Word*, and then Patrick Mahony, note what they consider to be the "literary banality" of the Wolf-Man's *Memoirs*. Says Mahony, "If we recognize traits of the protaganist's affability and dependence on others' decisions, we nonetheless search in vain for his instinctual life, which was portrayed by Freud as lacking any control. . . . The 'Memoirs' throughout are rather drab. There is scant evidence, moreover, of any deep self-awareness and analytical insight such as one might expect from a polylingual, well-educated aristocrat who had been analyzed so many years by Freud"

(13). Now Mahony will later argue that the "instinctual life" documented in Freud's case history is in fact Freud's own, superimposed through fantasy by means of reconstruction, onto the Russian. And Abraham and Torok will treat this "banality and moral conventionalism" as a symptomatic caricature of the conventional "truths" of the self-righteous. "In every line he writes," they claim, "and in all that he chooses not to write, one hears the cry: you don't really want to know anything about what I am!" (30).

Now when I read this passage, and others from Mahony—we will return later to both—I was stunned for two reasons. First, such a statement strikes me as the height of psychoanalytic and/or critical arrogance, as though the writers took their position as the "subject who is supposed to know" so seriously that they became "he who knows better than the subject." Rather than respecting the intention of the *Memoirs'* author to write something of importance to him, something that he in fact desires to be heard, they claim that he is deleting the stuff of his life; the stuff of real psychoanalytic weight. Rather than considering that the *Memoirs* represent the Wolf-Man's final chance to be understood, his last opportunity to provide us the missing pieces to decipher a truth which has been obscured by endless sheaves of psychoanalytic chaff, they reject his statements and regard him with pity. Second, my own reaction to the *Memoirs* was quite different. Rather than finding them "banal," I was carried along by their simplicity and found that I could barely put the book down. The more I read, the more I agreed with the cover comment of *New York Times* critic Christopher Lehmann-Haupt that appeared on the book jacket. Says Lehmann-Haupt: "It assumes the urgency of a detective thriller. Far more compelling and instructive than any of the recent popular treatments of Freud's life and theories." As I approached the final pages, although I already knew the nature of the ending, I had a sense of dread thinking that I had to confront, on an unyielding printed page, the last facts in this man's life. I had the familiar catch in my breath as I laid the book to rest.

We have here what might be called, at least, a "discrepancy" in reader response. A "literary effort" which was empty and without power to some moved me deeply. The unadorned rendering of the events of Sergei Pankiev's life carried an impact similar to the list of names of the dead which the TV news programs silently provide after a jumbo jetliner goes down. The very absence of predication allows Death to speak. And in *The Memoirs of the Wolf-Man*, Death makes it point.

Let me tell you how. Without providing the medium of the narrative, the people, the places, the circumstances of the Russian's life, I will chronicle some of the events and facts which organize Pankiev's *Memoirs*, chapter by chapter.

Chapter 1: *Recollections of my Childhood*

- Sergei's near death from pneumonia at a few months of age.
- His misery from malaria early in his childhood.
- His attachment to his nurse, his Nanya, whose infant son had died.
- The death of 200,000 sheep on his father's estate after an innoculation which was to have protected them from an epidemic which had infected the farm animals in the area.
- The deaths of his parents' siblings. Each had many brothers and sisters, most of whom had died during childhood or youth.
- The loss of contact with his father's favorite brother Pinya after he moved to Moscow.
- The psychotic deterioration of his father's brother Peter, who was confined to an institution.
- The death of his paternal grandfather, 1 year after Sergei's birth.
- The death of his paternal grandmother, Irina Petrovna, several years before.
- The alcoholic deterioration of his paternal grandfather after the death of his wife.
- The death of his aunt, Irina Petrovna's daughter Lyuba, at the age of 8 or 9 from scarlet fever. It had been Irina's dearest wish to have a daughter because she had many boys. Lyuba was her last child.
- That Irina Petrovna's death was caused by an overdose of some dangerous medicine. Whether accidental or intentional was never clarified.
- That his French tutor "Mademoiselle" lived in their villa until she died.
- That Nanya lived until she died on the family estate in the South of Russia.
- A. J., the Dutch tutor of the children, suddenly disappeared from sight one day after several years of service to the family.

Chapter 2: *Unconscious Mourning 1905–1908*

- The suicide of Sergei's sister Anna. Sergei was 19. She was 21.
- Sergei's visit to the Caucasus the following fall. While there he visited the site where the poet Lermontov fought the fated duel which brought about his death.

- The attacks of melancholia which beset Sergei's father at intervals of 3–5 years, requiring that he spend several months in a sanitarium.

Chapter 3: *Castles in Spain 1908*

- Sergei meets his future wife Teresa. She has a "sorrowful" look. Both of her parents were dead. (Mahony indicates that she furthermore had lost one of her two children by a previous marriage at this point [52].)
- The death of a Russian colonel at the sanitarium in Munich where Sergei spent some time as a patient.
- The early death of Aunt Eugenia's husband from TB.
- The sudden and unexpected death of Sergei's father at the age of 49, perhaps due to an overdose of sleeping medication. Many suspect that this was a suicide.
- Father's burial next to Sergei's sister Anna in the family tomb.

Chapter 4: *Shifting Decisions 1909–1914*

- "There were two deaths which touched us in 1909," writes Pankiev (Gardiner, 80).
- Here he describes the death of Uncle Peter, his favorite uncle, the one who became paranoid. After his institutionalization, he lived alone on his estate in the Crimea. He had been dead for several days before he was found. At the time of his discovery rats had been gnawing on his cadaver for some time.
- The other death of 1909, the Wolf-Man's painting teacher and friend G., of cancer of the larynx, after a brief illness.

Chapter 5: *After My Analysis: 1914–1919*

- The coincidence of Pankiev's last day of his first analysis with Freud with the assassination of Archduke Ferdinand and his wife (28 June 1914). He made it a point to follow the funeral procession. The assassination heralded World War I.
- The death of his mother's youngest brother at the age of 8. He was one of three brothers who had died in early youth. Writes Pankiev: "These deaths seem to have had a great impact on her young mind and to have left deep traces. She talked about them frequently" (93).
- The death of cousin Sasha's wife at the age of 36 from cancer of the breast.
- Teresa's remaining child Else fell ill with pneumonia. She was taken to a sanitarium for pulmonary diseases.
- The Russian Revolution (October, 1917).
- The death of Else in June, 1919.

Chapter 6: *Everyday Life 1919–1938*

- The death of Captain L, a friend and a colleague at the insurance office where Pankiev was employed in Vienna, of lung cancer.

Chapter 7: *The Climax 1938*

- Hitler's march on Austria in 1938. Mass psychosis and epidemic suicides take place.

- March 31, 1938 for Pankiev, the "most disastrous day" of his "whole life" (120). Teresa turns on the gas and kills herself in their Vienna apartment.

- His efforts to find therapeutic assistance to come to terms with his wife's suicide. His travels to Paris and London for treatment by Ruth Mack Brunswick.

Pankiev's *Memoirs* end in 1938, despite the fact that he lived for many, many more years. He died one day after Freud's birthday in 1979 (May 7). He makes eminently clear that in a very real sense his own life ended with Teresa's. Nonetheless, 1939 was a year not without consequence for him, so it might have seemed reasonable for him to have extended the perimeter of his pen by a few more months. One has to ponder why he did not. 1939 marked the death of yet another person of immeasurable importance to him: Sigmund Freud died on the 23rd of September of that year.

Pankiev does not give his analysis and relationship with Freud detailed attention as such in the *Memoirs*. In a way, the analysis is present as it should be, as part of the sweep of a much larger stroke in life. But occasionally he makes a comment about the Professor. The very scarcity of these comments makes each of them reverberate with significance. One of particular interest is as follows: "When we come to talk about the events of the war, Professor Freud remarked that we had 'a wrong attitude toward death,' from which I had to conclude that he saw these experiences from an entirely different angle from the usual one" (110). This same anecdote appeared in a similar form in a piece written by the Wolf-Man in 1952, entitled *My Recollections of Sigmund Freud*: "When I saw Freud again after World War I, in the spring of 1919, and spoke of how absolutely incomprehensible it was that such a mass slaughter could take place in the twentieth century Freud did not pursue this theme but remarked, somewhat resignedly, that we have 'a wrong attitude' toward death" (Gardiner, 151). On the same page, Pankiev wrote: "In the winter of 1919–1920 Freud suffered an extremely painful loss through the death of his older daughter to whom, I have heard, he was especially attached. I saw him the day following this tragic event. He was calm and composed as usual, and did not betray his pain in any way" (151).

The Memoirs of the Wolf-Man clearly puts the fact of Death-in-life squarely in front of the mind's eye, and these are the very pages which are read as banal by the analyst in search of the exuberant instinct of which Freud wrote. The continuance of this discrepancy demands that the Freudian text be re-examined. Let us therefore take a look at Freud's *History of an Infantile Neurosis* and then proceed to Ruth Mack Brunswick's "A Supplement to Freud's *History of an Infantile Neurosis*" to try to make some sense of the incongruity.

Freud writes:

> The case upon which I propose to report in the following pages (once again only in a fragmentary manner) is characterized by a number of peculiarities which require to be emphasized before I proceed to a description of the facts themselves. It is concerned with a young man whose health had broken down in his eighteenth year after a gonorrheal infection, and who was incapacitated and completely dependent upon other people when he began his psychoanalytic treatment several years later. He had lived an approximately normal life during the ten years of his boyhood that preceded the date of his illness, and got through his studies at secondary school without much trouble. But his earlier years were dominated by a severe neurotic disturbance, which began immediately after his fourth birthday as an anxiety-hysteria (in the shape of an animal phobia), then changed into an obsessional neurosis with a religious content, and lasted with its offshoots as far as into his tenth year. . . . [He] spent a long time in German sanatoria, and was at that period classified in the most authoritative quarters as a case of "manic-depressive insanity." This diagnosis was certainly applicable to the patient's father, whose life, with its wealth of activity and interests, was disturbed by repeated attacks of severe depression. But in the son I was never able to detect any changes of mood which were disproportionate to the manifest psychological situation either in their intensity or in the circumstances of their appearance. I have formed the opinion that this case, like many others which clinical psychiatry has labeled with the most multifarious and shifting diagnosis, is to be regarded as a condition following on an obsessional neurosis which has come to an end spontaneously but has left a defect behind it after recovery (Gardiner, 154).

Freud makes clear that he believes himself to be working with a patient with an obsessional structure who had obvious evidence of neurosis in childhood, which resolved but left its mark in the residual symptomatology that brought him to see Freud in 1910. At the time of that presentation, his chief complaint was chronic severe constipation and a feeling that "the world was hidden in a veil, or that he was cut off from the world by a veil. This veil was torn only at one moment—when, after an enema, the contents of the bowel left the intestinal canal; and he then felt well and normal again."

While presumably working upon the presenting symptoms, Pankiev reported to Freud a dream which he clearly dated to his birthday, Christmas Eve, at the age of 4. This dream, which provided Freud's patient with his famous appelation, was concurrent with the first among many outbursts during a naughty period in his life. These outbursts receded only after his mother introduced him to religious practices such as the veneration of icons, and together with his Nanya, schooled him in the story of Christ's passion. According to Freud, the dream followed his sister Anna's seduction of the boy into the pleasures of passive sexual experience by touching him on the penis. Freud recounts Pankiev as saying: "I dreamt that it was night and that I was lying in my bed. (My bed stood with its foot against the window; in front of the window there was a row of old walnut trees. I know it was winter when I had the dream and night time.) Suddenly the window opened of its own accord, and I was terrified to see some white wolves were sitting on the big walnut tree in front of the window. There were six or seven of them. The wolves were quite white, and looked more like foxes or sheep-dogs, for they had big tails like foxes and they had their fears pricked like dogs when they pay attention to something. In great terror, evidently of being eaten up by the wolves, I screamed, and woke up" (Gardiner, 173). At the time of the dream, Sergei's sister Anna was given to tormenting him with a picture book which represented a wolf standing upright. "Whenever he caught sight of this picture he began to scream like a lunatic that he was afraid of the wolf coming and eating him" (161).

It is through his extensive analysis of this dream that Freud reconstructed the Wolf-Man's exposure to the primal scene at the age 1 1/2 and thereby introduces the concept of "deferred action" into psychoanalytic theory. This notion—in effect, the psychological capacity to endow events with significance retrospectively—was received skeptically by Anna Freud and various British and American analysts (Mahony, 55). In contrast, it was elaborated by Lacan as the *après-coup*.

Freud's analysis went as follows: The wolves represented the Wolf-Man's father. His anxiety emerged from a repudiation of a wish to take his mother's place in the primal scene to copulate with his father. This "passive attitude" toward the father succumbed to repression because "his narcissistic genital libido, which, in the form of concern for his male organ, was fighting against a satisfaction whose attainment seemed to involve the renunciation of that organ" (Freud, 46). Freud continues: "Through the process of the dream he understood that castration is the necessary condition of femininity" (78). The fear of the father, having undergone a regressive transformation, appeared as a fear of wolves. "From the time of the dream onwards, in his unconscious he was homosexual, and in his neurosis he was at the level of cannibalism; while the earlier masochistic attitude remained the dominant one" (64).

As Freud continued his work upon Pankiev's obsessional neurosis he considered this "masochistic attitude" to be the motive for an identification with Christ which seemed to surface in the material. Although no longer religious, the Wolf-Man had been known during his youthful obsessional period to ruminate about whether Christ had a behind, whether or not he shit. Despite his Nanya's assurances that Christ as a man did everything that humans do, little Sergei concluded that this was untrue. If Christ could make food from nothing he could turn it into nothing inside of his body. These concerns, for Freud, contain the child's repressed homosexual desire, for they contain the question of "whether he himself could be used by his father like a woman—like his mother in the primal scene" (Freud, 64), which Freud believed to have taken place *a tergo*, from behind. What Freud calls Pankiev's feminine attitude is used by the Professor to explain the bowel symptoms with which the patient presented.

These bowel symptoms proved to be extremely tenacious despite what was in those days a very lengthy analysis. And Freud saw no progress. To move the patient along, so to speak, Freud set an arbitrary termination date, telling the patient that by the end of his analysis, his symptom would be cleared up. Obediently, the "Hysterical constipation" responded to the pressure. It nevertheless returned and was the reason for Pankiev's resumption of treatment with Freud for a few months in 1919. We recall that Teresa's Else died in June of that year. The Wolf-Man states that he completed his treatment on Easter of 1920.

The events of the Russian Revolution and the Great War left Pankiev impoverished. So Freud saw him without fee during 1919 and 1920. Furthermore, Freud collected an annual stipend from the analytic community which the Wolf-Man received for six years. During most of this time, Pankiev was, by the description of Freud and others, relatively well. His state of calm seemed to last, according to Ruth Mack Brunswick, until the summer of 1923, when he started to masturbate with obscene pictures. This seemed to initiate a period of increasingly loose sexual behavior, as well as an obsessional preoccupation with his teeth and nose. He sought, in a rather pressured way, opinions and treatments from dermatologists for blackheads, swellings, wounds from picking pimples, and imaginary scars. Every opinion was followed by a second opinion and then a great quandary about whom to trust. Although these preoccupations had notable quiescent periods, his illnesses and symptoms seemed to reappear on Easter and on Pentecost. For example, on Easter of 1925, the Wolf-Man discovered a large painful pimple on his nose. Despite its size, he expected it to disappear of its own accord. As Pentecost approached, he became impatient. On that very day he attended the cinema and saw *The White Sister*. This film reminded him of his dead sister and her complaints about her pimples. In despair, he consulted a dermatologist the next day. The latter reassured him that it would disappear in due course. When it did not, Pankiev returned in two weeks to be told that the pimple was an infectious sebaceous gland for which there was no treatment. He asked how he could be asked to be condemned to live with a disease for which there was no treatment. How could he go on living thus mutilated? From this doctor he rushed to a certain Professor X, whom he had previous consulted, and who was to figure prominently in Mack Brunswick's later work with the Wolf-Man. With an instrument, Professor X pressed the infected spot. Blood flowed out from the place of the gland. At the sight of his own blood flowing, Pankiev experienced an acute ecstasy (Gardiner, 273). Some claim he had an orgasm.

The Wolf-Man's joy was short-lived. He soon became obsessed with the residual swelling and concluded that pustules on his gums must have been the source of the problem. He sought a dentist who confirmed his own opinion and had an immediate extraction. This cycle of frenzied concern over his nose and teeth, marked by repetitive consultations with physicians and dentists who recommended contradictory remedies, eventuated in a visit with Freud on June 16, 1926. Freud sent him on to Mack Brunswick, herself in analysis with Freud at the time, for further analysis. It is important to note here that the Wolf-Man's spiral into hypochrondriasis and sexual misconduct began after a visit to Freud. Freud had just had the first of what were to be multiple surgeries on his mouth for the cancer that was to mutilate him and take his life. That operation was performed by a dental surgeon. By the Fall of that year (1923), everyone in the analytic community was well aware of the serious nature of Freud's illness.

When she received Pankiev for re-analysis, Mack Brunswick confronted a man whose character to her seemed changed. Although he frenetically checked his nose in the mirror, obsessed with a tiny scar which had assumed gargantuan psychological proportions, he refused to address this issue in treatment. Obsequious with her in the analytic setting, he praised her skills, favorably comparing her to Freud. He discussed his reaction to Freud's illness and revealed, only through a dream, that he was concealing the fact that he had recently acquired family jewels which he believed to be valuable, lest his stipend from Freud stop. Believing that the Wolf-Man was suffering from an unresolved, and presumably negative transference to Freud, Mack Brunswick chose to challenge the Wolf-Man's picture of himself as Freud's special patient/son. Mercilessly, she countered his notions that he had a social relationship with Freud, that he was the only case written up, that his analysis was the longest running. Furthermore, rather than waiting until the Wolf-Man learned by ordinary means of the death of Professor X, the dermatologist whom the Wolf-Man held responsible for the irreparably scarred nose, she announced it to him at the beginning of an analytic hour. What she uncovered, or perhaps precipitated, was a homicidal rage—at Freud, at herself, and at Professor X, whom Pankiev could no longer kill. Mack Brunswick found him to be psychotic with ideas of persecution that were delusional in nature. She explained all of this in the following way.

Pankiev identified the ailing and mutilated Freud with the dead and castrated father. The Wolf-Man, in turn, identified himself with the crucified Christ. As a protection against his own castration, he erected a megalomania. This, however, was insufficient to ward off his castration anxiety. The latter broke through in the form of the *idée fixe* about his nose. The nasal symptoms were a more extreme repetition of ones suffered as an adolescent, similarly an expression of castration fears. By his own admission, the Wolf-Man's contemplation of Freud's impending death brought with it the thought that he might be heir to an inheritance, however small. In keeping with Freud's original formulation of the primal scene, the gift, like the Christmas presents he demanded as a child, would provide the passive homosexual satisfaction he desired. You see, in the famous wolf-dream, the wolves in the tree were said to have condensed the representation of the desired father with the packages traditionally hung from the Christmas tree. Pankiev's rage was generated by his unrequited love for Father/Freud, not by competitive hostility. So, in the face of a dying Freud, the fantasy of symbolic satisfaction of his homosexual desire drove this man crazy. After all of this was worked through, he rather suddenly recovered.

Mack Brunswick's formulation poses a question: why didn't the yearly stipends, which perhaps maintained a passive homosexual transference to Freud, create an equally regressive picture? How can we understand the special power of Freud's illness and portended death? Furthermore, what accounts for the rather dramatic resolution of what Mack Brunswick declared to have been a psychosis?

Mack Brunswick's account rests upon the validity of Freud's primal scene reconstruction. Daring and brilliant though it was, it seems not to have withstood the critical eye of more recent generations of analysts and commentators. To uncover what *"really"* happened during the Wolf-Man's early life, the Derridans Abraham and Torok boldly undertake a "cryptographic analysis" of the available texts. Offering what has been hailed as a new "theory of readability" (Abraham and Torok, li), they phonetically re-analyze the Wolf-Man's dreams. Claiming that English was Pankiev's first language, they utilize artful combinations of sounds derived from three languages, Russian, German, and English, to decipher underlying meanings. For example, in the wolf-dream, "It was night" is taken for *nochu* in Russian and then said to stand for the phonetically similar "not you" in English. Similarly *zimoi* (winter), is read as "it's a boy." Further, they combine both Cyrillic and Latin alphabets in this enterprise.

By means of the application of this method to all of the available dreams of the Wolf-Man, they conclude the following: The scene of consequence to which he bore witness was not the primal one but rather one between father and sister. There were 6 or 7 wolves in the dream. The Russian word for 6 is *shiest* which phonetically suggests *siestorka* the word they take for "sister" in Russian. *Vidient san*, the Russian for "to dream," contains a notion of witness. So they read "At night I witnessed my sister." The "TR" sound in *siestorka* is repeated in *Tepek (Tierek)*, the mountain which he chose to visit in the Caucasus after his sister's death, and in Teresa, his wife's name. Further, it appears in *natieret* and *tieret*, meaning to scrub, rub, or rub oneself. For the Wolf-Man rubbing and scrubbing were linked to an early childhood memory of the servant girl, Grusha, on her knees, "her buttocks projecting" (Freud 92), during which time the boy was "seized with excitement owing to the activation [of the primal scene]" (Freud 43). Grusha, meaning pear, is the diminutive of Agripina. Abraham and Torok dramatically conclude that the hidden, "encrypted," sentence of the Wolf-Man's desire that could never be spoken was, "Come Sis, rub me ..." (24). Through the Russian *tierebit*, which Abraham and Torok translate as "rip off," they re-analyze the Wolf-Man's famous dream of the Wasp. Here I quote from Freud:

> He confirmed the connection between the Grusha scene and the threat of castration by a particularly ingenious dream, which he himself succeeded in deciphering. "I had a dream," he said, "of a

man tearing off the wings of an *Espe.*" "*Espe?*" I asked. "What do you mean by that?" "You know; that insect with yellow stripes on its body, that stings." This must be an allusion to Grusha, the pear with the yellow stripes." I could now put him right: "So what you mean is a *Wespe* [wasp]." "Is it called a *Wespe?* I really thought it was called an *Espe.*" "But *Espe,* why that's myself: SP" (which were his initials). The *Espe* was of course a mutilated *Wespe.* The dream said that he was avenging himself on Grusha for her threat of castration (Gardiner 236).

In this Abraham and Torok read: "Come Professor (Freud), do these words to me. 'Cut me,' Oh! 'Cut Me,' 'pull me,' 'rip me,' Oh confounded words, unsayable words, oh! yes, but, cut my genitals for me so they stand up on two paws like a wolf disguised as a grandmother with a white bonnet on its head. Oh, yes 'rip off (*tierebit*) the wings of this wasp, of the S.P.' (Wasp), rub, rub it for he cannot stand it—but. . . ." (25).

Mahony is in essential accord with Abraham and Torok's assessment of the Wolf-Man's memoirs. He is less certain of their methodology in re-translating Freud's German texts into a semiotic structure of confluent childhood languages. On the one hand, struck by the "awesomeness of their enterprise" (38), he, on the other hand, considers it "wild analysis" (65). He himself is more interested in analyzing Freud. He underscores the centrality of phonemes to do so and asserts that Freud and Pankiev shared important signifiers. He asks, "Since the navel of the dream is undecipherable, might we say that phonemes at times are closer than words to that navel?" (120). Using, for instance, the famous "Irma" dream, Mahony points out that the day residue for the "trimethylamin" was a gift bottle of liquor with the name *Ananas.* At the time of the dream Freud's wife Martha was pregnant with a child to be named *Anna* if a girl. Pankiev's sister's name was *Anna.* Further, the *Espe* (S.P.) of the *Wespe* dream contains a reversal of the initials of *Professor Sigmund,* founder of *p*sychoanalysis. Mahony's elaboration of this idea is both extensive and impressive.

Agreeing with Mack Brunswick's diagnosis of psychosis, Mahony has this to say about the Wolf-Man:

In resume then: he finished a second analysis with Freud in 1920; two years later he underwent a character change; the next year saw the outbreak of paranoia, and in 1924 hypochondria. When he began analysis with Brunswick in October 1926, he brought into it several recent years of manifest psychic degeneration, but it was Freud's illness that mainly precipitated the patient's paranoia. The effects were multiple: regressive decompensation, personality fragmenta-

tion, lack of self-cohesiveness, the retrogression of mature narcissistic cathexis into parts of the body self, a raging relation to frustrating
objects, a disruption of the narcissistic transference and merger
with the idealized parental Freud and disillusionment with his om-
nipotence. In the face of this onslaught, even the magical mirror did
not suffice in its regressive use for maintaining self-object ties and
its defensive purpose against maternal re-engulfment and diffusion
of self-object boundaries (137–38).

Among all these words there seems to be no room for a mention of
this man's *suffering* in the face of a dying Freud.

In 1962 an analyst named Albert Lubin published in *Psychoanalytic
Forum* a paper entitled, "The Influences of the Russian Orthodox
Church on Freud's Wolf-Man: A Hypothesis (With an Epilogue Based
on Visits with the Wolf-Man)." His discussants, among them Muriel
Gardiner, were kind but dismissive. Apparently impressed with the
persistence and power of the Christ identification which both Freud
and Mack Brunswick had observed, he was not satisfied that an understanding of the Wolf-Man's passive homosexual and masochistic striv-
ings sufficiently accounted for its particularity. He seemed to be grappling with what some might call the "cultural factors" in the
production of a neurosis. Through interviews with the Wolf-Man,
Lubin documented that both Pankiev's mother and Nanya were pious
women. His Nanya in fact took him to the Russian Orthodox Liturgy
with regularity on Sundays. During the interviews Pankiev showed
Lubin his baptismal cross, which he claimed to have worn daily until
he was twenty years old. Lubin was impressed with the veneration
with which he seemed to regard it. He believed that Pankiev's attitude
and behavior belied his frequent pronouncements that he'd aban-
doned his religious faith before puberty.

Girded with this information, Lubin found religious imagery in the
wolf-dream, among others. Utilizing a painting of the wolf nightmare
that Pankiev had done, Lubin saw the similarity of the tree to the
traditional Russian 3-bar Cross. Citing both the epistle of Peter and
the Orthodox vespers of Good Friday, he noted the identification of
the cross and the tree. The white wolves, he continued, suggest sheep,
and Jesus is the Lamb of God. The white could represent the white
loin cloth of the crucified Christ (156). Furthermore, a "veil" is used
to cover the Eucharistic gifts. Lubin concluded therefore that the
Russian Orthodox Church was neurosogenic in its own right. And
there he stopped. Lubin did not consider the psychological aim or the
point or the purpose of the neurotic integration of the religious themes
in Pankiev's life. Neither did he consider just how such a linkage

between the cultural and the libidinal, the spirit and the flesh, might have taken place.

Now how are we to make sense of all this? We learn through the Wolf-Man's pen that his life proceeded in Death. We find that his psychoanalysts, commentators, and critics find his own view of his life unimpressive and disappointing. They are more interested in his homosexuality, his masochism, his paranoia, and his narcissism. Some old duck named Lubin attempts to expand the horizon of consideration while still committed to Freud's original formulation. He finds that the imagery of the Wolf-Man's dreams is shared by his Church. Perhaps the ideas of Lacan can help us sort all of this out.

It seems to me that the place to begin is with the question of diagnosis. Most analysts are persuaded, with Mack Brunswick, that the Wolf-Man was psychotic. They take the degree of what they consider to be his hypochondrical preoccupation with his nose, and the intensity of his affective expression of persecutory ideas, as sufficient evidence of a seriously compromised reality testing. Mack Brunswick emphasized, which I have not, the Wolf-Man's identification with his mother, which seemed to overtake him completely during his psychotic enactment of the feminine position. But this raises the question of whether one need be crazy in order to be crazed. In the absence of an examination of the underlying structure, the question cannot be addressed. Sheep can after all wear the clothing of a wolf.

For Lacan, the *sine qua non* of psychosis is a "foreclosure" of the Name-of-the-Father. The Name-of-the-Father, the bearer of the Law of the Father and therefore the structuring principle of the symbolic order, of civilization itself, must find its place in the Other, in the Unconscious. Should it not, psychosis, an idiosyncratic and personalized relationship to one's name, and to the world of unanchored meanings, results. Another way to put this is that the paternal metaphor, itself on a vertical axis of substitution, must have its place on a signifying chain which can be located in the Other. Now if we can demonstrate that a signifying of the Name-of-the-Father, through some sort of phonetic elision or metonymic displacement, found a habitat under repression, we would have a strong argument favoring a neurotic diagnosis.

First, let us consider whether the paternal metaphor functions. The father, not necessarily the real father but the symbolic father, must *have* a place in order for that place to be occupied by a substitute. Successful substitution would imply that this be the case. Such a notion addresses the concept of transference. Psychoneurotics are capable of forming transferences. Psychotics are not.

In the Wolf-Man's case, Mack Brunswick provides material which

182 / Lila Kalinich

speaks to this very point. Professor X was an obvious "substitute for Freud." "The patient blamed Freud for the loss of fortune in Russia, but laughed at the idea that Freud's advice could have been intentionally malicious. It was necessary for him to seek out an indifferent but equally symbolic persecutor, to whom he could consciously and wholeheartedly ascribe the most vicious motives" (Gardiner 299). By this account, the Wolf-Man sounds somewhat like a psychoanalytic candidate in training: the negative transference to the analyst is held under repression in the analytic setting, while it is split and displaced onto a teacher or a supervisor. Mack Brunswick seems to indicate, then, that the paternal metaphor does function in the Wolf-Man.

Another way to approach the question is to consider how the Wolf-Man's mother regarded the Name, or the Law of the Father. Writers have emphasized the probable inadequacy of Pankiev's real father—his serious mood swings, his long absences from home, etc. From a Lacanian point of view, the situation and personality of the actual (or imaginary) father is less important than the mother's role in the structuring process. To quote Stuart Schneiderman's book *Rat Man*, on the topic of the Rat Man's mother: "Certainly his mother referred to such a Law, thus leaving a place for its articulation and making it functional. This means that the Law is not foreclosed as it is with the psychotic, where the mother does not open a place for its articulation" (97).

Pankiev informed us that the "naughty period" contemporaneous with his wolf-dream ended when his mother introduced him to religion. Religious practice functioned as a "No" to his naughtiness. Each night young Pankiev had to kiss and pray before icons. In the tradition of the Russian Orthodox Church, an icon is never kissed without the believer making the sign of the cross, or crossing himself, while saying the words:

"In the Name of the Father, the Son, and the Holy Spirit, Amen."

In Russian this begins:

Vo Imja Otsa

Otsa. Now consider this. Taken as phonemes, as a Signifier, *otsá*, the genitive case of *otets*, meaning *father*, is barely a sound away from *ocá/osá*, which in Russian means wasp!

I must add that according to Gardiner, the Wolf-Man "had the idea that years containing the figure 8 were always bad years in his life" (*Memoirs*, 335). The number 8 in Russian is *òcam* (*osam*).

We see here, then, something other than a foreclosure in the Other, which according to Lacan in "On the possible treatment of psychosis" (*Ecrits* 81), would create "the inadequacy of the metaphoric effect" present in psychosis. Instead, we see not only a place but indeed a famous place for the Name-of-the-Father in the signifying chain. To finally put to rest the question of the Wolf-Man's psychosis, I must quote Lacan: "Not only can man's being not be understood without madness, it would not be man's being if it did not bear madness within itself as the limit of his freedom" (*Ecrits*, 215).

One more small point might be made about the *Wespe*. Pankiev was very much involved with images. He was a painter by avocation, he dreamed of icons, and during the extremity of his nasal preoccupation, he looked again and again into the mirror. So it may be of some interest that *Wespe*, in addition to functioning as a signifier, as an acoustic image, functions as an icon as well. Observe the following transformation of the word Wespe $\rightarrow$ Sepew. Treating it as an anagram, substitute the Cyrillic ●● for the Latin S and the Cyrillic ■■ for the Latin W. E remains an E in Cyrillic. P in Cyrillic is the letter "R."

We now have

 C E P E ■■

Add

 C E P Ё ■■

This is *Seriëzh*, a mutilated version of *Seriëzha* (pronounced *Seryozha*); the diminutive of the name Sergei. *Wespe* is an icon of the mutilated (name of the) son.

Let us return now to the questions implied by Lubin's paper on the religious influences of the Russian Orthodox Church and attempt to explore the psychological gain of Pankiev's powerful identification with Christ.

We know from Pankiev through his *Memoirs* that Death was a powerful presence in his life. Not only did he himself experience repetitive and tragic losses, those closest to him did as well. Nanya and Mother seemed especially marked by their histories of grief. For Nanya, little Sergei, Seriëzha, was the reincarnation of her dead son; for Mother, perhaps, of her dead little brother, among others. For the Orthodox Christian, reincarnation really means resurrection, and perhaps here is the point. Little Sergei, born on Christmas Eve, born with a cawl which signified to him a special destiny, believed he was given the task of restoring these dead. From the perspective of Lacan we can say that the Wolf-Man's desire is the desire of the Other. This means also that his desire is for her desire. By accomplishing the resurrection of the dead, Pankiev can fulfill his mother's/Nanya's desire. He can *be* the mother's phallus and in that sense sacrifice his own. Put another way, he attempted to be the Logos rather than the subject through whom the Logos speaks.

Perhaps an analysis of yet another key signifier which we know the Wolf-Man to have uttered during his analysis will support such a hypothesis; Grusha—the young scrubwoman whom little Seriëzha loved, and who Freud believed threatened the child with castration. Upon his first recollection of her, he thought her name to have been the same as his mother's. Later he realized that in his memory he had fused the two of them (*S.E.* Freud XVII, 90). Couldn't it be that this fusion represents yet another metonymic displacement along a signifying chain? In Slavic languages, an adjective may be used as a noun and a name when it refers to an essentially identifying quality. Here the phonemes "Grusha" easily slide into *Grustnaja*, which means "the sad one." The threat of castration comes from her who has known Death, *Grustnaja*. Let us reconsider here Abraham and Torok's "Magic Word" *tieret*. Phonetically it is one vowel sound away from *tieriat*, which means "to lose." Is Sergei's desire for Grusha, who scrubs, or for the Sad One who loses? And does not the illness and portended death of Freud assert the Desire of the Other in an imperious way, thereby evoking Christ, crucified and resurrected, yet again?

Although Freud was not unmindful of the role of Death in neurosis, he subordinated it to instinctual factors. A tension existed in his writing between a preoccupation with organ loss and the scope of the larger issues of existence. In contrast, for Lacan, castration embodies the ordering principle of the symbolic, from which none of us is exempt. Existence by its nature prescribes castration, and Death is its sharpest scapel. Language is the medium through which the symbolic order returns to the flesh and writes its messages. In this way the *Drives* are transformed into *Desire*. The messages thus inscribed are the particular ones of our linguistic and acoustic experience, not simply fantasmagoric creations of our own solipsistic and individual lives. In other words, we are what we hear. And Sergei Pankiev heard the language, the music of the language, of the Church. That language informed him and provided a scaffold around which he could erect his mother's Desire. And this is what he would have heard:

> From a Troparion from the Royal Hours on Christmas Eve: ". . . The Tree of Life blossoms forth from the virgin in the cave. Christ is coming to restore the image which he made in the beginning."

Followed by the Christmas Eve vespers and the Divine Liturgy of St. Basil the Great, read every year for the 1000 years that the Orthodox Christian Church has existed in Russia, the reading from the Prophet Isaiah:

> He shall smite the earth with the word of his mouth, and with the breath of his lips. He shall slay the wicked. His loins will be girded with righteousness, and his sides will be clothed with the truth. And the wolf shall feed with the lamb, and the leopard shall lie down with the kid, and the young calf, the bull, and the lion shall feed together, and a little child shall lead them. And the infant shall play over the serpent's hole and the weaned child shall put his hand in the adder's den.

And from the Pascha service, the Easter Resurrection Matins, from the Sermon of St. John Chrysostom, preached each Easter for that same thousand years:

> Let no one fear death, for the Savior's death has set us free. He that was held prisoner of it has annihiliated it. By descending into Hell, He made Hell captive. He embittered it when it tasted of his flesh. And Isaiah foretelling this, did cry: Hell, said he, was embittered, when it encountered thee in the lower regions. It was embittered, for it was mocked. It was embittered, for it was slain. It was embittered, for it was overthrown. It was embittered, for it was fettered in chains. It took a body and met God face to face. It took earth, and encountered heaven. It took that which was seen and fell upon the unseen.
> O, Death, where is thy sting?
> O, Hell, where is thy victory?
> Christ is risen and thou art overthrown.
> Christ is risen, and the demons are fallen.
> Christ is risen, and the angels rejoice.
> Christ is risen, and not one dead remains in the grave.

The *Memoirs of the Wolf-Man* can be taken as banal only by someone who believes that he has a privileged access to the Wolf-Man's truth. This is the sense imparted by the Abraham and Torok book. They stand almost in disbelief and awe of their own genius, intuition, and good luck as they pour over the Russian dictionary for the secret sounds of the Wolf-Man's inner sanctuary. They impart their own *jouissance* in their enterprise very effectively. I was impressed here, bewildered there, sometimes enraged, but never indifferent. And although the territory the work is said to occupy is the space between fantasy and trauma, fiction and reality (lvi), Abraham and Torok communicate a certainty about the Wolf-Man's Truth, a certainty that I will call a "delusional certainty." Their *jouissance* is like a *psychotic* symptom, an experience which, I will assert, is at the heart of this approach to criticism. Abraham and Torok scoured *Freud's* texts. Freud was dead, Pankiev was dead, and the text clearly silent. The silence of the text tricked them, mocked them as it watched them make translating errors, methodological errors, and weave, over five tedious years of labor and love, a well-organized delusional system in which they rejoiced. Were time to allow it, I could provide you with examples which would substantiate a claim that they misapplied their sparse knowledge of Russian. Further, we might explore their arbitrary omission of French from the Young Wolf-Man's lexicon.

About midway into their task their certainty was threatened with an interruption. Lo, the Wolf-Man returned from the dead and had something to say. Abraham and Torok discovered Muriel Gardiner and the Wolf-Man's *Memoirs*. They found them banal, self-righteous, hiding the truth. "Go back to the grave, old man. We don't care what you have to say. Why should you be heard when we can speak in your place. In our mouths you are a tasty subject. In your own, chewed cud. Poor fellow, go home." They close his book, nail his coffin, and return to their frenzied and certain interpreting of the text.

The joy of this certainty is extraordinary. I knew it myself in the preparation of this paper. While on the one hand comprehending that the whole enterprise of seeking quasi-analytic truths from a *text* about a patient, in the absence of the patient, is extremely questionable, on the other I was swept away by the sense of having found something *right*. I had to restrain increasingly absurd leaps in my thinking.

The "reality" from which the critical experience can be cut is that of death. Under ordinary circumstances, the text offers no surprises. No contingencies exist. In that it is dead, it can create the illusion in the critic of a mastery of Death.

Now, in contrast, if in psychoanalysis the discourse can be said to constitute a text, it is a text which lives, precisely because it speaks back and corrects the steering when the analyst's certainty threatens to lose the road. The power of existence over both analyst and patient, the castration of *both* analyst and patient by the Real, ultimately structures the discourse. In that psychoanalysis proceeds in the Real, it walks in the Valley of the Shadow of Death. This stands in contradistinction to the experience of the critic who may carry the beacon of

his own illumination in order momentarily to believe that the Shadow
has passed away.

Works Cited

Abraham, Nicolas and Maria Torok. *The Wolf Man's Magic Word: A Cryptonomy*. Trans.
Nicholas Rand. *Theory and History of Literature* 37. Minneapolis: University of Min-
nesota Press, 1986.

Freud, Sigmund. *The Standard Edition of the Complete Psychological Works of Sigmund
Freud* 17 (1917–1919). Ed. James Strachey. London: Hogarth Press, 1955.

Gardiner, Muriel, Ed. *The Wolf-Man by the Wolf-Man*. New York: Basic Books, 1971.

Lacan, Jacques. "On the possible treatment of psychosis." *Ecrits: A Selection*. Trans.
Alan Sheridan. New York: W.W. Norton and Co., 1977.

Lubin, A. (1967a), "The Influences of the Russian Orthodox Church on Freud's Wolf-
Man: A Hypothesis." *Psychoanalytic Forum* 2:145–62. (1967b).

———. "Lubin's Response to his Discussants." *Psychoanalytic Forum* 2:170–174.

Mahony, Patrick J. *Cries of the Wolf Man, History of Psychoanalysis*. Monograph 1. Ed.
The Chicago Institute for Psychoanalysis. New York: International Universities
Press, Inc., 1984.

Schneiderman, Stuart. *Rat Man*. New York: New York University Press, 1986.

10

The Truth Arises from Misrecognition

Slavoj Žižek

I The Dialectics of the Symptom

Back to the future

The only reference to the domain of science fiction that we find in Lacan's work concerns the time-paradox. In his first *Seminar*, Lacan uses the metaphor, invented by Norbert Wiener, of the inverted direction of time, to explain the symptom as a "return of the repressed."

Wiener posits two beings each of whose temporal dimension moves in the opposite direction from the other. To be sure, that means nothing, and that is how things which mean nothing all of a sudden signify something, but in a quite different domain. If one of them sends a message to the other, for example a square, the being going in the opposite direction will first of all see the square vanishing before seeing the square. "That is what we see as well. The symptom initially appears to us as a trace, which will only ever be a trace, one which will continue not to be understood until the analysis has got quite a long way, and until we have discovered its meaning" (*Seminar I*, 159).

Analysis is thus conceived as a symbolization, a symbolic integration of meaningless imaginary traces; this conception implies a fundamentally imaginary character of the unconscious. It is made of "imaginary fixations which couldn't have been assimilated to the symbolic development" of the subject's history; consequently, "it is something which will be realized in the symbolic or, more precisely, something which, thanks to the symbolic progress which takes place in the analysis, will [retroactively] become what it was" (future anterior: *aura été*) (I, 158, translation modified). The Lacanian answer to the question, from where does the repressed return, is then paradoxically: from the future. Symptoms are meaningless traces; their meaning is not discovered, excavated from the hidden depth of the past, but constructed retroactively. The analysis produces the truth, i.e., the signifying frame which gives to the symptoms their symbolic place and meaning. As soon as we enter the symbolic order, the past is always present in the form of historical tradition, of interwoven traces which constitute a synchronic network of signifiers. The meaning of these traces is not given; it changes continually with the transformations of the signifier's network. Every historical rupture, every advent of a new master signifier, changes retroactively the meaning of all tradition, restructures the narration of the past, makes it readable in another, new way. Thus things which don't make any sense suddenly mean something, but in an entirely other domain. What is a journey into the future if not this "overtaking" by means of which we suppose in advance the presence in the other of a certain knowledge—knowledge about the meaning of our symptoms.

What is it, then, if not the transference itself? This knowledge is an illusion. It does not really exist in the other, the other does not really possess it. It is constituted afterwards, through our—the subject's—signifier's working. But it is at the same time a necessary illusion, because we can paradoxically elaborate this knowledge only by means of the illusion that the other already possesses it and that we are only discovering it. If, as Lacan is pointing out, the repressed content in the symptom is returning from the future and not from the past, then the transference—the actualization of the reality of the unconscious—must transpose us into the future and not into the past. And what is the journey into the past if not this retroactive working-through, the elaboration of the signifier itself: a kind of hallucinatory *mise-en-scène* of the fact that, in the field of the signifier and only in this field, we can change, we can bring about the past? The past exists as it is included, as it enters (into) this synchronous net of the signifier, i.e., as it is symbolized in the texture of the historical memory. That is why we are "rewriting history" all the time, retroactively giving the elements their symbolic weight by including them in new textures. It is this elaboration which decides retroactively what they "will have been (*auront été*)."

The Oxford philosopher Michael Dummett has written two very interesting articles included in his collection of essays, *Truth and Other Enigmas*: "Can an Effect Precede its Cause?" and "Bringing About the Past." The Lacanian answer to these two enigmas would be "yes", because the symptom as a "return of the repressed" is precisely such an effect which precedes its cause (its hidden kernel, its meaning). In working through the symptom, we are precisely "bringing about the past." That is, we are producing the symbolic reality of the past, long-forgotten traumatic events. One is then tempted to see in the time-paradox of science-fiction novels a kind of hallucinatory apparition in the real of the elementary structure of the symbolic process, the so-called internal, internally inverted eight: a circular movement, a kind of snare where we can progress only in such a manner that we "over-take" ourselves in the transference, to find ourselves later at a point at which we have already been. The paradox consists in the fact that this superfluous detour, this supplementary snare of overtaking ourselves (voyage into the future) and then reversing the time-direction (voyage into the past) is not just a subjective illusion/perception of an objective process taking place in so-called reality, independently of these illusions. This supplementary snare is rather an internal condition, an internal constituent of the so-called "objective" process itself. It is only through this additional detour that the past itself, the "objective" state of things, becomes retroactively what it always was. Transference is then an illusion, but the point is that we cannot bypass it and reach directly for the truth. The truth itself is constituted through the illusion proper to the transference—"the truth arises from misrecognition" in Lacan's words.

If this paradoxical structure is not yet clear, let us take another science-fiction example, the well-known story by William Tenn, *The Discovery of Morniel Mathaway*. A distinguished art historian takes a journey with a time-machine from the twenty-fifth century to our days to visit and study *in vivo* the immortal Morniel Mathaway, a painter not appreciated in our time but who was later discovered to have been the greatest painter of our era. When he encounters him, the art historian finds no trace of a genius, just an imposter who is a megalomaniac and even a swindler who steals his time-machine from him and escapes into the future, so that the poor art historian stays tied to our time. The only thing open to him is then to assume the identity of the escaped Mathaway and to paint under his name all his masterpieces that he remembers from the future. It is himself who is really the misrecognized genius he was looking for!

This is then the basic paradox we are aiming at. The subject is confronted with a scene from the past that he wants to change, to meddle with, to intervene in. He takes a journey into the past, inter-venes in the scene and—it is not that he "cannot change anything," quite the contrary—it is only through his intervention that the scene from the past becomes what it always was. His intervention was from the beginning comprised, included. The initial "illusion" of the subject consists in simply forgetting to include in the scene his own act, i.e., in overlooking how "it counts, it is counted, and the one who counts is already included in the account" (Lacan, *Seminar* XI, 20; translation modified).

This introduces a relationship between truth and misrecognition/ misapprehension by which the truth, literally, arises from misrecognition, as in the well-known story about the "appointment in Samarra" (from **W. S.** Maugham's play *Sheppey*)

> *Death*: "There was a merchant in Baghdad who sent his servant to market to buy provisions and in a little while the servant came back, white and trembling, and said, Master, just now when I was in the marketplace I was jostled by a woman in the crowd and when I turned I saw it was death that jostled me. She looked at me and made a threatening gesture; now, lend me your horse, and I will ride away from this city and avoid my fate. I will go to Samarra and there death will not find me. The merchant lent him his horse, and the servant mounted it and he dug his spurs in its flanks and he went as fast as the horse could gallop. Then the merchant went down to the market-place and he saw me standing in the crowd and he came to me and said, Why did you make a threatening gesture to my servant when you saw him this morning? That was not a threatening gesture, I said, it was only a start of surprise. I was astonished to see him in Bagdad, for I had an appointment with him tonight in Samarra.

Before we ask ourselves what this story has to do with psychoanalysis, we ought to remind ourselves that we find the same structure in the myth of Oedipus. It is *predicted* to Oedipus's father that his son will kill him and marry his mother, and the prophecy realizes itself, "becomes true," through the father's attempt to evade it. He exposes his little son in the forest, etc., and Oedipus, not recognizing him twenty years later when he encounters him, kills him. In other words, the prophecy becomes true by means of its being communicated to the person it affects and by means of his or her attempt to elude it. One knows one's destiny in advance, one tries to evade it, and it is by means of this attempt itself that the predicted destiny realizes itself. Without the prophecy, the little Oedipus would have lived happily with his parents and there would be no "Oedipus complex."

Repetition in history

The time-structure with which we are concerned here is such that it is mediated through subjectivity: the subjective "mistake," "fault," "error," "misrecognition," arrives paradoxically *before* the truth in relation to which we are designating it as "error," because this "truth" itself becomes true only through—or, to use a Hegelian term, by mediation of—the error. This is the logic of unconscious cunning, the way the unconscious deceives us. The unconscious is not a kind of transcendent, unattainable thing that we are unable to take cognizance of. It is rather—to follow Lacan's word play—his translation of *Unbewusste—une bévue*, an overlooking: we overlook the way our act is already part of the state of things we are looking at, the way our error is part of the truth itself. This paradoxical structure in which the truth arises from misrecognition also gives us the answer to the question: why is the transference necessary? Why must the analysis go through it? The transference is precisely an illusion by means of which the final truth (the meaning of a symptom) is produced.

We find the same logic of the error as an internal condition of truth with Rosa Luxemburg, with her description of the dialectics of the revolutionary process. I am alluding here to her argument against Edward Bernstein, against his revisionist fear of seizing power too soon, "prematurely," before the so-called "objective conditions" had ripened. This was, as is well known, Bernstein's main reproach to the revolutionary wing of social democracy: they are too impatient, they want to hasten, to outrun the objective logic of historical development. The answer of Rosa Luxemburg is that the first seizures of power *are necessarily "premature"*. The only way for the working class to reach its "maturity," to await the arrival of the "appropriate moment" for the seizure of power, is to form itself, to educate itself for this act of seizure. And the only possible way of achieving this education is precisely by "premature" attempts. If we just wait for the "appropriate moment," we will never live to see it, because this "appropriate moment" cannot arrive without the subjective conditions of the maturity of the revolutionary force (subject) being fulfilled. That is, it can arrive only after a series of "premature," failed attempts.

The opposition to the "premature" seizure of power is thus revealed to be opposition to the seizure of power as such, *in general*. To repeat the famous phrase of Robespierre, the revisionists want a "revolution without revolution." If we look at this argument closely, we perceive that what is at stake in Rosa Luxemburg's argument is precisely the impossibility of metalanguage in the revolutionary process. The revolutionary subject does not "conduct," "direct" this process from an objective distance. He is constituted through this process, and because of this—because the temporality of the revolution passes through subjectivity—we cannot "make the revolution at the right moment" without previous "premature," failed attempts. Here, in the opposition between Bernstein and Luxemburg, we have the opposition between the obsessional (man) and the hysterical (woman): the obsessional is delaying, putting off the act, waiting for the right moment, while the hysterical, so to speak, overtakes herself in her act and thus unmasks the falsity of the obsessional's position. This is also what is at stake in Hegel's theory of the role of repetition in history: "a political revolution is generally sanctioned by the opinion of the people only when it is renewed" (Hegel)—i.e., it can succeed only as a repetition of a first failed attempt. Why this necessity of a repetition?

Hegel developed his theory of repetition through the case of Caesar's death. When Julius Caesar consolidated his personal power and strengthened it to imperial proportions, he acted "objectively" (in itself) in accordance with historical truth, historical necessity. The Republican form was losing its validity, and the only form of government which could save the unity of the Roman state was monarchy, a state based upon the will of a single individual. But it was still the Republic which prevailed formally (for itself, in the opinion of the people). The Republic "was still alive only because she forgot that she was already dead," to paraphrase the famous Freudian dream of the father who did not know that he was already dead. (We find the same paradoxical place "in between two deaths" occupied by Napoleon at Elba: his role was already finished, i.e., he was already dead without knowing it, and that's why he had to die for the second time: at Waterloo, he died also "for himself,") To the "opinion" which still believed in the Republic, Caesar's amassing of personal power, which was of course contrary to the spirit of the Republic, appeared an arbitrary act, an expression of contingent individual self-will. The conclusion they drew was that if this individual (Caesar) were to be removed, the Republic would regain its full splendor. But it was precisely the conspirators against Caesar (Brutus, Cassius, etc.) who—following the logic of the "cunning of reason"—attested the truth (i.e. the historical necessity) of Caesar. The final result, the outcome of Caesar's murder, was the reign of Augustus, the first *caesar*. The truth thus arose from the failure itself. In failing, in missing its express goal, the murder of Caesar fulfilled the task which was, in a Machiavellian way, assigned to it by history: to exhibit the historical necessity by denouncing its own non-truth, i.e., its own arbitrary, contingent character.

The whole problem of repetition is here: in this passage from "Caesar" the name of an individual to "caesar," title of the Roman emperor. The murder of Caesar, historical personality, provoked as its final result the installation of *caesarism*: Caesar-person repeats itself as caesar-title. What is, then, the reason, the driving force of this repetition? At first sight, the answer seems to be clear: the delay of con-

194 / Slavoj Žižek

sciousness of the "objective" historical necessity. A certain act through which the historical necessity breaks through is perceived by consciousness (the "opinion of the people") as arbitrary, as something which also could have *not* happened. Because of this perception, people try to do away with its consequences, to restore the old state of things, but when this act repeats itself, it is finally perceived as an expression of the underlying historical necessity. In other words, repetition is the way historical necessity asserts itself in the eyes of "opinion."

But such an idea of repetition rests upon the epistemologically naive presupposition of an objective historical necessity, persisting independently of consciousness (of the "opinion of the people") and asserting itself finally through repetition. What is lost in this notion is the way so-called historical necessity itself is constituted through misrecognition, through the initial failure of opinion to recognize its true character, i.e., the way truth itself arises from misrecognition. The crucial point is here the changed symbolic status of an event. When it erupts for the first time, an event is experienced as a contingent traumatism, as an intrusion of a certain non-symbolized real. It is only through its repetition that this event is recognized in its symbolic necessity—i.e., that it finds its place in the symbolic network, that it is realized in the symbolic order.

But as with Moses in Freud's analysis, this recognition-through-repetition necessarily presupposes the crime, the act of murder. To realize himself in his symbolic necessity, i.e., as a power-title, Caesar has to die as an empirical, flesh-and-blood personality, precisely because the "necessity" in question is a *symbolic* one. It is not, then, only that people need time to understand, to grasp, it is not only that in its first form of appearance, the event (for example Caesar's amassing of individual power) was too traumatic for people to grasp its real signification. The misrecognition of its first advent is immediately "internal" to its symbolic necessity, it is an immediate constituent of its final recognition. To put it in a traditional way: the first murder (the parricide of Caesar) opened up the guilt, and it was this guilt, this debt, which was the real driving force of the repetition—the event did not repeat itself because of some objective necessity, independent of our subjective inclination and thus irresistible, but because its repetition was a repayment of our symbolic debt. In other words, repetition announces the advent of the Law, of the Name-of-the-Father in place of the dead, assassinated father. The event which repeats itself receives its law retroactively through its repetition. That is why we can grasp Hegelian repetition as a passage from a lawless series to a lawlike series, as the inclusion of a lawless event in a lawlike series—i.e., as a gesture of interpretation par excellence, a symbolic appropriation of a traumatic, non-symbolized event. (Lacan says somewhere that the interpretation always proceeds under the sign of the Name-of-the-Father.) Hegel was thus probably the first to articulate the *delay* which is constitutive of the act of interpretation. The interpretation always sets in too late, with some delay, when the event which is to be interpreted repeats itself. The event cannot already be lawlike in its first advent. This same delay is also formulated in the preface of Hegel's *Philosophy of Law*, in the famous passage about the owl of Minerva (i.e. the philosophical comprehension of a certain epoch) which takes flight only in the evening, after this epoch has already come to its end.

The fact that the "opinion of the people" was to see in Caesar's action an individual contingency and not an expression of historical necessity is then not a simple case of delay of consciousness in relation to effectivity. The point is that this necessity itself which was misrecognized by opinion in its first manifestation—i.e., which was mistaken for a contingent self-will—constitutes itself, realizes itself *through* this misrecognition.

And we should not be surprised to find the same logic of repetition also in the history of the psychoanalytic movement: it was necessary for Lacan to *repeat* his split with the IPA. The first split (the one of 1953) was still experienced as a traumatic contingency. Lacanians were still trying to patch things up with the IPA, to regain admission to the IPA, but in 1964, it also became clear to their "opinion" that there was a logical necessity in this split, so they cut their links with the IPA and Lacan constituted his own School.

Hegel with Austen

Jane, not John L.: it is Jane Austen who is perhaps the only counterpart to Hegel in literature: *Pride and Prejudice* is the literary *Phenomenology of the Spirit*, *Mansfield Park* the *Science of Logic*, and *Emma* the *Encyclopaedia*. No wonder, then, that we find in *Pride and Prejudice* the perfect case of this dialectics of truth arising from misrecognition. Although they belong to different social classes—he is from an extremely rich aristocratic family, she from the impoverished middle class—Elizabeth and Darcy feel a strong mutual attraction. Because of his pride, his love appears to Darcy as something unworthy; when he asks for her hand, he confesses openly his contempt for the world to which she belongs and expects her to accept his proposition as an unheard-of honor. But because of her prejudice, Elizabeth takes him for an ostentatious, arrogant, and vain type. His condescending proposal humiliates her, and she refuses him. This double failure, this mutual misrecognition, possesses a structure of a double movement of communication where each subject receives from the other its own message in inverse form. Elizabeth wants to present herself to Darcy as a young cultivated woman, full of wit, and she gets from him the message, "You're nothing but a poor empty-minded creature, full of false finesse." Darcy wants to present himself to her as a proud gentleman, and he gets from her the message, "Your pride is nothing but a contemptible arrogance." After the break in their relations, each discovers—through a series of accidents—the true nature of the other: she the sensitive and tender nature of Darcy, he her real dignity and wit. The novel ends as it should, with their marriage.

The theoretical interest of this story is in the fact that the failure of their first encounter, the double misrecognition concerning the real nature of the other, functions as a positive condition of the final outcome: we cannot go directly for the truth, we cannot say "if, from the very beginning, she had recognized his real nature and he hers, their story could have ended at once with their marriage." Let's take as a comical hypothesis that the first encounter of the future lovers was a success, i.e., that Elizabeth had accepted the first proposal of Darcy. What would happen in this case? Instead of a couple bound together in true love, they would become a vulgar everyday couple, a liaison of an arrogant rich man and a pretentious empty-minded young girl. If we want to spare ourselves the painful roundabout route through the misrecognition, we miss the truth itself: only the "working through" of the misrecognition allows us to accede to the true nature of the other and at the same time to overcome our own deficiency— for Darcy, to free himself of his false pride, and for Elizabeth, to get rid of her prejudices. These two movements are interconnected because Elizabeth encounters in Darcy's pride the inverse image of her own prejudices and Darcy in the vanity of Elizabeth the inverse image of his own false pride. In other words, Darcy's pride is not a simple positive state of things existing independently of his relationship to Elizabeth, an immediate property of his nature: it takes place, it appears, only from the perspective of her prejudices. And vice versa, Elizabeth is a pretentious empty-minded girl only for Darcy's arrogant view. To articulate things in Hegelian terms: in the perceived deficiency of the other, each perceives—without knowing it—the falsity of his/her own subjective position. The deficiency of the other is just an objectification of the distortion of our own point of view.

The two Hegelian jokes

There is a well-known, very Hegelian joke that illustrates perfectly the way truth arises from misrecognition, i.e., the way our path towards truth coincides with the truth itself. In the beginning of this century, there were a Pole and a Jew sitting in a train, facing each other. The Pole was shifting nervously, watching the Jew all the time. Something was irritating him. Finally, being unable to restrain himself anymore, he exploded: "Tell me, how do you Jews succeed in extracting from people the last small coin and in this way accumulate all your wealth?" The Jew replied: "Okay, I will tell you, but not for nothing; first give me five zloty" (Polish money). After receiving the required amount, the Jew began: "First, you take a dead fish; you cut off her head and put her entrails in a glass of water. Then, around midnight, when the moon is full, you must bury this glass in a churchyard." "And," the Pole interrupted him greedily, "if I do all this, will I also become rich?" "Not too quickly," replied the Jew, "this isn't all you must do; but if you want to hear the rest, you must pay me another five zloty!" After receiving the money again, the Jew continued his story. Soon afterwards, he again demanded more money, etc., till finally the Pole exploded in fury: "You dirty rascal, do you really think that I didn't notice what you were aiming at? There is no secret at all! You simply want to extract the last small coin from me!" The Jew answered him calmly and with resignation: "Well, now you see how we, the Jews . . ."

In this little story, all is to be interpreted, starting with the curious, inquisitive way the Pole looks at the Jew. It means that from the very beginning, the Pole is caught in a relationship of transference, i.e., that the Jew embodies for him the "subject supposed to know"—to know the secret of how to extract money from people. The point of the story is of course that the Jew has *not* deceived the Pole: he kept his promise and taught him how to extract money from people. What is crucial here is the double movement of the outcome, i.e., the distance between the moment when the Pole breaks out in fury and the final answer of the Jew. When the Pole blurts out, "There is no secret at all! You simply want to extract the last small coin from me!," he is already telling the truth without knowing it. That is, he sees in the handling of the Jew a simple deception—what he misses is that through this very deception, the Jew kept his word, delivered him what he was paid for (the secret of how the Jews . . .). The Pole's error is simply his perspective: he looks forward for the "secret" to be revealed somewhere at the end. He situates the narration of the Jew as a path to the final revelation of the "secret," but the real secret is already in the narration itself, in the way the Jew, through his narration, captures the desire of the Pole, in the way the Pole is taken in by this narration and is prepared to pay for it.

The "secret" of the Jew lies then in our own (Pole's) desire: in the fact that the Jew knows how to take our desire into account. That is

198 / Slavoj Žižek

why we can say that the final turn of the story, with its double scan-
sion, corresponds to the final moment of the psychoanalytic cure, the
dissolution of transference and "going through the fantasy." When the
Pole breaks out in fury, he has already stepped out of the transference,
but he has yet to traverse his fantasy. This is achieved only by realizing
how, through his deception, the Jew has kept his word. The fascinating
"secret" which drives us to follow carefully the narration of the Jew
is precisely the Lacanian *object petit a*, the chimerical object of fantasy,
the object causing our desire and at the same time—this is its paradox—posed retroactively by this desire. In "going through the fantasy," we experience how this fantasy-object (the "secret") only materi-
alizes, positivizes the void of our desire.

It is usually overlooked how another well-known joke possesses
exactly the same structure. We are referring, of course, to the joke
about the Door of the Law from the ninth chapter of Kafka's *Trial*, to
its final turnaround when the dying man from the country asks the
doorkeeper: "Everyone strives to attain the Law—how does it come
about, then, that in all these years no one has come seeking admittance
but me?" The doorkeeper perceives that the man is at the end of his
strength and that his hearing is failing, so he bellows in his ear: "No
one but you could gain admittance through this door, since this door
was intended only for you. I am now going to shut it."

This final turn is perfectly homologous to that at the end of the story
about the Pole and the Jew: the subject makes the experience of how
he (his desire) was from the very beginning part of the game, how the
entrance was meant only for him, how the stake of the narration was
only to capture his desire. We could even invent another ending for
Kafka's story to bring it nearer to the joke about the Pole and the Jew.
After the long wait, the man from the country broke out in fury and
began to scream at the doorkeeper: "You dirty rascal, why do you
pretend to guard the entrance to some enormous secret, when you
know very well that there is no secret beyond the door, that this door
is intended only for me, to capture my desire!"—and the doorkeeper
(if he were an analyst) would answer him calmly: "You see, now,
you've discovered the real secret: beyond the door is only what your
desire introduces there."

In both cases, the nature of the final turn follows the Hegelian logic
of surmounting, of abolishing "bad infinity." That is to say, in both
cases, the starting point is the same: the subject is confronted with
some substantial Truth, Secret from which he is excluded, which
evades him *ad infinitum*—the inaccessible heart of the Law beyond
the infinite series of doors, the unattainable last answer, or the last
secret of how the Jews extract money from us, awaiting us at the end

of the Jew's narration (which could go on *ad infinitum*). And the solution is in both cases the same: the subject has to grasp how, from the very start of the game, the door concealing the secret was meant only for him, how the real secret at the end of the Jew's narration is his own desire—in short, how his external position in relation to the Other (the fact that he experiences himself as excluded from the secret of the Other) is internal to the Other itself. Here, we encounter a kind of "reflexivity" which cannot be reduced to philosophical reflection: the very feature which seems to exclude the subject from the Other (his desire to penetrate the secret of the Other—the secret of the Law, the secret of how the Jews . . .) is already a "reflexive determination" by the Other. Precisely as excluded from the Other, we are already part of its game.

A timetrap

The positivity proper to the misrecognition—i.e. the fact that the misrecognition functions as a "productive" instance—is to be conceived in an even more radical way: the misrecognition is not only an immanent condition of the final advent of the truth, but it already possesses in itself so to speak a positive ontological dimension. It founds, it renders possible, a certain positive entity. To exemplify it, let's refer again to science fiction, to one of the classic science-fiction novels, *The Door into Summer*, by Robert A. Heinlein.

The hypothesis of this novel (written in 1957) is that in 1970, hibernation has become an ordinary procedure, managed by numerous agencies. The hero of the novel, a young engineer by the name of Daniel Boone Davis, hibernates himself as a professional deception for a period of 30 years. After his awakening in December 2000, he encounters—among other adventures—the old Dr. Twitchell, a kind of "mad genius" who has constructed a time-machine; Davis persuades Dr. Twitchell to use this machine on him and to transpose him back into the year 1970. There our hero arranges his affairs (by investing his money in a company that he knows—from his voyage to 2000—will be a great success in 30 years time, and even by arranging for his own wedding in 2000; he also organizes the hibernation of his future bride), and then hibernates himself again for 30 years. The date of his second awakening is April 27th 2001. This way, all ends well. There is just a small detail annoying the hero. In the year 2000, the newspapers publish, beside "Births," "Deaths," and "Marriages," also the column "Awakenings," listing the names of all persons roused from hibernation. His *first* stay in the years 2000 and 2001 lasted from December 2000 till June 2001; this means that Doc Twitchell has transposed him back to the past *after* the date of his second awakening in April 2001. In the *Times* for Saturday, 27 April 2001, there was of course his name in the list of those awakened on Friday, 25 April: "D. B. Davis." Why did he, during his *first* stay in 2001, miss his own name among the "Awakenings," although he had all the time been a very attentive reader of this column? Was this an accidental oversight?

"But what would I have done if I *had* seen it? Gone there, met myself—and gone stark mad? No, for if I *had* seen it, I wouldn't have done the things I did afterward—'afterward' for me—which led up to it. Therefore it could never have happened that way. The control is a negative feedback type, with a built-in 'fail safe,' because the very existence of that line of print depended on my not seeing it; the apparent possibility that I might have seen it is one of the excluded 'not possibles' of the basic circuit design. 'There's a divinity that shapes our ends, rough-hew them how we will.' Free will and predestination in one sentence and both true."

Here we have the literal definition of the "agency of the letter in the unconscious": the line "the very existence of [which] depended on my not seeing it." If, during his first stay in 2001, the subject had perceived his own name in the newspaper, i.e. if he had perceived—during his first stay—the trace of his *second* stay in 2001, he would have acted thereupon in a different manner (he would not have traveled back into the past, etc.), i.e., *he would have acted in a way that would have prevented his name from appearing in the newspaper*. The oversight itself has then, so to speak, a negative ontological dimension: it is the "condition of the possibility" of the letter that it must be overlooked, that we must not take notice of it—its very existence depends on its not being seen by the subject. Here, we have a kind of inversion of the traditional *esse percipi*: it is the *non-percipi* which is the condition of *esse*. This is perhaps the right way to conceive the "pre-ontological" status of the unconscious (evoked by Lacan in his *Seminar* XI): the unconscious is a paradoxical letter which *insists* only insofar as it does not *exist* ontologically.

In a homologous way, we could also determine the status of knowledge in psychoanalysis. The knowledge that is at work here is knowledge concerning the most intimate, traumatic being of the subject. It is the knowledge about the particular logic of his enjoyment. In his everyday attitude, the subject refers to the objects of his *Umwelt*, of the world that surrounds him, as to some given positivity. Psychoanalysis brings about a dizzying experience of how this given positivity exists and retains its consistency only insofar as somewhere else (on another scene, *an einem anderen Schauplatz*) some fundamental non-knowledge insists. It brings about the terrifying experience that if we come to know too much, we may lose our very being. Let us take, for example, the Lacanian notion of the imaginary self. This self exists only on the basis of the misrecognition of its own conditions. It is the effect of this misrecognition. So Lacan's accent is not on the supposed incapacity of the self to reflect, to grasp its own conditions, i.e., on its being the plaything of inaccessible unconscious forces. His point is that the subject can pay for such a reflection with the loss of his very ontological consistency. It is in this sense that the knowledge which we approach through psychoanalysis is impossible-real. We are on a dangerous ground: in getting too close to it, we observe suddenly how our consistency, our positivity is dissolving itself.

In psychoanalysis, knowledge is marked by a lethal dimension: the subject must pay for the approach to it with his own being. In other words, to abolish the misrecognition means at the same time to abolish, to dissolve, the "substance" which was supposed to hide itself behind the form-illusion of misrecognition. This "substance"—the only one recognized in psychoanalysis—is, according to Lacan, enjoyment (*jouissance*). Access to knowledge is then paid for with the loss of enjoyment. Enjoyment in its stupidity is possible only on the basis of certain non-knowledge, ignorance. No wonder, then, that the reaction of the analysand to the analyst is often paranoid: by driving him towards knowledge about his desire, the analyst wants effectively to steal from him his most intimate treasure, the kernel of his enjoyment.[1]

II The Symptom as Real

The Titanic as symptom

This dialectics of overtaking ourselves towards the future and at the same time of retroactive modification of the past—dialectics by which error is internal to the truth, by which misrecognition possesses a positive ontological dimension—has its limits, however. It stumbles onto a rock upon which it becomes suspended. This rock is of course the real, that which resists symbolization: the traumatic point which is always missed but which nonetheless always returns, although we try—through a set of different strategies—to neutralize it, to integrate it into the symbolic order. In the perspective of the last stage of Lacanian teaching, it is precisely the symptom which is conceived as such a real kernel of enjoyment which persists as a surplus and returns through all attempts to domesticate it, to gentrify it (if we may be permitted to use this term adopted to designate strategies to domesticate the slums as symptoms of American cities), to dissolve it by means of explication, of putting its meaning into words.

To give an example of this shift of accent in the concept of the symptom which occurs in Lacan's teaching, let us take a case which is today again attracting public attention: the shipwreck of the Titanic. Of course, it is already a commonplace to read the Titanic as a symptom in the sense of a "knot of meanings." The sinking of the Titanic had a traumatic effect, it was a shock, "the impossible happened," the unsinkable ship had sunk. But the point is that precisely as a shock, this sinking arrived at its proper time—"the time was waiting for it," even before it actually happened, there was already a place opened, reserved for it in fantasy-space. It had such a terrific impact on the "social imaginary" precisely because it was expected. It was foretold in amazing detail by Walter Lord:

> In 1898 a struggling author named Morgan Robertson concocted a novel about a fabulous Atlantic liner, far larger than any that had ever been built. Robertson loaded his ship with rich and complacent people and then wrecked it one cold April night on an iceberg. This somehow showed the futility of everything, and in fact, the book was called *Futility* when it appeared that year, published by the firm of M. F. Mansfield. Fourteen years later a British shipping company named the White Star Line built a steamer remarkably like the one in Robertson's novel. The new liner was 66,000 tons displacement; Robertson's was 70,000. The real ship was 882:5 feet long; the fictional one was 800 feet. Both vessels were triple screw and could make 24–25 knots. Both could carry about 3000 people, and both had enough lifeboats for only a fraction of this number. But, then, this didn't seem to matter because both were labeled "unsinkable." On April 10, 1912, the real ship left Southampton on her maiden voyage to New York. Her cargo included a priceless copy of the *Rubaiyat* of Omar Khayyam and a list of passengers collectively worth two hundred fifty million dollars. On her way over she too struck an iceberg and went down on a cold April night. Robertson called his ship the *Titan;* The White Star Line called its ship the *Titanic.* (Lord, xi–xii)

The reasons, the background for this incredible coincidence are not difficult to guess. At the turn of the century, it was already part of the *Zeitgeist* that a certain age was coming to an end—the age of peaceful progress, of well-defined and stable class distinctions, etc., i.e., the long period from 1850 till the First World War. New dangers were hanging in the air (labor movements, irruptions of nationalism, anti-semitism, the danger of war) which would soon tarnish the idyllic image of Western civilization, releasing its "barbaric" potentials. And if there was a phenomenon which, at the turn of the century, embodied this age coming to an end, it was the great transatlantic liners, floating palaces, wonders of technical progress, an incredibly complicated and well-functioning machine, and at the same time, the meeting-place of the cream of society. It was a kind of microcosm of the social structure, an image of society, not as it really was, but seen as society wanted to be seen, i.e., as a stable totality with well-defined class distinctions, etc.—in brief, the ego ideal of society. In other words, the shipwreck of the Titanic made such a tremendous impact, not because of the immediate material dimensions of the catastrophe, but because of its symbolic overdetermination, because of the ideological meaning invested in it. It was read as a "symbol," as a condensed, metaphorical representation of the approaching catastrophe of European civilization itself. The shipwreck of the Titanic was a form in which society lived the experience of its own death. And it is interesting to note how both the traditional rightist and leftist readings retain this same perspective, with only the accent shifted. From the traditional perspective, the Titanic is a nostalgic monument of a bygone era of gallantry lost in today's world of vulgarity. From the leftist view, it is a story about the impotence of an ossified class society.

But all these are commonplaces that could be found in any report on the Titanic. This way, we can easily explain the metaphorical overdetermination which confers its symbolic weight on the Titanic. The problem is that this is not all. We can easily convince ourselves that this is not all by taking a look at the photos of the wreck of the Titanic made recently by undersea cameras. Where does the terrifying power of fascination exercised by these pictures lie? It is, so to speak, intuitively clear that this fascinating power cannot be explained by symbolic overdetermination, by the metaphorical meaning of the Titanic. Its last resort is not that of representation, but that of a certain inert presence. The Titanic is a Thing in the Lacanian sense: the material left-over, the materialization of the terrifying, impossible *jouissance*. By looking at the wreck, we gain an insight into the forbidden domain, into a space that should be left unseen. Fragments that we see are a kind of coagulated remnant of the liquid flux of *jouissance*, a kind of petrified forest of enjoyment. This terrifying impact has nothing to do with meaning, or, more precisely, it is a meaning permeated with enjoyment, a Lacanian *jouis-sens*. The wreck of the Titanic thus functions as a sublime object: a positive, material object elevated to the status of the impossible Thing. And perhaps all the effort to articulate the metaphorical meaning of the Titanic is nothing but an attempt to escape this terrifying impact of the Thing, an attempt to domesticate the Thing by reducing it to its symbolic status, by providing it with a meaning. We usually say that the fascinating presence of a thing obscures its meaning; here, it is rather the opposite which is true. The meaning obscures the terrifying impact of the thing's presence.

From the symptom to the sinthome

This, then, is the symptom, and it is on the basis of this notion of the symptom that we must locate the fact that in the final years of Lacan's teaching we find a kind of universalization of the symptom: almost everything that is becomes in a way symptom, so that finally even woman is determined as the symptom of man. We can even say that "symptom" is Lacan's final answer to the eternal philosophical question, "Why is there something instead of nothing?" This "something" which "is" instead of nothing is precisely the symptom. The general reference of the philosophical discussion is usually the triangle world-language-subject, the relation of the subject to the world of objects, mediated through language; Lacan is usually reproached for his "absolutism of the signifier." That is, the reproach is that he doesn't take into account the objective world, that he limits his theory to the interplay of subject and language as if the objective world did not exist, as if it were only the imaginary effect/illusion of the signifier's play. But Lacan's answer to this reproach is that not only does the world—as a given whole of objects—not exist, but that neither do language and subject exist. It is already a classical thesis of Lacan that "the great Other (i.e. the symbolic order as a consistent, closed totality) does not exist," and the subject is noted as $, the crossed, blocked S, a void, an empty place in the signifier's structure. At this point, we must of course ask ourselves the naive, but necessary question: if neither the world nor language nor subject exists, what *does* then exist? More precisely: what confers on existing phenomena their consistency? Lacan's answer is, as we have already indicated, the symptom.

To this answer we must give its whole anti-poststructuralist accent. The fundamental gesture of poststructuralism is to deconstruct every substantial identity, to denounce behind its solid consistency an interplay of symbolic overdetermination—briefly, to dissolve the substantial identity into a network of non-substantial, differential relations. The notion of symptom is the necessary counterpoint: the substance of enjoyment, the real kernel around which this signifying interplay is structured.

To seize the logic of this universalization of the symptom, we must connect it with another universalization, that of foreclosure (*forclu-sion/Verwerfung*). Jacques-Alain Miller ironically spoke of the passage from a specific to a general theory of foreclosure (referring, of course, to Einstein's passage from a specific to a general theory of relativity). When Lacan introduced the notion of foreclosure in the fifties, it designated a specific phenomenon: the exclusion of a certain key signifier (*point de capiton*, Name-of-the-Father) from the symbolic order, which triggered the psychotic process. Here, foreclosure was not proper to language as such, but was a distinctive feature of the psychotic phenomena. In Lacan's reformulation of Freud, what was foreclosed from the symbolic returned in the real—in the form of hallucinatory phenomena, for example.

But in the last years of his teaching, Lacan gave universal range to this function of foreclosure: there is a certain foreclosure proper to the order of the signifier as such. Whenever we have a symbolic struc-ture, it is structured around a certain void; it implies the foreclosure of a certain key signifier. For example, the symbolic structuration of sexuality implies the lack of a signifier of the sexual relationship. It implies that "there is no sexual relationship," that the sexual relation cannot be symbolized, i.e., that it is an impossible, "antagonistic" relation. And to seize the interconnection between the two universal-izations, we must simply again apply the proposition that "what was foreclosed from the symbolic returns in the real of the symptom": Woman does not exist; her signifier is originally foreclosed, and that is why she returns as a symptom of man.

The idea of the symptom as real seems directly opposed to the classic Lacanian thesis that the unconscious is structured like a lan-guage. Is the symptom not a symbolic formation par excellence, a cyphered, coded message that can be dissolved through interpretation because it is already in itself a signifier? Is the whole point of Lacan not that we must detect, behind the corporeal-imaginary mask (e.g., of a hysterical symptom) its symbolic overdetermination? To explain this apparent contradiction, we must take into account the different stages of Lacan's development.[2]

We can use the concept of the symptom as a kind of clue or index, allowing us to differentiate the main stages of Lacan's theoretical development. At the beginning, in the early fifties, the symptom was conceived as a symbolic, signifying formation, a kind of cypher, a coded message addressed to the great Other which was supposed to confer on it its true meaning, retroactively. The symptom arises where the word failed, where the circuit of the symbolic communication was broken. It is a kind of "prolongation of the communication through other means." The failed, the repressed word articulates itself in a coded, cyphered form. The implication of this is that the symptom not only can be interpreted but is, so to speak, already formed in view of its interpretation: it is addressed to the great Other supposed to contain its meaning. In other words, there is no symptom without its addressee. In the psychoanalytic cure, the symptom is always addressed to the analyst: it is an appeal to him to deliver its hidden meaning. We can also say that there is no symptom without transference, without the position of some subject supposed to know its meaning. Precisely as an enigma, the symptom is, so to speak, overtaking itself to its dissolution through interpretation. The aim of psychoanalysis is to reestablish the broken network of communication by allowing the patient to verbalize the meaning of his symptom, and through this verbalization, the symptom is automatically dissolved. This, then, is the basic point. In its very constitution, the symptom implies the field of the great Other as consistent and complete, because its very formation is an appeal to the Other containing the meaning of it.

But it was here that the problems began. Why, in spite of its interpretation, does the symptom not dissolve itself? Why does it persist? The Lacanian answer is, of course: enjoyment. The symptom is not only a cyphered message, it is at the same time a way for the subject to organize his enjoyment. That is why, even after a completed interpretation, the subject is not prepared to renounce its symptom. That is why he "loves his symptom more than himself." In locating this dimension of enjoyment in the symptom, Lacan proceeded in two steps.

First, he tried to isolate this dimension of enjoyment as that of *fantasy*, and to oppose symptom and fantasy through a whole set of distinctive features. Symptom is a signifying formation which is overtaking itself toward its interpretation, i.e., which can be analyzed. Fantasy is an inert construction which cannot be analyzed, and which resists interpretation. Symptom implies and addresses some non-blocked great Other which will retroactively confer on it its meaning. Fantasy implies a crossed, blocked, barred, non-whole, inconsistent Other, i.e., it is filling out a void in the Other. A symptom (e.g., a slip of the tongue) causes discomfort and displeasure when it occurs, but we embrace its interpretation with pleasure. We gladly explain to others the meaning of our slips; their "intersubjective recognition" is usually a source of intellectual satisfaction. When we give ourselves to fantasy (e.g., in daydreaming), we feel immense pleasure, but, on the contrary, it causes us great discomfort and shame to confess our fantasies to others.

This way, we can also articulate two steps of the psychoanalytic process: interpretation of symptoms and going through fantasy. When

we are confronted with the patient's symptoms, we must first interpret them and penetrate through them to the fundamental fantasy as
the kernel of enjoyment which is blocking the further movement of
interpretation. Then we must accomplish the crucial step of going
through the fantasy, of obtaining distance from it, of experiencing
how the fantasy-formation is just masking, filling out a certain void,
lack, empty place in the Other.

But here, again, another problem arose: how to account for patients
who have, beyond any doubt, gone through their fantasy, who have
obtained distance from the fantasy-framework of their reality, but
whose key symptom still persists? How do we explain this fact? What
do we do with a symptom, with this pathological formation, which
persists not only beyond its interpretation, but even beyond fantasy?
Lacan tried to answer this challenge with the concept of the *sinthome*,
a neologism containing a set of associations (synthetic-artificial man,
synthesis between symptom and fantasy, Saint Thomas, the saint . . .).
Symptom as *sinthome* is a certain signifying formation penetrated
with enjoyment. It is a signifier as a bearer of *jouis-sens*, enjoyment-
in-sense. What we must bear in mind, here, is the radical ontological
status of the symptom. Symptom, conceived as *sinthome* is literally
our only substance, the only positive support of our being, the only
point that gives consistency to the subject. In other words, the symptom is the way we—the subject—"avoid madness," the way we "choose
something (the symptom-formation) instead of nothing (radical psychotic autism, the destruction of the symbolic universe)" through the
binding of our enjoyment to a certain signifying, symbolic formation
which assures a minimum of consistency to our being in the world. If
the symptom in this radical dimension is unbound, it means literally
"the end of the world." The only alternative to the symptom is nothing:
pure autism, a psychic suicide, surrendering to the death drive to the
point of the total destruction of the symbolic universe. That is why
the final Lacanian definition of the end of the psychoanalytical process
is: *identification with the symptom*. The analysis achieves its end when
the patient is able to recognize in the real of his symptom the only
support of his being. That is how we must read Freud's *wo es war, soll
ich werden*. You, the subject, must identify yourself with the place
where your symptom already was. In its "pathological" particularity
you must recognize the element which gives consistency to your being.

This is, then, a symptom: a particular, "pathological," signifying
formation, the binding of enjoyment, an inert stain resisting communication and interpretation, a stain which cannot be included into the
circuit of discourse, of social bond/network, but which is at the same
time a positive condition of it. Now it is perhaps clear why woman is,

according to Lacan, a symptom of man. To explain this we need only remember the well-known male-chauvinist wisdom already quoted by Freud: women are impossible to bear, a source of eternal nuisance, but still, they are the best thing we have of their kind; without them, it would be even worse. So, if Woman does not exist, man is perhaps simply a woman who thinks that she does exist.

"In you more than yourself"

Insofar as the *sinthome* is a certain signifier which is not enchained in a network but immediately filled, penetrated with enjoyment, its status is by definition "psychosomatic," that of a terrifying bodily mark which is just a mute attestation bearing witness to a disgusting enjoyment, without representing anything or anyone. Is Franz Kafka's story "A Country Doctor" not, then, the story of a *sinthome* in its pure, so to speak, distilled form? The open wound growing luxuriantly on the child's body, this nauseous, verminous aperture, what is it if not the presentification of vitality as such, of the life-substance in its most radical dimension of meaningless enjoyment?

> In his right side, near the hip, was an open wound as big as the palm of my hand. Rose-red, in many variations of shade, dark in the grooves, lighter at the edges, softly granulated, with irregular clots of blood, open as a surface-mine to the daylight. That was how it looked from a distance. But on a closer inspection there was another complication. I could not help a low whistle of surprise. Worms, as thick and as long as my little finger, themselves rose-red and blood-spotted as well, were wriggling from their fastness in the interior of the wound towards the light, with small white heads and many little legs. Poor young man, he was past helping. I had discovered his great wound; this blossom in his side was destroying him.

"In his right side, near the hip"; exactly like Christ's wound, although its closest forerunner is rather the suffering of Amfortas in Wagner's *Parsifal*. The problem of Amfortas is that as long as his wound bleeds *he cannot die*, he cannot find peace in death; his attendants insist that he must do his duty and perform the Grail's ritual, regardless of his suffering, while he is desperately asking them to have mercy on him and put an end to his suffering by simply killing him—just like the child in "A Country Doctor," who addresses the narrator-doctor with the desperate request: "Doctor, let me die."

At first sight, Wagner and Kafka are as far apart as is imaginable. On the one hand we have the late romantic revival of a medieval legend, and on the other, the description of the fate of the individual in contemporary totalitarian bureaucracy. But if we look at things closely we perceive that the fundamental problem of *Parsifal* is eminently a *bureaucratic* one: the incapacity, the incompetence of Amfortas in performing his ritual-bureaucratic duty. The terrifying voice of Amfortas's father Titurel, this superego-injunction of the living dead, addresses his impotent son in the first act with the words: "Mein Sohn Amfortas, bist du am Amt?" To which we have to give all the bureaucratic weight: are you at your post; are you ready to officiate? In a somewhat perfunctory sociological manner, we could say that Wagner's *Parsifal* is staging the historical fact that the classical Master (Amfortas) is no longer capable of reigning in the conditions of totalitarian bureaucracy and that he must be replaced by a new figure of a Leader (Parsifal).

In his film-version of *Parsifal*, Hans-Jürgen Syberberg demonstrated—by a series of changes introduced into Wagner's original—that he was well aware of this fact. First of all, there is his manipulation of the sexual difference: at the crucial moment of inversion in the second act—after Kundry's kiss—Parsifal changes his sex, i.e., the male actor is replaced by a young, cold female. What is at stake here is not any ideology of hermaphroditism but precisely the insight into the "feminine" nature of totalitarian power: totalitarian Law is an obscene Law, penetrated by filthy enjoyment, a Law which has lost its formal neutrality. But what is crucial for us here is another feature of Syberberg's version: the fact that he has *externalized* Amfortas's wound—it is carried on a pillow beside him, as a nauseous partial object out of which, through an aperture resembling vaginal lips, trickles blood. Here we have the contiguity with Kafka: it is as if the wound of the child from "A Country Doctor" had externalized itself, becoming a separate object, gaining independent existence or, to use Lacan's writing, ex-sistence. That's why Syberberg stages the scene where, just before the final denouement, Amfortas desperately begs his attendents to run their swords through his body and so relieve him of his unbearable torments, in a way which differs radically from the customary:

> Already I feel the darkness of death enshroud me,
> And must I yet again return to life?
> Madmen! Who would force me to live?
> Could you but grant me death!
> (*He tears open his garment.*)
> Here I am—here is the open wound!
> Here flows my blood, that poisons me.
> Draw your weapons! Plunge your swords
> In deep—deep, up to the hilt!

The wound is Amfortas's symptom. It embodies his filthy, nauseous enjoyment; it is his thickened, condensed life-substance which does not let him die. His words, "Here I am—here is the open wound!" are thus to be taken literally: all his being is in this wound. If we annihilate it, he himself will lose his positive ontological consistency and cease to exist. This scene is usually staged in accordance with Wagner's instructions: Amfortas tears open his garment and points at the bleeding wound on his body. With Syberberg, who has externalized the wound, Amfortas points at the nauseous partial object outside himself—i.e., he does not point back at himself but there outside, in the sense of, "there outside I am; in that disgusting piece of the real consists all my substance!"

How should we read this externality? The first, most obvious solution is to conceive this wound as a *symbolic* one: the wound is externalized to show that it does not concern the body as such, but the symbolic network in which the body is caught. To put it in a simple way: the real reason for Amfortas's impotence and therewith for the decay of his kingdom is a certain blockage, a certain derailment in the network of symbolic relations. "Something is rotten" in this country where the ruler has trespassed a fundamental prohibition (he allowed himself to be seduced by Kundry). The wound is then just a materialization of a moral-symbolic decay.

But there is another, perhaps more radical, reading. Insofar as it sticks out from the (symbolic and symbolized) reality of the body, the wound is "a little piece of real," a disgusting protuberance which cannot be integrated into the totality of "our own body," a materialization of that which is "in Amfortas more than Amfortas" and which is thereby—according to the classic Lacanian formula—destroying him. It is destroying him, but at the same time it is the only thing which gives him consistency. This is the paradox of the psychoanalytic concept of the symptom. The symptom is an element sticking on as a kind of parasite and "spoiling the game," but if we annihilate it, things get even worse. We lose all we had, i.e., even the rest which was threatened but not yet destroyed by the symptom. When confronted with the symptom, we are always in a position of a certain impossible choice, of an unbearable *vel* illustrated by a well-known joke about the chief editor of one of Hearst's newspapers. In spite of persuasion from Hearst, he did not want to take a well-deserved leave. When Hearst asked him why he did not want to go on his holiday, the editor's answer was, "I'm afraid that if I were absent for a couple of weeks, the sales of the newspaper would fall; but I'm even more afraid that in spite of my absence, the sales would *not* fall!" This is the symptom: an element causing a great deal of trouble, but the absence of which would mean even greater trouble, total catastrophe.

Take as a final example, Ridley Scott's movie *Alien:* the disgusting parasite which jumps out of the body of poor John Hurt. Is it not precisely such a symptom, is its status not precisely the same as that of Amfortas's externalized wound? The cave on the desert planet into which the space travelers enter when the computer registers signs of life in it and where the polyp-like parasite sticks onto Hurt's face has the status of the pre-symbolic Thing, i.e. of the maternal body, of a living substance of enjoyment (the uterus-vaginal associations aroused by this cave are almost too intrusive). The parasite stuck on Hurt's face is thus a kind of a "sprout of enjoyment," a leftover of the maternal Thing which then functions as a symptom—the real of enjoyment—of the group marooned in the wandering spaceship: it threatens them and at the same time constitutes them as a closed group. The fact that this parasitical object incessantly changes its form just confirms its *anamorphotic* status: it is a pure being of semblance. The "alien," the eighth supplementary passenger, is an object which, being nothing at all in itself, must nonetheless be added, annexed as an anamorphotic surplus. It is the real in its purest: a semblance, something which, on a strict symbolic level, does not exist at all, but at the same time, the only thing in the whole film which actually exists, the thing against which the whole reality is utterly defenseless. One has only to remember the shivering scene, when the liquid pouring from the polyp-like parasite after the doctor makes an incision with a scalpel, dissolves the metal floor of the spaceship.

From this perspective on the *sinthome*, we could give a different reading to our title: truth and enjoyment are radically incompatible; the dimension of truth is opened through our misrecognition of the traumatic Thing, embodying the impossible *jouissance*.

Notes

(1) This is also the way *ideology* functions. Ideology is not an illusionary, false representation of reality but (social) *reality it-self* based upon an illusion, structured by an illusion, i.e. reality which can reproduce itself only through a certain non-knowledge of subjects. Cf. our essay "The Real in Ideology," in *PsychCritique* 2; no. 3 (1987).

(2) For this account of the concept of the symptom, the author is indebted to Jacques-Alain Miller's seminar *Ce qui fait insigne* (Paris 1986–1987).

Works Cited

Austen, Jane. *Emma*. New York: Oxford University Press, 1971.

———. *Mansfield Park*. New York: Harcourt, Brace & World, 1967.

———. *Pride and Prejudice*. Ed. with intro. Frank W. Bradbrock. Text, notes and bibliography James Kinsley. New York: Oxford University Press, 1970.

Dummett, Michael. *Truth and Other Enigmas.* Cambridge, Mass.: Harvard University Press, 1978.

Hegel, G. W. F. *Philosophy of the Law.* Philadelphia: University of Pennsylvania Press, 1975.

———. *Science of Logic.* New York: Humanities Press, 1976.

———. *The Logic of Hegel.* Trans. from *The Encyclopedia of the Philosophical Sciences.* London: Oxford University Press, 1968.

Heinlein, Robert A. *The Door Into Summer.* New York: Bantam, 1986.

Kafka, Franz. *The Trial.* Trans. Willa and Edwin Muir. New York: Vintage Books, 1965.

Lord, Walter, *A Night to Remember.* New York: Bantam, 1983.

Lacan, Jacques. *Seminar XI: The Four Fundamental Concepts* (1964). Ed. Jacques-Alain Miller. Trans. Alan Sheridan. New York: W. W. Norton & Co., 1978.

———. *The Seminar of Jacques Lacan, Book I: Freud's Papers on Technique* (1953–1954). Ed. Jacques-Alain Miller. Trans. with Notes by John Forrester. New York: W. W. Norton & Co., 1988.

Maugham, W. Somerset. *Sheppey in Acting.* London: S. French, 1948.

Robertson, Morgan. *Futility.* London: M. F. Mansfield, 1898.

11

Literature as Symptom

Colette Soler

When Lacan gave a year-long Seminar on "Joyce the Symptom" in 1975–1976, he wrote the word symptom as it used to be written in French—"*sinthome*"—introducing thereby the enigma of a translinguistic equivocation. We hear in it the English words "sin" and "home," as well as the French words *saint* (saint) and *homme* (man)." This playing with the mother tongue sets the tone. We must try to estimate the importance of the possible effects of this way of handling the letter. But don't think that this is a literary question. Rather, we will see that it is an analytic question. Moreover, it will come as no surprise to you that this question concerns the psychoanalyst, for the agency of the letter can be found in the unconscious, as Lacan put it back in 1956. Here, in fact, we have a question: how is psychoanalysis allowed to speak of a work of art, here of literature?

Freud, for his part, would not have been likely to say "Joyce the symptom," but rather, "Goethe [or Jansen] the fantasy." Do these phrases imply a belittling of the work of art? We are aware of what Freud did with literature. In artists he saw his precursors, and in literary texts he saw an opportunity to verify the analytic method. From Sophocles to Goethe, via Jansen and Dostoyevsky, he found in literary fiction an anticipation of the discovery of the unconscious; and thus for Freud it is the neurotic who seems to be copying the fable in telling his family history, which he calls the "family novel" to say that his fantasy is structured like a novel. In any case, Freud lapsed into applied psychoanalysis, treating the artist's know-how as equivalent to what he himself called the work of the unconscious, putting artistic and literary works on the same level as dreams, slips of the tongue, bungled actions, and symptoms, all of which are interpretable.

Lacan reverses Freud's position concerning this point: it is not that the written text must be psychoanalyzed; rather, it is that the psychoanalyst must be well read. Psychoanalysis does not apply to literature. Its attempts in doing so have always manifested their futility, their unfitness to lay the grounds for even the most meager literary judgment. Why? Because artistic works are not products of the unconscious. You can well interpret a novel or poem—i.e., make sense of it—but this sense has nothing to do with the creation of the work itself. This sense has no common measure with the work's existence, and an enigma remains on the side of the existence of the work of art. This would even be a possible definition of the work in its relation to sense: it resists interpretation as much as it lends itself to interpretation. Nevertheless, if psychoanalysis does not apply to literature, psychoanalysis can learn a lesson from literature, taking a page out of its book, as it were. More precisely, the teaching of Lacan displays that we can learn either from his work or from his person, from his life, but without deducing one from the other. Thus a psychobiography is possible, but it does not explain the work of art, which is impossible to deduce from the author's life. Anyway, following Lacan's numerous literary references we could say: "Hamlet, desire;" "Antigone, beauty;" "Gide, the fetish;" "Sade and Kant, the will to *jouissance;*" "Edgar Allan Poe, the letter;" and finally "Joyce and his literature, the symptom."

Lacan's recourse to literature follows in the line of his recourse to linguistics. You know that people—not everyone, but the people of the IPA—have wanted to denounce therein a tendency towards intellectualism and verbalism. But this early recourse of Lacan's was necessary and inevitable for a simple reason: linguistics delivers the "material" of analysis, and even the "apparatus with which one operates in analysis," which is nothing other than the statements proferred either by the analysand or the analyst.

But the analytic operation itself is not a linguistic one, for it attests to language's hold on the symptom, the symptom as it presents itself in analysis. For the moment I am thinking of the symptom in its clinical sense, as it is presented to the analyst as that which does not stop from imposing itself on you. It is a not being able to refrain from thinking, or from feeling in the body, or from experiencing affects, and it is only through speaking that you can change the thought, the feeling in the body, and the affect.

Let us return to literature. In psychoanalysis, language operates on the symptom, and the question at hand is to know how the literary use of language can be said to be a symptom. Is it enough to drop speech in favor of writing? And how can literary creation—the spice, as it is often thought, of civilization—be placed on the same level as the symptom, when, by its very definition, a symptom is what is a bit "fishy," or doesn't quite "fit in"? First let me point out the general direction of the solution: literary creation can be a symptom because a symptom is itself an invention. What does it mean to create? The answer is: to bring something into being where there was nothing before. But saying "where there was nothing," I already imply a place. And there is no such thing as a place without the symbolic and its marks, and every symbolic mark engenders as empty the place that it creates.

Allow me on a lighter tone to recount a personal memory which comes from my years of supposed religious education. I must have been about nine or ten years old when an old canon came up to me during an examination, with great pomp and ceremony, and asked me a banal question of catechism: "What was there before God created the earth?" What would you answer? For my part, I answered with the greatest self-assurance: nothing. Note that "nothing" is nothing other than what remains when the signifier "earth" is barred. But my answer was not correct, to my astonishment and sanction. The answer was "nothingness." That had a great effect on me. I even stirred up the people around me, trying out the problem on them, but the old canon turned out to be right. Nothingness is not nothing. It is the word which was invented to speak about the unthinkable pre-symbolic void, which, compared with "nothing"—the result of the elision of something—is a horse of a different color, though that in no way dispels the aporias of divine creation! What is clear is that all creation supposes that the Symbolic has brought forth a lack in the real, where by definition nothing can lack.

I can complete my first statement: creation brings something into being, where there was nothing before, nothing but a hole, which is not nothing. This void is found in analytic experience at every level— first of all as the subject's lack, the first effect of speech being to transform the living being into the subject of the want-to-be, which we symbolize with the minus phi $(-\Phi)$ of castration. It is also found, as a consequence of this first level, as the lack of the object which would plug up this crack or fissure. This is what Freud closes in on with his theory of an object which is always substituting for an originally lost object. We recognize in this formulation that it is simply the subject's lack which gives the object its importance.

This is what Lacan takes up, grounding it with his logic of the signifier in the statement: "there no such a thing as a sexual relationship." What does it mean? There are certainly bodies, biological bodies of different genders, and signifiers related to sex: man and woman, father and mother, as well as all those which erect sexual ideals, such as "virgin," "whore," "wife," and so on. None of these inscribes the object which would annul the sexual lack, and they all fail to compensate for the hole, for "the partner of *jouissance* is unapproachable in language." The result is that one seeks; that's why one speaks and why there is even satisfaction in blah blah blah, unless one finds a . . . replacement.

That is what the symptom does: it plugs up the "there is no such a thing" of the no-relationship with the erection of a "there is." Given that the appropriate partner for *jouissance* is lacking, a symptom puts in place something else, a substitute, an element proper to incarnate *jouissance*. The first consequence is that there is no subject without a symptom. Its function is to fix the mode of the privileged *jouissance* of the subject. It is the symptom that makes the singularity of the subject, subjected otherwise to the great law of the want-to-be. The symptom is a function—a logical function—of exception relative to the infinite work, the infinite ciphering of the unconscious. A symptom snows in, nails in, *jouissance*, while the unconscious displaces *jouissance*.

Now how did we get from the Freudian discovery to these last formulas about symptom? In Freud's terms the deciphering of the symptom reveals the fantasm and the libidinal satisfaction that it engenders. The Freudian notion of compromise formation implies that the symptom constitutes the return of repressed *jouissance*. It is not simply a memory of *jouissance*, it is *jouissance* forever current, unchangeable in its core. Now if it can be deciphered, and its transformation brought about, for us Lacanians it can be deduced that it is of the same nature as language—which accounts for the thesis that the unconscious is structured as language. But on the other hand, its inertia contrasts with what is proper to language, namely the substitution of signs, substitution by which meaning is engendered. This contradiction is resolved by Lacan in the following way: in the symptom, the signifier is married, so to speak, to something else, and finds itself transformed accordingly.

And what would this something else be, if not what is manifested in suffering, and dwells in fantasy, namely what we call *jouissance?* Cathecting a term, a signifier, which is subtracted from signifying substitution, from the incessant ciphering of the unconscious *jouissance*, turns it into a letter which is outside of meaning and therefore real, a letter which alone is able to always fix or tie down the same being of *jouissance*. This is why Lacan says that the signifier returns in experience like a letter.

But then how could literature be a symptom? Literature serves, of course, as a vehicle of *jouissance*. But which *jouissance?* It is most often the *jouissance* of meaning, especially in the case where literature is novelistic and makes use of fiction, in other words, of the imaginary. Is not this a contradiction? Here let us consider Lacan's examples of symptomatic invention. It is not only Joyce's literature which can be called symptom according to Lacan. It is also a woman, or to take another example, the masochistic scenario, or even the Lacanian invention of the real. When a man is compliant with the paternal model, a woman (with the "a" underlined) can be his symptomatic invention, because Woman (with a capital "W") does not exist. Which is to say that supposed normality, heterosexuality—which Lacan writes *"norm-mâle,"* or *"père-version"* (since in French "père" means father— in English you could say "version of the father")—is itself a symptom. A symptom which Freud renders in the Oedipus myth.

Here we can see that perhaps invention is not creation. The symptom invents—that is to say, chooses, selects—the singular term which is not programmed by the Other, and which fixes *jouissance*. But this term is not necessarily an original one. In this sense, if creation—true creation, which produces a radical novelty—is a symptom, it is a special one, and we could say that the artist/creator is always without a father. Even if always dated, his work does not have filiation. He is always "son of his work," as Cervantes said. And therefore it is always foolish to look for the key to a work of art in its sources. The masochistic scenario as a symptom is something else. But its case is an instructive one for us, since it indicates that a scenario—i.e., the imaginary— can be the variable of the symptom. Therefore why not speak in the same way of the novelistic symptom? Clinical experience provides examples among readers, but also among artists/creators. Read again for example the account of Jean-Jacques Rousseau regarding the composition of the *Nouvelle Héloïse,* the novel that made all Europe tremble. Certainly a novel is dedicated to meaning, while a symptom is real, outside of meaning. But this is a paradox only in appearance, since nothing opposes a unity of meaning as a novel does the one of the symptom.

It is in this context that Lacan invokes Joyce, using *Finnegans Wake* to illustrate Edgar Allan Poe's message about the letter-object, the litter. What was, according to Lacan, the message of Poe when he wrote "The Purloined Letter"? A letter is not only a vehicle of a message; a letter is also an object. Joyce took equivocation, which is the essence of poetry, to an exponential power excluding meaning, pushing it to the power of the unintelligible. Before Joyce, one could not say that poets, even at the height of their art of the letter, demonstrated anything more than the efficacy of the letter in the genesis of meaning. The poet makes clear the joint or seam at which the audacity of the letter engenders something new in meaning. That is the operation by which the poet subverts so-called common sense. His operation certainly produces a *jouissance* to which the Kantian antinomy of taste/judgment is no objection, for this *jouissance* need not be universal for it to be attested to. Nonetheless, this *jouissance* is not pure *jouissance* of the letter. It does not go beyond the *jouissance* of the pun, which in playing on literality, produces an effect of meaning, sometimes brought as far as non-meaning. Its *jouissance* emerges at the joint at which meaning wells up out of the literal, going far beyond, and thus short-circuiting, the subject's intention.

Poetry and puns thus use a know-how of the letter, but it is to move the unconscious. Joyce takes an additional step with *Finnegans Wake*. He manages to use language—where unconscious knowledge rests—without making the meaning vibrate. This is why Lacan says of Joyce that he is "*désabonné à l'inconscient*"—i.e., not registered in the unconscious. This work, characterized by something like elation, something very close to what in psychiatry is called mania, unburdened of the weight of meaning, belongs to the scientific era. It fascinates by the *jouissance* to which it attests, and has a greater affinity with the *jouissance* that the mathematician finds in figures than with that of the classical novelist. And maybe he even signals the end of the classical literary symptom. But note that Joyce does not shut himself within the unintelligible: another of Joyce's accomplishments is to have succeeded in imposing on his commentators, for centuries to come, the weight of meaning that his work forecloses.

Now what in the symptom of Joyce interests the analyst? More precisely, what in his know-how interests the analyst? What interests the analyst is the limit of the analytic action. The symptom of Joyce is the unanalyzable symptom; it is in its own *jouissance* closed to the effects of sense, let us say outside of transference. And psychoanalysis is precisely a practice which operates by sense. It assumes that the subject lets itself be seduced and captivated by meaning, as an effect of the signifying articulation. Well, this limit, which probably explains why Joyce did not undergo analysis, appears to Lacan as the model for the end of a psychoanalysis. Joyce went straight to the best that could be expected at the end of a psychoanalysis, says Lacan. Why? What is the analytic problem at play here? It is the problem of putting a term to the transferential relationship with the analyst, which is itself a new symptom. It is a problem of disengaging the analysand from the *jouis-sens* of the unconscious. On this point Joyce is an example. This is what Lacan teaches us with Joyce. Here, you can see, that each one learns to the extent of his own knowledge. And I believe that we are far from catching up with Lacan.

Works Cited

Lacan, Jacques. *Le Séminaire de Jacques Lacan. Livre* XXIII: *Le Sinthome* (1975–1976). Unpublished text.

———. "The agency of the letter in the unconscious or reason since Freud" (1954). Trans. Alan Sheridan. *Ecrits: A Selection.* New York: W. W. Norton & Co., 1977.

Poe, Edgar Allen. "The Purloined Letter," in *The Purloined Poe: Lacan, Derrida, and Psychoanalytic Reading.* Eds. John P. Muller and William J. Richardson. Baltimore: Johns Hopkins University Press, 1988.

Rousseau, Jean-Jacques. *La Nouvelle Héloïse.* Paris: Librairie Larousse, 1937.

Index

Gaze, the, 13, 73, 78, 148–151: the gaze
of the other(s), 64, 74; of the Other,
74; and the void, 76
Gender ideologies, 50
Genet, Jean, 88
Grice, Paul, 22

Hartmann, Heinz, 95
Hegel, Georg Wilhelm Friedrich, 5, 15,
98, 192–211 passim; The Phenomenol-
ogy of Spirit, 29, 30, 31; Philosophy of
Law, 195
Heidegger, Martin, 27, 30, 77
Heinlein, Robert A., The Door into Sum-
mer, 199
Hermaphroditism, 209
Heterosexuality, 72, 217
Holmes, Sherlock, 161, 162
Homosexuality, 72
Husserl, Edmund, 98
hypokeimon, 13, 97
Hysteria, 11, 75, 90

Ideal ego, the, 70, 73
Identity: agencies of causality, 3; gender
identity, 7, 12, 55, 60; and phallic signifier, 51; and desire, 62; and sexual
difference, 66; and style, 147
Ideology, 55, 56, 211n: gender as, 62
Imaginary order, the, 16, 40, 51, 154,
217: and objet a, 1; imaginary function of the language of bees, 37; Derridean primacy of, 154
Imaginary self, 201
Indart, Juan-Carlos, 40
International Psychoanalytic Association, 94, 96, 195
Interpretation, 16, 56, 73, 87, 88, 133,
163, 214: analysis as, 91, 125
Irigaray, Luce, 53–55, 71

Jardine, Alice, 65
Johnson, Barbara, "The Frame of Reference: Poe, Lacan, Derrida", 154
Jones, Ernest, "The Concept of a Normal
Mind", 108
Jouissance 2, 4, 7, 11, 15, 16, 17, 30, 51–
52, 55–56, 61, 62, 65, 78, 86, 95, 97,
145, 146, 211, 218: and the analyst, 2;
and the feminine, 7; surplus, 11; of
the body, 16; and truth, 16; links to
repetition and death, 70; as enjoyed

meaning, 92; of the (great) Other, 116;
unconscious displacement of, 216; and
literature, 216; and transference, 218
Joyce, James, 87; his literature as symptom, 214; Finnegans Wake, 218

Kafka, Franz, 98; Trial, 198; "A Country
Doctor", 208
Kant, Immanuel, 5
Kernberg, Otto, 34
Klein, Melanie, 113; theory of object
loss, 113
Kreisel, George, 98
Kripke, Saul, 27, 160

Lacan, Jacques Émile Marie: passim;
L'acte psychoanalytique 1, 3; compari-
son of Lacan's structuralism with the
structuralism of Levi-Strauss and
Saussure, 4; theory of language, 8;
Seminar on the Purloined Letter, 9, 37;
"Discourse on Rome", 37; L'Ethique de
la psychanalyse, 41, 111; The Four
Fundamental Concepts of Psychoanalysis, 42, 159; "The agency of the letter
in the unconscious or reason since
Freud", 49, 52, 110; "A Love Letter",
52; "Of Structure as an Inmixing of an
Otherness Prerequisite to Any Subject
Whatever", 52; "The Formations of the
Unconscious", 59; "Desire and the Interpretation of Desire in Hamlet", 59,
Television, 76; "La psychanalyse et son
enseignement", 103; "Function and
field of speech and language in psychoanalysis", 110; "Le cas Aimee",
124; "Le president Schreber", 124;
"Joyce, le sinthome" ("Joyce the
Symptom"), 124, 213; "On the possible treatment of psychosis", 183
Lack, 4, 8, 17, 37, 55, 150: differing position of masculine and feminine regarding, 75; in the (great) Other, 120
Language, 24, 31: and sexual identity, 3;
and referentiality, 27–34 passim, 51,
149; and correspondence, 29, 49; theory of language as disappearance theory, 29; and creation, 32; and desire,
43, 125; as castration, 61; truth in, 93;
and the body, 118; and the sexual division, 117–118; and intersubjectivity,

Contributors

Willy Apollon is Professor of Philosophy, Laval University, and Director of GIFRIC (Freudian Interdisciplinary Group of Research and Intervention), Quebec City, Canada.

Russell Grigg is Professor of Humanities and Philosophy, Deakin University, Australia.

Lila Kalinich is Associate Clinical Professor of Psychiatry, Training and Supervising Analyst, Columbia Psychoanalytic Center for Training and Research.

Jacques-Alain Miller is a practising psychoanalyst, and Professor and Director of the Department of Psychoanalysis, Paris VIII.

Judith Miller is Professor of Philosophy, Paris VII.

Stuart Schneiderman, Ph.D., is a practising psychoanalyst in New York City.

Colette Soler is a practising psychoanalyst, and Professor of Psychoanalysis, Paris VIII.

Ellie Ragland-Sullivan is Professor of French and English and Chair of English, University of Missouri, Columbia.

Henry W. Sullivan is Middlebush Professor of Romance Languages, University of Missouri, Columbia.

Slavoj Žižek is Professor of Philosophy, University of Ljubliana, Yugoslavia.